The Teaching Portfolio

The Teaching Portfolio

A Practical Guide to Improved Performance and Promotion/Tenure Decisions

THIRD EDITION

Peter Seldin

Lubin School of Business
Pace University
Pleasantville, New York

ANKER PUBLISHING COMPANY, INC.
Bolton, Massachusetts

The Teaching Portfolio

A Practical Guide to Improved Performance and Promotion/Tenure Decisions
Third Edition

ISBN 1-882982-69-X

Composition by Deerfoot Studios
Cover design by Jennifer Arbaiza Graphic Design

Anker Publishing Company, Inc.
176 Ballville Road
P.O. Box 249
Bolton, MA 01740-0249 USA

www.ankerpub.com

About the Author

Peter Seldin is Distinguished Professor of Management at Pace University in Pleasantville, New York. A behavioral scientist, educator, author, and specialist in the evaluation and development of faculty and administrative performance, he has been a consultant on higher education issues to more than 300 colleges and universities throughout the United States and 40 countries around the world.

A well-known speaker at national and international conferences, Seldin regularly serves as a faculty leader in programs offered by the American Council on Education, the American Association for Higher Education, and the Association to Advance Collegiate Schools of Business.

His well-received books include:

The Administrative Portfolio (2002, with Mary Lou Higgerson)

Changing Practices in Evaluating Teaching (1999, with associates)

The Teaching Portfolio, second edition (1997)

Improving College Teaching (1995, with associates)

Successful Use of Teaching Portfolios (1993, with associates)

The Teaching Portfolio (1991)

How Administrators Can Improve Teaching (1990, with associates)

Evaluating and Developing Administrative Performance (1988)

Coping with Faculty Stress (1987, with associates)

Changing Practices in Faculty Evaluation (1984)

Successful Faculty Evaluation Programs (1980)

Teaching Professors to Teach (1977)

How Colleges Evaluate Professors (1975)

He has contributed numerous articles on the teaching profession, student ratings, educational practice, and academic culture to such publications as *The New York Times, The Chronicle of Higher Education,* and *Change* magazine. For his contributions to the scholarship of teaching, he has received honorary degrees from Keystone College (Pennsylvania) and Columbia College (South Carolina).

About the Contributors

SHIVANTHI ANANDAN is assistant professor in the Department of Bioscience and Biotechnology at Drexel University. Her teaching and research interests are in the areas of microbiology, genetics, and biotechnology.

LINDA ANSTENDIG is professor of English and communications at Pace University, Pleasantville, New York, where she teaches freshman and advanced writing and American literature. She is also codirector of the Pforzheimer Center for Faculty Development.

MARY BARROWS has been a full-time instructor of English and literature at Barton County Community College (Kansas) for over 15 years. Her graduate school training is in student learning disabilities.

KATHRYN A. BALLOU is assistant professor in the School of Nursing at the University of Missouri, Kansas City. She specializes in health systems research and critical feminist qualitative methodologies.

ABBEY L. BERG is assistant professor in the Department of Communication Studies/Communication Sciences and Disorders at Pace University, New York City. Her research interests include early detection and identification of hearing loss.

CURTIS C. BRADLEY is assistant professor of physics at Texas Christian University. A specialist in atomic physics, he worked for two years at the National Institute of Science and Technology as a National Research Council postdoctoral fellow.

JANE COLLINS is associate professor of English at Pace University, New York City, where she directs the Poets at Pace reading series. Her teaching interests include core literature courses as well as modern American drama, Chaucer, Shakespeare, and the American short novel.

MILTON D. COX is university director for teaching effectiveness programs at Miami University, Oxford, Ohio, where he founded and continues to direct the national Lilly Conference on College Teaching. He is also founder and editor-in-chief of the *Journal on Excellence in College Teaching*.

MONICA A. DEVANAS is director of faculty development and assessment programs at the Rutgers University Teaching Excellence Center. She has been recognized as a national model developer for Science Education and Civic Engagements by the Association of American Colleges and Universities.

JOSEPH G. DONELAN is professor of accountancy at the University of West Florida. His teaching and research interests are in managerial uses of information for planning, control, and decision-making.

KAY L. EDWARDS is assistant professor of music education and supervises student teachers at Miami University, Oxford, Ohio. Her primary interests are early childhood elementary music, multicultural music education, and the use of guided listening materials to enhance children's response to music.

SALLY L. FORTENBERRY is associate professor and department chair of design, merchandising, and textiles in the AddRan College of Humanities and Social Sciences at Texas Christian University, where she also coordinates the internship program.

MYRA FRADY is associate dean of finance, operations, and information technology and senior lecturer of mathematics at Oxford College of Emory University. She is actively involved in innovative approaches to assessing student learning and faculty development.

STEPHEN W. HENDERSON is associate professor of geology at Oxford College of Emory University. (From a young age he wanted to become a paleontologist.) His primary areas of interest are taphonomy and the connection between geology and culture.

SUSAN KAHN is director of the Office of Institutional Effectiveness at Indiana University–Purdue University Indianapolis. She speaks and consults widely about assessment, faculty development, and electronic portfolios.

CONSTANCE A. KNAPP is associate professor of information systems and codirector of the Pforzheimer Center for Faculty Development at Pace University, Pleasantville, New York.

JEAN E. L. LAYNE is program coordinator for faculty learning communities—a collaborative project of the Center for Teaching Excellence and the Dwight Look College of Engineering—at Texas A&M University. She works in faculty development and teaches learning strategies courses.

SAUNDRA K. LIGGINS is assistant professor of English at the State University of New York, College at Fredonia. She teaches courses in African American literature, contemporary American literature, gothic literature, and the Harlem Renaissance.

TECK-KAH LIM is professor of physics at Drexel University. He was in the first cohort of faculty inducted into the Teaching Portfolio Program in 1998 and now serves as an in-house mentor for other Drexel faculty as they prepare their portfolios.

JANET LIOU-MARK is assistant professor of mathematics at New York City College of Technology, City University of New York. She is blessed with a department that supports her creative teaching style and appreciates the opportunity to mentor faculty in writing their teaching portfolios.

KATHLEEN A. McDONOUGH is assistant professor of communication at the State University of New York, College at Fredonia. An award-winning documentary filmmaker, she teaches video production, multimedia, and applied media aesthetics.

MARGARET MITCHELL is associate professor of theatre arts at the University of the Incarnate Word. She teaches courses in costume design, costume history, introduction to theatre design, scenic design, and theatre practicum.

BARBARA A. B. PATTERSON is senior lecturer in the Department of Religion at Emory University. Her research explores the relationship between spiritual practices and social change. An advocate of scholar citizenship, she directs Emory's Experiential Learning Program.

KAREN L. RASMUSSEN is associate professor and associate chair of the Division of Instructional and Performance Technology in the College of Professional Studies at the University of West Florida. She consults in the design and development of a variety of products including webquests for Quick Science, a tool for teachers supporting science and technology initiatives.

WILLIAM ROBINSON is a mathematics instructor at Barton County Community College (Kansas). He has been teaching all levels of mathematics at the community college level for 20 years.

AMY E. SELDIN is a professional development teacher of reading/language arts for the Springfield Public Schools in Massachusetts. Prior to this she had a one-year appointment at Westfield State College where she taught courses in reading and literacy.

CLEMENT A. SELDIN is professor of education at the University of Massachusetts, Amherst. Recipient of his university's Distinguished Teaching Award, he is currently working with Columbia University (Teachers College) on a nationwide study of schools of education.

ALAN SHEPARD is professor and director of the School of Literatures and Performance Studies in English at the University of Guelph, Ontario, Canada. He is the author of *Coming to Class: Pedagogy and the Social Class of Teachers,* a collection devoted to the effects of social class on teaching, and *Marlowe's Soldiers.*

ARTHUR B. SHOSTAK is professor of sociology at Drexel University. A professional futurist, he specializes in industrial sociology and has written, edited, or coauthored 24 books and over 150 articles.

NANCY J. SIMPSON is director of the Center for Teaching Excellence at Texas A&M University. She has worked in faculty development for ten years and, in addition, teaches courses in mathematics.

BRIDGET THOMAS is assistant professor of classics at Truman State University. She teaches the languages, literatures, and cultures of the ancient Greeks and Romans. Her research focuses on gender and ethnic identity in ancient Greek literature.

TAMARA L. WANDEL is assistant professor of public relations at the University of Southern Indiana. Prior to this, she served as an assistant dean at the University of Evansville, where she coordinated the teaching portfolio project.

JOHN ZUBIZARRETA is professor of English and director of honors and faculty development at Columbia College, Columbia, South Carolina. Selected as a Carnegie Foundation/C.A.S.E Professor of the Year, he has published and presented widely on teaching, learning, and portfolios.

Table of Contents

xi

PART IV: KEEPING THE PORTFOLIO CURRENT

John Zubizarreta

PART V: SAMPLE PORTFOLIOS FROM ACROSS DISCIPLINES

Accounting

Bioscience and Biotechnology

Communication Studies/Communication Sciences and Disorders

Classical Languages and Literature

Design, Merchandising, and Textiles

Education

English

Preface to the Third Edition

Since 1991, when the first edition of *The Teaching Portfolio* was published, I have visited hundreds of colleges and universities and talked with faculty groups, department chairs, deans, and promotion and tenure committees about the portfolio and its place in the evaluation and improvement of teaching. I've also had the distinct pleasure of working one-on-one as a mentor to more than 500 faculty members as they prepared their personal teaching portfolios.

This extensive involvement as a practitioner has enabled me to gain new perspectives and new ideas, as well as refine and modify what has already been learned about portfolios. The new edition of *The Teaching Portfolio* puts much of this into practice.

Although this book provides readers with a distillation of the relevant research literature, it also does much more in that it reflects my personal experience over three decades as an academic dean, department chair, professor of management, and consultant on teaching and learning issues to institutions of higher education throughout the United States and in 40 countries around the world. This edition also includes important contributions by prominent educators who have prepared their own exemplary teaching portfolios, worked with others who have done so, and engaged in seminal work in the field.

Like the first and second editions, this one keeps the focus on self-reflection and documenting teaching performance. Part One sets forth the what, why, and how to develop teaching portfolios. It includes an extensively tested step-by-step approach to create a portfolio, discusses in detail how to prepare it for use in tenure and promotion decisions and to improve teaching, provides answers to common questions, discusses the role of the portfolio mentor, and describes how to prepare a portfolio if no mentor is available.

In this edition, considerable substance has been added to Part One through:

- An expanded list of items that might appear in portfolios.

- An enhanced section on the process of self-reflection.

- A new section on cautions to consider in preparing portfolios.

- A new set of specific suggestions for improving portfolios.

- An expanded section on updating the portfolio.

- A new section providing key resources for portfolio development from three institutions.

Part Two is new and addresses web-based electronic teaching portfolios. It describes how hyperlinks, menus, and other navigational tools, as well as hierarchical arrangements of information and materials and the availability of multimedia, can stimulate new thinking, perspectives, and insights. Screen shots are included.

Part Three is also new and describes in important detail how seven colleges and universities—large, small, public, and private—have implemented portfolios. It takes a hard, real-world look at purposes, strategies, tough decisions, what worked, and what didn't.

Part Four provides specific strategies for updating and improving portfolios. Since portfolios are living process documents, it also contains a current portfolio draft that includes numbered items that correspond to a list of changes made after self-reflection and collaboration with a mentor.

Part Five, also new, contains the actual teaching portfolios of 22 faculty members from an array of disciplines and a wide range of institutions. All were developed under the guidance of a skilled portfolio mentor. None of these portfolios appeared in the first or second editions of this book.

This new edition also identifies key issues, red-flag warnings, and benchmarks for success. It carefully differentiates between portfolios prepared for personnel decisions and those prepared for teaching improvement. It lists 31 possible portfolio items from which faculty can choose the ones most personally relevant.

In short, *The Teaching Portfolio,* third edition, offers the kind of ready-to-use, hands-on information required to foster the most effective use of portfolios. It is written for faculty members, department chairs, deans, and members of promotion and tenure committees, and should also be helpful to graduate students, especially those planning careers as faculty members. The straightforward language, practical suggestions, and field-tested recommendations should prove valuable.

The Teaching Portfolio was published in its first edition 13 years ago. Since then, the book has gained tenure as perhaps the most widely used and all-time bestseller in the teaching portfolio field. It has succeeded not only in the United States but also in many countries around the world.

I am humbled by this overwhelming show of trust and approach this latest edition with renewed enthusiasm, determined to build on the solid foundation that made the first two editions such highly regarded tools for self-reflection and for documenting teaching effectiveness.

Peter Seldin
Pleasantville, New York
October 2003

Part I

THE TEACHING PORTFOLIO: PURPOSE, PROCESS, AND PRODUCT

1

The Teaching Portfolio

An important and welcome change is taking place on college and university campuses: Teaching is being taken more seriously. Countless institutions are reexamining their commitment to teaching and exploring ways to improve and reward it. And faculty are being held accountable, as never before, to provide solid evidence of the quality of their classroom teaching.

The familiar professorial paradox is crumbling on many campuses. For years, professors were hired to teach, but were rewarded for research and publication. This is still true, of course, in many institutions—especially those with strong graduate schools—but it has been largely swept away on campuses stressing undergraduate education.

What is behind the new emphasis on teaching? Strident demands for teaching accountability from newly aroused legislatures and governing boards, and the insistent viewpoint that teaching is actually an expression of scholarship—that scholarship is not confined to the cutting edge of research but also lives in intimate knowledge and teaching of the research in the classroom—added to the pressure on campuses. But perhaps the most compelling force was the growing chorus of complaints from professors, themselves, that they had little solid evidence about what they did in the classroom and how well they did it. True, they probably had student ratings but that's about all, and student ratings alone fall far short of a complete assessment of one's classroom performance.

Yet in the absence of factual information about teaching, how can it be evaluated? How can it be rewarded? How can it be improved? And how can institutions give the teaching function its proper role and value?

Is there a way for colleges and universities to respond simultaneously to the movement to take teaching seriously and to the pressures to improve systems of teaching accountability? The answer is yes. A solution can be found by looking outside higher education.

Architects, photographers, and artists all have portfolios in which they display their best work. The teaching portfolio would do the same thing. It would enable faculty members to display their teaching accomplishments for the record. And, at the same time, it would contribute to more sound personnel decisions as well as the professional development and growth of individual faculty members.

What Is a Teaching Portfolio?

A teaching portfolio is a collection of materials that document teaching performance. It brings together in one place information about a professor's most significant teaching accomplishments. The portfolio is to teaching what lists of publications, grants, and honors are to research and scholarship. It is flexible enough to be used for tenure and promotion decisions or to provide the stimulus and structure for self-reflection about areas in need of improvement.

An important point: The teaching portfolio is *not* an exhaustive compilation of all of the documents and materials that bear on an individual's teaching performance. Rather, it presents thoughtfully chosen information on teaching activities along with indisputable evidence of their effectiveness. Just as in a curriculum vita, all claims made in the portfolio must be supported by empirical evidence. An effective portfolio requires careful selection and thoughtful organization and must give an accurate, well-rounded picture of teaching effectiveness in order to be convincing to those who read it.

Why should a skeptical professor spend valuable time preparing a portfolio? For this reason: As faculty, we typically document our research and publication activities. But we don't document our teaching. It makes good sense to document teaching activities with the same care and vigor we document research and scholarship.

The logic behind portfolios is straightforward. Earlier assessment methods, such as student ratings or peer observations, were like flashlights. That is, they illuminated only the teaching skills and abilities that fell within their beams. As such, they shed light on only a small part of a professor's classroom performance. But with portfolios, the flashlight is replaced by a searchlight. Its beam discloses the broad range of teaching skills, abilities, attitudes, and values.

The national movement in higher education toward using portfolios is now at an unprecedented high. Although reliable numbers are hard to come by, it is estimated that as many as 2,000 colleges and universities in the United States and Canada (where it is called a teaching dossier) are now using or experimenting with portfolios. That is a stunning jump from the ten or so institutions thought to be using portfolios in 1990.

The portfolio movement is not restricted to North America. In fact, it is a world-wide movement. Portfolios are being used to document teaching effectiveness in such diverse locations as Australia, Kenya, England, South Africa, Finland, Israel, and Malaysia.

WHY PREPARE A TEACHING PORTFOLIO?

Why would very busy—even harried—faculty members want to take the time and trouble to prepare a teaching portfolio? Seldin (2003) offers the following reasons:

- To gather and present hard evidence and specific data about their teaching effectiveness to tenure and promotion committees.

- To provide the needed structure for self-reflection about areas of their teaching needing improvement.

- To provide evidence in applications for grants or released time.

- To foster an academic environment where discussion about teaching practices becomes the norm.

- To apply for teaching awards.

- To present as part of documentation submitted for a job search.

- To provide evidence for post-tenure review.

- To share teaching expertise and experience with younger faculty members.

- To leave a written legacy within the department or institution so that future generations of teachers who will be taking over the courses of about-to-retire professors will have the benefit of their thinking and experience.

It is vital to bear in mind that the purpose for which the portfolio is to be used determines what is to be included and how it is to be arranged. This point will be discussed in detail later.

2

Preparing the
Teaching Portfolio

In theory, a teaching portfolio can be prepared by the professor working alone, but this isolated approach has limited prospects for contributing to personnel decisions or improving classroom performance. This is because portfolios prepared by the professor working alone provide none of the control or corroboration of evidence that may be needed to sustain personnel decisions. It also enlists none of the collegial or supervisory support needed in a program of teaching improvement. That is why portfolio development *should* involve interaction and mentoring in the same way that a doctoral dissertation reflects both the efforts of the candidate and the advice of the mentor.

Who might serve as a portfolio mentor? A department chair, a colleague, or a faculty development specialist could fill the role. They discuss with the professor such guiding questions as:

- Which areas of the teaching-learning process are to be examined?

- What kinds of information do they expect to collect?

- How is the information to be analyzed and presented?

- Why are they preparing the portfolio?

One caution: Whoever serves as portfolio mentor (or coach) must have a wide knowledge of procedures and current instruments to document effective teaching. In this way, the mentor can assist the faculty member by providing suggestions and resources and maintaining steady support during the preparation of the portfolio.

A second caution: Because faculty members and institutional contexts differ widely, there is no one best way to structure the collaboration. But there are several approaches which have proven useful:

- An older, more experienced professor who works directly with a younger colleague from the same or another discipline.

- A trained group of in-house faculty who, in exchange for a course reduction in teaching load, mentor several professors as they prepare their portfolios.

- An outside consultant either from one's own discipline or from another.

A third caution: The mentor must remember that the portfolio is owned by the faculty member who prepares it. Decisions about what goes into it are generally cooperative ones between the mentor and the professor. But the final decision about what to include, its ultimate use, and the retention of the final product all rest with the professor. In short, no matter how tempting it might be, the mentor must refrain from imposing his or her assumptions, purposes, form, or style. The mentor role is that of guide, not director.

THE KEY ROLE OF THE CHAIR

When used for personnel decisions, a teaching portfolio will have genuine value only when those who make tenure, promotion, and retention decisions learn to trust the approach. Important to the development of trust is the periodic exchange of views between the department chair and professor about teaching responsibilities, duties ancillary to teaching, and specific items for the portfolio.

The discussion between the department chair and professor should address expectations and how teaching performance is to be reported. Otherwise, there is a danger that the data submitted may overlook areas of prime concern. Open discussion largely eliminates possible misunderstandings. The goal is for the portfolio to attain the status of an important and trusted instrument that accurately captures the complexity and individuality of teaching.

STEPS TO CREATE A TEACHING PORTFOLIO

Most faculty members rely on the following step-by-step approach in creating their portfolios. It is based on the work of the Pennsylvania State University Center for Excellence in Learning and Teaching (*Designing a Teaching Portfolio,* 1997), Haugen (1998), Knapper and Wright (2001), Seldin (1997), and Seldin (2003).

Step 1: Planning

Before assembling the portfolio, the faculty member needs to think about purpose and audience. As mentioned earlier, there are many different reasons for developing a portfolio—personnel decisions, improvement, a job search, an award nomination, a legacy. To a large degree, the purpose drives the content. So does the audience that will read it. That is why reflecting on purpose and audience helps give shape to the portfolio. Some guiding questions to consider:

- What is your primary purpose in creating the portfolio?
- Who are your primary readers?
- What evidence will they expect to find?
- What types of evidence will be most convincing to those readers?
- Who will you ask for what information?

Step 2: Summarize Teaching Responsibilities

Portfolios often begin with a two- or three-paragraph statement covering such topics as courses currently taught or taught in the last few years, whether the courses are required or elective, graduate or undergraduate. It might also cover activities ancillary to teaching such as serving as faculty advisor to student organizations or advising individual graduate or undergraduate students. The focus here is on what the faculty member is responsible for as a teacher. It sets the framework for everything that follows.

Step 3: Describe Your Approach to Teaching

This is typically the longest section in the portfolio. Based on the teaching responsibilities described in Step 2, the faculty member prepares a two- to two-and-one-half-page reflective statement describing his or her teaching philosophy, objectives, methodologies, and strategies. The statement addresses the issue of *how* faculty members carry out teaching responsibilities from the standpoint of *why* they do *what* they do in the classroom. Some guiding questions to consider:

- What are your beliefs about teaching?
- What are your aims for students, and why are these aims important to you?
- How do your actions as a teacher reflect your beliefs about teaching and learning?
- What evidence will show that your actions reflect your beliefs?

- What specific examples can you provide?

- How do you apply your knowledge of pedagogy to your subject area specialization?

- How have your teaching methods changed in response to changes in students, course materials, curriculum changes?

- What is your role in fostering critical thinking skills? in facilitating the acquisition of lifelong learning skills?

- How do you make decisions about content, resources, methods?

- How do you decide whether/when to use active learning? student-centered learning principles?

- What instructional materials have you developed?

- What innovative activities have you designed?

Step 4: Select Items for the Portfolio

From a list of possible items for a portfolio, the faculty member selects those items for inclusion which are most applicable to his or her teaching responsibilities and approach to teaching. The choice of items should reflect the professor's personal preferences, style of teaching, academic discipline, and particular courses. Being creative and thoughtful in itemizing teaching accomplishments and presenting reflections on teaching will help faculty members to create a personalized portfolio.

What determines the selection of items for the portfolio? It depends on the purpose for which the portfolio is prepared as well as the audience who will read it. Other factors include the teaching style of the faculty member, the courses taught, and any content requirement of a professor's department or institution. As long as they are allowed by the department and institution, individual differences in portfolio content and organization should be encouraged.

Step 5: Prepare Statements on Each Item

Statements are prepared by the professor on activities, initiatives, and accomplishments on each item. Some guiding questions to consider:

- Do you have a variety of measures of your teaching effectiveness?

- Have you taken part in programs designed to improve teaching?

- Have you included the dates and topics of each?

- Do your course syllabi coalesce around a specific theme reflected in your teaching?
- Have you provided support documentation for every claim made?
- Have you cross-referenced your narrative with the appendices?

Step 6: Arrange the Items in Order

The sequence of statements about accomplishments in each area is determined by their intended use. For example, if the faculty member intends to demonstrate teaching improvement, activities such as attending faculty development workshops and seminars would be stressed. Another example: If the faculty member intends to demonstrate curricular revision, previous and current syllabi as well as an explanation of why the curricular revisions were made would be stressed.

Step 7: Compile the Supporting Data

Evidence supporting all items mentioned in the portfolio is retained by the faculty member and made available for review. These would include, for example, letters from colleagues or the department chair, original student evaluations of teaching, samples of student work, invitations to contribute articles on teaching one's discipline, a colleague evaluation. This evidence is back-up material and is placed in the appendix or made available upon request.

Step 8: Housing the Portfolio

All of the portfolio material is housed in a single one-and-one-half- or two-inch, three-ring binder. It is secure and flexible and permits the efficient arrangement of material in separate sections labeled with identification tabs.

3

Choosing Items
for the Teaching Portfolio

The teaching portfolio is a highly personalized product. No two are exactly alike. Both content and organization differ widely from one professor to another (see the sample portfolios in Part V of this volume). Different fields and courses cater to different types of documentation. For example, an introductory course in calculus is far removed from an advanced course in landscape design. A freshman geology course is worlds apart from a graduate course in genetics.

From personal review of more than 1,000 portfolios prepared by professors in institutions representing all sectors of higher education, I can say with confidence that certain items appear again and again. They fall into three broad categories.

Material From Oneself

- A statement of teaching responsibilities, including course titles, numbers, enrollments, and an indication about whether the course is required or elective, graduate or undergraduate.

- A reflective statement by the professor, describing his or her personal teaching philosophy, strategies and objectives, and methodologies.

- Instructional innovations and assessment of their effectiveness.

- A description of curricular revisions, including new course projects, materials, and assignments.

- Course and instructional materials developed, including study guides, manuals, case studies, annotated bibliographies, course booklets, and computer-aided learning programs.

- A representative course syllabi detailing course content and objectives, teaching methods, readings, and homework assignments.
- A description of how audiovisual or computer-based materials were used in teaching.
- Research that directly contributes to teaching.
- Participation in programs on sharpening instructional skills.
- A description of steps taken to evaluate and improve one's teaching.
- Success at securing grants for teaching-related activities.
- A personal statement by the professor, describing teaching goals for the next five years.
- Graded appraisal tools showing a clear relationship between appraisal methods and course objectives.
- Committee work relating to teaching and learning.

Material From Others

- Student course or teaching evaluation data which produce an overall rating of effectiveness or satisfaction or suggest improvements.
- Honors or other recognition from colleagues or students, such as a distinguished teaching or student advising award.
- Statements from colleagues who have systematically reviewed the professor's classroom materials (such as the course syllabi, assignments, the reading list, and evidence of testing and grading practices) or have observed the faculty member in the classroom.
- Invitations from outside agencies to teach or present a paper at a conference on teaching one's discipline or teaching in general.
- Documentation of teaching development activities through the campus center for teaching and learning.
- Statements from colleagues at other institutions on how well students have been prepared for graduate school.
- Statements by alumni on the quality of instruction.
- Evidence of help given to colleagues on course development or teaching improvement.
- Statements from colleagues with regard to program design, program materials, study guides, and online instruction.

Products of Teaching/Student Learning

- Student scores on pre- and post-course examinations as evidence of student learning.

- Student essays, fieldwork reports, laboratory workbooks, or logs.

- Examples of graded student essays showing excellent, average, and poor work.

- A record of students who succeed in advanced study in the field.

- Student publications or conference presentations on course-related work prepared under the direction of the faculty member.

- Evidence of influence on student career choice or help given by the professor to secure student employment or graduate school admission.

- Successive drafts of student papers along with the professor's comments on how each draft could be improved.

- Evidence of student early semester learning versus end of term performance.

These are the most commonly selected items but by no means are they the only ones to appear in portfolios. Some professors, for reasons of academic discipline, teaching style, or institutional preference, choose a different content mix. Items that sometimes appear in portfolios are:

- A videotape of the faculty member teaching a typical class.

- Participation in off-campus activities relating to teaching.

- A description of how technology is used in the classroom.

- A self-evaluation of teaching-related activities.

- Contributing to, or editing, a professional journal on teaching the professor's discipline.

- A statement by the department chair assessing the professor's teaching contribution to the department.

- Performance reviews as a faculty advisor.

How Many Pages? How Much Time?

How much information and evidence is needed to fairly represent a professor's teaching performance? There is no simple answer. Experience suggests that a thoughtful, selective document of eight to ten pages plus supporting appendix material is sufficient for the vast majority of faculty members. In fact, to keep the portfolio at a manageable length, an increasing number of colleges and universities are putting a ceiling on the number of pages they permit in order to prevent data overkill.

How long does it take to put a portfolio together? Again, there is no simple answer. But for most professors—especially those working with a skilled mentor—12 to 15 hours spread over several days seems sufficient to get to third draft stage.

THE APPENDIX

Just as information in the narrative part of the portfolio should be selective, so, too, the appendices should consist of judiciously chosen evidence that adequately supports the narrative section of the portfolio. Sometimes evidence is too large or bulky to include in the appendices. In that case, the professor may briefly discuss such materials in the narrative and make them available upon request.

Many professors weave references to appendices within the narrative portion of their portfolio. In other words, the narrative is cross-referenced to the appendices. Why? Because this approach strengthens coherence (see the sample portfolios in Part V of this volume). Typically included in the appendices are supporting documents such as student ratings of instruction, peer reviews, syllabi, invitations to speak at a conference on teaching one's discipline, and graded student papers.

The appendices must be of manageable size if they are to be read. For most professors, six to ten categories of appendix items is sufficient.

Bear in mind that the best sequence of portfolio development is to first reflect on one's underlying teaching philosophy, then describe the teaching strategies and methodologies that flow from that philosophy (*why* you do *what* you do in the classroom), and only then to select documents and materials which provide the hard evidence of one's teaching activities and accomplishments.

THE VALUE OF SELF-REFLECTION

One of the most significant parts of the portfolio is the faculty member's self-reflection on his or her teaching. Preparing it can help professors unearth new discoveries about themselves as teachers. Here are some questions that may assist in the process of self-reflection:

• What is your greatest strength as a teacher? Why?

- What is the one thing you would most like to change about your teaching? Have you taken any steps to bring about this change?

- What has been your most significant teaching accomplishment?

- What new teaching strategies have you tried in the last year?

- What did you learn from the strategies that succeeded? From the ones that did not?

- What do your syllabi say about your teaching style?

- How do you motivate superstar students? How do you motivate those who are struggling?

- How would you describe the feeling between you and your students?

- What are the three most important things that new teachers in your discipline should know to be effective teachers?

- How would you describe your attitude toward teaching? Has it changed in recent years? In what ways?

UPDATING THE TEACHING PORTFOLIO

The teaching portfolio is a living document. It changes over time. New items are added. Others—now outdated or no longer relevant—are removed (see Part IV in this volume). What span of time should the portfolio cover? It depends on the purpose for which it is to be used. For improvement purposes, a two- to four-year look back is sufficient. But if the professor faces a personnel decision for tenure or promotion, the time span covered in the portfolio will be longer, perhaps six years. Documenting teaching accomplishments from the distant past (for example student ratings or classroom observations from many years ago) becomes less pertinent with the passage of time.

Updating a portfolio annually becomes a simple matter of placing items pertaining to teaching into a file drawer just as faculty now do for research and service. Any evidence that might be useful when the portfolio is updated is put in the drawer. If that is done, data collection becomes ongoing and, on an annual basis, the procedure of revising the portfolio should not take the faculty member more than one day.

4

Using the Teaching Portfolio

B ecause the teaching portfolio provides tangible evidence of teaching effectiveness, there are different purposes for which professors decide to prepare portfolios. Some do so in order to take on the road as they seek a different or first teaching position. Others prepare them for consideration of teaching awards or merit pay. Still others do so in support of faculty grant applications or to leave as a legacy within their department or institution.

By far, though, the two most often cited reasons for preparing teaching portfolios are to provide evidence for use in personnel decisions and to improve teaching performance.

USING THE PORTFOLIO FOR PERSONNEL DECISIONS

Why should professors want to give evaluation committees their teaching portfolios? Doing so provides the committee with hard to ignore information on what faculty members do in their classroom and how they do it. In addition, a portfolio enables evaluators to go far beyond student ratings in examining teaching effectiveness because it gets at both the individuality and the complexity of teaching.

Because they are based on triangulation of data, teaching portfolios are the fairest way that I know to evaluate teaching. They allow those who evaluate teaching for promotion or tenure decisions to counter possible biases in student evaluation data, readily see teaching improvement over time, and recognize the full range of what faculty members do as teachers inside and outside of the classroom. For the professor, providing several perspectives on the same courses provides a far more complete and accurate picture of teaching effectiveness than could be achieved with only one source.

Some argue that professors should be given unrestricted freedom to select the items that best reflect their teaching performance. This approach may work reasonably well if the portfolio is used for improving performance. But it works less well if the portfolio is used for personnel decisions. Because each portfolio is unique, the lack of standardization makes comparability very difficult for faculty members from different teaching contexts.

One answer that has been adopted by many institutions using portfolios for tenure and promotion decisions is to require that they include certain mandated items along with the elective ones. Such mandated items might include, for example, summaries of student evaluations on global questions, representative course syllabi, the department chair's assessment of the professor's teaching contribution to the department, innovative course materials, evidence of efforts to improve one's teaching, and a reflective statement in which the faculty member describes his or her teaching philosophy, objectives, and methodologies. All additional items in the portfolio would be chosen by the professor.

A typical table of contents for a portfolio prepared for *evaluation* purposes might include the following entries:

TEACHING PORTFOLIO
Name of Faculty Member
Department/College
Institution
Date

Table of Contents
1) Teaching Responsibilities
2) Teaching Philosophy
3) Teaching Objectives, Strategies, Methodologies
4) Student Evaluations for Multiple Courses Using Summative Questions
5) Classroom Observations by Faculty Peers or Administrators
6) Review of Teaching Materials by Colleagues Inside or Outside the Institution
7) Representative and Detailed Course Syllabi
8) Evidence of Student Learning (Cognitive or Affective)
9) Teaching Recognition and Rewards
10) Short-Term and Long-Term Teaching Goals
11) Appendices

What should personnel committees look for when evaluating teaching from a portfolio? Appendix Three provides a helpful checklist, and the following general guidelines will also prove useful:

First, portfolios should not demand an inordinate amount of time or energy to read and evaluate. One way to assure this is to put a page limit on the length of portfolios. Whatever the limit—seven, eight, even ten pages, plus appendix—the figure should be clearly known by all professors and personnel committee members.

Second, the portfolio program must have the unqualified support of the evaluators and those being evaluated. This means that academic administrators and faculty leaders must build support for the program on its attitudinal and interpersonal aspects.

Third, portfolios should be unified as a construct. The collection and selection of materials should be tied together with a reflective commentary since it is through reflection and commentary that faculty members make their thinking visible.

Fourth, in the interest of fairness and rigor, standard criteria should be used to evaluate portfolios. Guiding principles might include completeness of documentation, clarity of organization, broad selection of evidence from multiple sources, and connection between the reflective statement (including teaching philosophy, objectives, and methodologies) and the evidence.

Fifth, there needs to be general agreement about what constitutes teaching effectiveness. At the same time, Knapper and Wright (2001) rightly warn against trying to force portfolios into a quantitative paradigm when one of their strengths is providing rich qualitative data that will differ somewhat from person to person and discipline to discipline.

Sixth, evaluators must focus attention on the *evidence* supporting teaching effectiveness and ignore fancy covers, dazzling computer graphics, and attractive printer fonts. Those things cannot overcome weak performance for a professor in a portfolio any more than they can for a student in a term paper.

It is important to bear in mind that the use of portfolios for personnel decisions is only occasional. Its primary purpose is to improve teaching effectiveness.

USING THE PORTFOLIO TO IMPROVE TEACHING

Can preparation of a teaching portfolio help the professor to improve the quality of teaching performance? Seldin (2003) points out that the very process of creating the collection of documents and materials that comprise the portfolio stimulates the professor to ponder personal teaching activities, organize priorities, rethink teaching strategies, and plan for the future.

Portfolios possess a special power to involve faculty members in reflecting on their own classroom practice and how to improve it.

Just as students need feedback to correct errors, faculty members need factual and philosophical data to improve their teaching performance. Feedback from a range of sources can produce in the professor the kind of dissonance or dissatisfaction that sets the psychological stage for change.

The portfolio is a particularly effective tool for instructional improvement because it is grounded in discipline-based pedagogy. That is, the focus is on teaching a particular subject to a particular group of students at a particular time.

As a vehicle for structured reflection about teaching, the portfolio gives professors the opportunity to think about why they do certain things in class and to consider what works and what doesn't. As a result, it encourages professors to become more self-aware about their teaching and to engage in classroom research.

When used for *improvement* purposes, the portfolio contains no mandated items. Instead, it contains only items chosen by the professor working in collaboration with a consultant/mentor.

Sometimes, a professor will decide not to do a teaching portfolio that covers an array of courses but rather to do a portfolio that focuses on a single course. The goal is to improve his or her teaching of that particular course. A *course* portfolio might include:

- A summary of instructional methods used.

- Specific course objectives and the degree of student achievement of those objectives.

- Student ratings on diagnostic questions.

- A full-period classroom observation by several trained observers.

And sometimes a professor will decide to do a course portfolio in an *electronic* rather than a paper version. A portfolio constructed in this way includes technologies that allow the developer to collect and organize the contents in many formats, including audio, video, graphical, and text. As Barrett (2001) points out, the electronic portfolio typically uses hypertext links to organize the material, connecting it to appropriate goals and standards (see Part II in this volume).

Whether electronic or paper, when the purpose of the portfolio is to improve teaching, a typical table of contents might look like this:

TEACHING PORTFOLIO
Name of Faculty Member
Department/College
Institution
Date

Table of Contents

1) Teaching Responsibilities
2) Teaching Philosophy
3) Teaching Objectives, Strategies, and Methodologies
4) Description of Teaching Materials (Syllabi, Handouts, Assignments)
5) Efforts to Improve Teaching
   - Innovations in Teaching
   - Curricular Revisions
   - Teaching Conferences/Workshops Attended
6) Student Ratings on Diagnostic Questions
7) Evidence of Student Learning
8) Short-Term and Long-Term Teaching Goals
9) Appendices

SUGGESTIONS FOR IMPROVING PORTFOLIOS

Whether used for personnel decisions or improvement, the following is a list of suggestions that should be helpful to faculty members who prepare their portfolios. These elements, which may go unnoticed, are items of importance to every portfolio developer.

Include the Date of the Portfolio

Dating the portfolio helps the faculty member establish a baseline from which to measure development in teaching performance. That growth can be gauged by the degree to which the portfolio demonstrates instructional improvement resulting from a reexamination of his or her philosophy, objectives, strategies, and methodologies.

Include a Detailed Table of Contents

A table of contents enables portfolio readers to see the breadth and flow of information. It also serves as a reminder to the professor that the portfolio should be updated each year.

Add a List of Appendix Items
A list serves as a table of contents and makes it easier for readers to find specific evidence for claims made by the professor in the narrative.

Include Specific Dates for Courses Taught
If the portfolio is prepared for a personnel decision, dates should be given for all courses taught during the previous five or six years. For improvement purposes, the look back will be shorter, probably just two to four years.

Use Specific Examples, Not Generalities, to Illustrate Points
Instead of saying, "I attended a faculty development seminar," it is better to say, "In fall 2003, I attended a faculty development seminar on teaching using the case method at Harvard University. As a result of attending that seminar I now use the case method of instruction in teaching my Organizational Behavior course."

Seek Coherence Among Portfolio Sections
A well-developed portfolio integrates material from the faculty member, material from others, and the products of student learning. It offers a coherent teaching profile in that all parts support the whole. For example, the philosophy of teaching outlines a professor's belief in active learning. The methodology section describes how that philosophy is implemented in the classroom. Student rating forms would include a question or two relating to the student perspective on the faculty member's effectiveness in using active learning. And peer observers would comment on that effectiveness from their perspective.

Explain the Evidence in the Portfolio
Unexplained evidence is difficult for readers to understand and interpret. For example, two course syllabi from different years provide evidence of instructional change over time. But the significance of the change and why it took place are not apparent. That is why the addition of a commentary explaining why specific changes were made as well as the impact of those changes on student learning provides more convincing evidence of the professor's efforts to improve instruction.

Enhance the Student Evaluation Section
A graph or chart is an effective and interesting way to present student rating results. Be sure to include the number of students, course titles, and all core questions on the student rating form. (Core questions are looked at more closely than others by members of personnel committees.) Highlight the key

questions in the narrative section and refer readers to the appendix for complete student evaluation results.

Limit the Number of Student Comments

Some professors assume that the more favorable student comments they include, the better. But that is a mistaken assumption. In truth, just two or three student comments are sufficient, but be sure the comments are specific and are tied to the professor's methodology. For example, "The Socratic Method used by Professor Smith was very effective in engaging us in the material."

Include Names and Positions of People to Whom You Refer

If reference is made to a peer observation report or to an outstanding student achievement, be sure to include the name and position of that person. For example, "My department colleague, Harold Babb, professor of psychology, observed my Abnormal Psychology class on October 10, 2003. His report appears in Appendix B." Another example: "Lisa Stamatelos, a student in my Research Methods course during fall 2003, presented a poster session on Changing Practices in Business Survey Techniques at the 2003 annual meeting of the Academy of Management in Atlanta, Georgia."

Number the Pages in the Portfolio

Though this may seem self-evident, my experience as a mentor of more than 500 faculty members as they prepared their portfolios proved otherwise. Numbering pages is just as important in a teaching portfolio as it is in a student term paper.

Make Bulky Portfolio Items Available Upon Request

Some items—videotapes, large photographs, sculptures, musical scores—don't lend themselves to being placed in an appendix because they are unwieldy or too large and can be easily lost. For that reason, it is suggested that if the appendices contain nonprint materials or items that do not fit within the portfolio cover, such as supplementary descriptions, diskettes, or video/audiotapes, the faculty member may briefly discuss these materials in the narrative and make them available for inspection upon request.

Use a Three-Ring Binder With Tabs for Appendices

A binder is a useful and inexpensive way to secure material and makes it easy to add or delete items. The tabs serve to organize and neatly separate the appendix sections.

Gaining Acceptance of the Portfolio Approach

Some professors resist the portfolio approach. They say that they are not comfortable as self-promoters, that they have neither the time nor the desire to reflect on their teaching or to keep a record of their classroom achievements. But these concerns can be disposed of by pointing out that this is an age of accountability, and professors must produce better evidence of their teaching contribution. They also need to convey those accomplishments clearly and persuasively for third party inspection.

If the portfolio is ultimately to be embraced, an institutional climate of acceptance must first be created. How can that be done?

- The portfolio approach must be presented in a candid, complete, and clear way to every faculty member and academic administrator.

- Faculty members must have a significant role in developing and running the portfolio program. They must feel, with justification, that they "own" the program.

- The primary purpose of the portfolio program should be the improvement of teaching.

- If portfolios are used for tenure or promotion decisions, all professors must know the criteria and standards by which portfolios will be evaluated. Those who evaluate portfolios must also know the criteria and standards and must abide by them.

- It is wise to allow for individual differences in portfolio development. Disciplines differ. So do teaching styles.

- The portfolio approach should not be forced on anyone. It's better to use faculty volunteers.

- Top-level academic administrators must give their active support to the portfolio concept. They must be publicly committed to the program and provide the needed resources to assure that it operates efficiently.

- Allow sufficient time—a year, even two years—for acceptance and implementation. Use the time to modify techniques and standards, but keep moving forward.

5

Answers to Common Questions About the Teaching Portfolio

In the time I've been working with teaching portfolios, I have visited hundreds of colleges and universities of differing sizes and missions to talk with faculty members and administrators about the portfolio and its place in the evaluation and improvement of teaching. In the course of our discussions, certain questions have come up repeatedly. Those questions and my answers to them follow.

How does the teaching portfolio differ from the usual end-of-the-year faculty report to administrators?

First, the portfolio empowers faculty to include the documents and materials that they feel best reflects their performance in the classroom and is not limited just to items posed by administrators. Second, the portfolio is based on collaboration and mentoring, rather than being prepared by faculty working alone. Third, the purpose of the portfolio determines what is included and how it is arranged. Fourth, in the very preparation of the portfolio professors reflect on *why* they do *what* they do in the classroom. For many faculty—almost as a byproduct—this reflection results in improved teaching performance.

Is the portfolio restricted to traditional classroom teaching?

Not at all. The word *teaching* signifies all professional activity that provides direct support for student learning. That includes not only traditional classroom and laboratory teaching, but also instruction in computer laboratories and small-group settings, one-to-one teacher-student interactions, student advising, and the scholarship of teaching and communication of its results.

Don't all portfolios look alike?

Absolutely not. The portfolio is a highly personalized product. Both the content and organization differ widely from one professor to another. Varying importance is assigned by different professors to different items (see the sample portfolios in Part IV of this volume). Different courses and disciplines cater to different types of documentation. Individual differences in portfolio content and organization should be encouraged so long as they are allowed by the department and institution.

How long is the typical portfolio?

It has a narrative of seven to ten pages, followed by a series of appendices that document the claims made in the narrative. Often a three-ring binder holds the portfolio, and tabs identify the different appendices. Just as information in the narrative should be selective, so should the appendices consist of judiciously chosen evidence.

How much time does it take to prepare?

Most faculty members construct the portfolio in 12 to 15 hours spread over several days. Much of that time is spent in thinking, planning, and gathering the documentation for the appendices.

Who owns the portfolio?

The portfolio is owned by the faculty member who prepares it. Decisions about what goes into it are generally cooperative ones between mentor and professor. But the final decision on what to include, its ultimate use, and retention of the final product all rest with the professor.

Why are portfolio mentors so important?

Most faculty come to the portfolio process with no prior experience with the concept. That is why the resources of a trained mentor are so important. The mentor—who is comparable to a dissertation advisor—makes suggestions, provides resources, and offers steady support during the portfolio's development.

Should the mentor be from the same discipline as the professor who is preparing the portfolio?

The process of collaboration is *not* discipline specific. In fact, it is often advantageous for the mentor not to know the details of the teaching content. In that way, the mentor can concentrate on documenting teaching effectiveness instead of how the professor teaches a particular subject. And a wonderful byproduct of working with a colleague from a different discipline is that the mentor learns something about a new field.

Is there a way to self-mentor if there are no trained mentors available?

Although it is strongly recommended that portfolios be developed collaboratively, sometimes there are no willing and able mentors available. In that case, even though the important collaborative aspect of portfolio development will be lost, it is still possible to prepare a portfolio. The following self-assessment questions identified by Eison (1996) and Seldin (2003) may help.

- Is every claim made in the narrative supported by hard evidence in the appendices?

- Is the portfolio sufficiently reflective? Does it include a balance of items from oneself, from others, and from student learning?

- Does the portfolio clearly identify *what* you teach, *how* you teach it, and *why* you teach it as you do?

- Is a complete table of contents and appendices included?

- Does the portfolio contain reflective observations?

- Have efforts at growth and improvement been cited?

- Are numerical student rating results included for several courses over several years?

- Have any department or institutional factors influenced your teaching effectiveness?

- Would including some charts, tables, or graphs enhance the portfolio?

Is the syllabus actually inserted into the portfolio? Are student ratings? Peer observations?

These normally appear as appendices. But specific references to them are included in the body of the portfolio. For example, "Copies of my syllabi for all courses taught are found in Appendix A." For student ratings and peer observations, a slightly different approach is recommended: Place the actual material in the appendices but include some highlights of that material in the body of the portfolio. Figure 5.1 offers an example.

FIGURE 5.1

Highlights of Student Ratings in the Body of the Portfolio

My student ratings are consistently higher than the Department of History average. For the fall 2003 semester, the 22 students in my history course on the Civil War (History 322) rated my teaching as follows:

Questions	Dept. Average	My Score
Explains clearly	4.10	4.35
Stimulates student interest	3.98	4.10
Interesting assignments	3.99	4.22
Motivates students	4.23	4.28
Overall course quality	4.21	4.34
Overall instructor quality	4.33	4.41

Scale: one is low and five is high

Doesn't the subjectivity of the portfolio interfere with its use for personnel decisions or improvement of teaching?

Surprisingly, it doesn't because of the collaboration between a professor and a mentor who helps steer the portfolio toward meeting the needs of assessment or improvement. Collaboration ensures a fresh, vital, and critical perspective that encourages cohesion between the portfolio's narrative and appendices. The mentor's task is to flesh out objective data, provide balance and control, and corroborate evidence. That's why faculty are urged to enlist the creative and supportive help of a mentor in preparing a portfolio.

Can an impressive looking portfolio gloss over weak teaching?

Absolutely not because the portfolio is an evidence-based document. Supporting material must be included for every claim made. If a faculty member is weak in teaching, the evidence is just not available. For example, an instructor who claims that student evaluations rate class preparation as "outstanding" must provide numerical rating data that bear out this statement. Another example: An instructor who claims that a department chair rated his or her teaching as "exemplary" must provide substantive evidence to support that claim. A fancy cover and attractive printer fonts cannot overcome weak performance in the classroom for a professor any more than they can for a student.

What guidelines would you suggest for getting started with portfolios?
A climate of acceptance must first be built at the college or university. Here are some suggestions that should be helpful in doing so:

- Start small.

- Rely on faculty volunteers and don't force anyone to participate.

- Involve the institution's most respected faculty members from the outset.

- Obtain top-level administrative support for the portfolio approach and an institutional commitment for the necessary resources.

- Keep everyone informed about what is going on every step of the way.

- Allow room for individual differences in portfolios. Styles of teaching differ. So do disciplines.

- Permit sufficient time—a year, or even two—for acceptance and implementation.

Are the time and energy required to prepare a portfolio really worth the benefits?
In my view, and in the view of virtually every one of the 500 faculty members I've personally mentored as they prepared their portfolios, the answer is a resounding yes. It usually takes no more than a few days to prepare, and the benefits are considerable. The teaching portfolio allows professors to describe their teaching strengths and accomplishments for the record, a clear advantage when evaluation committees examine the record in making promotion and tenure decisions. But the portfolio does more than that. Many faculty members find that the very process of collecting and sorting documents and materials that reflect their teaching performance serves as a springboard for self-improvement. And, importantly, many colleges and universities find that portfolios help to underscore teaching as an institutional priority.

It is estimated that as many as 2,000 colleges and universities in the United States are now using or experimenting with portfolios. Considering the above benefits, it's not surprising that the teaching portfolio has proven to be one of the most popular and successful approaches in years.

The key to developing successful teaching portfolio programs is to proceed slowly, carefully, openly, and to lay the groundwork for each step. Success does not come automatically, but it comes. The proof is in the many successful programs operating around the country.

Part I: Appendices

Each of the following resources has been field-tested and adjusted for workability. They are intended to provide practical help in developing, maintaining, and evaluating teaching portfolios.

Appendix 1, developed at the University of Iowa, is a graphic organizer that puts the essential elements of a portfolio onto one page.

Appendix 2, developed at Texas A&M University, provides an overview of the topics addressed by portfolios. It also includes a suggested means of documentation and a set of questions that serve as reflective cues.

Appendix 3 is a checklist of general items for evaluating teaching portfolios. Developed at Columbia College, it provides specific guidelines for academic administrators and members of tenure and promotion committees for evaluating teaching from portfolios.

APPENDIX 1
Elements of the Teaching Portfolio

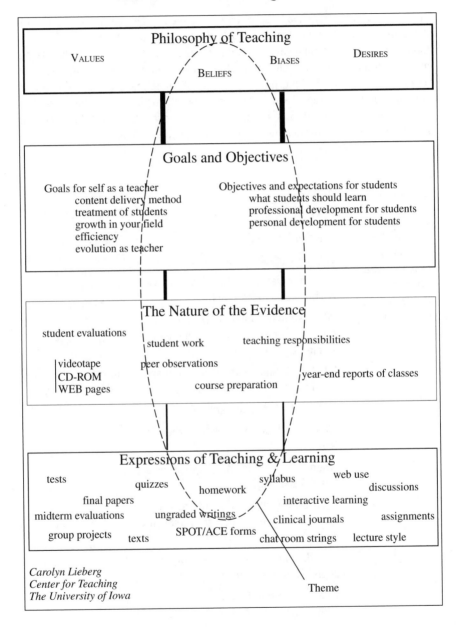

Philosophy of Teaching

VALUES   BELIEFS   BIASES   DESIRES

Goals and Objectives

Goals for self as a teacher
content delivery method
treatment of students
growth in your field
efficiency
evolution as teacher

Objectives and expectations for students
what students should learn
professional development for students
personal development for students

The Nature of the Evidence

student evaluations

student work   teaching responsibilities

videotape
CD-ROM
WEB pages

peer observations

course preparation

year-end reports of classes

Expressions of Teaching & Learning

tests   quizzes   homework   syllabus   web use   discussions
final papers   interactive learning
midterm evaluations   ungraded writings   clinical journals   assignments
group projects   texts   SPOT/ACE forms   chatroom strings   lecture style

Carolyn Lieberg
Center for Teaching
The University of Iowa

Theme

Appendix 2

Teaching Portfolio Reflection Process Guide

The teaching portfolio is made up of two components: 1) a narrative description of teaching, eight to ten pages in length, double spaced, and 2) a set of appendices containing information (artifacts of teaching) that support the claims made in the narrative. The following table provides an overview of the topics to be addressed in the teaching portfolio, a list of reflection cues to assist you in thinking about each topic, and suggestions for supporting documentation. This information is not intended as a template for portfolio production, but rather as a catalyst for your reflection and a framework for the process.

Reflection Topics	Reflection Cues	Process Documentation
Philosophy of learning and teaching that drives your classroom performance.	Why am I a teacher? Why do I teach the way I do? What motivated me to select a career path that includes teaching? What is my personal definition of a great teacher and what experience formed that definition? What do I believe about learning and teaching? How do I approach learning? What does learning look like when it happens? When learning does not happen, what has gone wrong? What do I want my students to know and be able to do when they leave my course? How do I hope that students are changed by experiencing my course? What do I want students to wonder about as a result of taking my course?	A description of materials that have helped to form your beliefs about teaching and learning. Materials that demonstrate growth and change in your thinking about teaching and learning.

Reflection Topics	Reflection Cues	Process Documentation
	Why do I choose the teaching strategies/methods that I use?	
	Why do I select particular assignments/experiences for my students?	
	What synonyms for "teacher" would accurately describe what I believe myself to be, or what I would like to be, for my students?	
Context and description of your courses.	What do I teach?	List of course titles, numbers, credit hours, and enrollments.
	How long have I been teaching?	
	What are the learning objectives of the courses I teach?	Record of supervision of honors or graduate courses.
	What level(s) are the students (undergraduate/graduate)?	
	How many students?	Course goals and objectives.
	Required/elective?	Course curriculum.
	Majors/nonmajors?	
	Do I supervise teaching assistants?	Articulation with other courses.
	Do I chair or serve on graduate committees?	
Your choices of methodologies/ strategies for learning and teaching.	How do I teach?	Course planning and teaching materials.
	What do I do in the classroom/outside the classroom?	
	What do I ask students to do in the classroom/outside the classroom?	Course materials prepared for students.
	What guidance do I give my students?	
	What kind of feedback do I give my students?	Examples of student assignments, projects, etc.
	How do I assess my students' learning?	Examples of exams.
	What do I ask my students to read?	Examples of feedback to students.
	What do I ask my students to do with what they read?	

Reflection Topics	Reflection Cues	Process Documentation
	What do I ask my students to write?	
	What do I ask them to do with what they write?	
	What kind of course materials do I prepare?	
	What kind(s) of exams do I give?	
Other activities that support/inform learning and teaching.	Outside of my actual classroom teaching, what do I do that is related to teaching?	Evidence of effectiveness working with students outside the classroom.
	Advising?	
	Textbook editing/consulting?	Evidence of other teaching-related activities.
	Serving on curriculum committees?	
	Presenter/facilitator for teaching workshops?	
	Mentoring?	
	Continuing education activities?	
Efforts to assess and improve learning and teaching effectiveness.	What do I know about my teaching effectiveness and how do I know it?	Student evaluation results.
	What do I know about how well my students are learning and how do I know it?	Peer observation/ evaluation reports.
		Midsemester evaluation results.
	Am I reaching all of my students or just the ones who learn the way I do?	Periodic one-minute evaluation results.
	Am I sensitive to differences (ability, culture, ethnicity, gender, learning styles, race, etc.) that may have an impact on learning in my classroom?	Course goals/ objectives and student performance.
	Do I need to update my course to reflect current research on learning?	Response to evaluation results.
	If I overheard my students talking about my class, what would I want them to be saying?	Participation in teaching improvement activities.
	What would they be saying?	

Reflection Topics	Reflection Cues	Process Documentation
	What, specifically, do I want to improve about my teaching?	Evidence of use of multiple teaching methods and strategies.
	What are my short-term and long-term goals with regard to improvement of my teaching?	
		Evidence of growth and change in teaching.
	What steps am I taking (or have I taken) to improve my teaching?	Pre-post tests/ attitude surveys.
	Where do I go from here?	Unsolicited letters regarding your teaching.
		Election/appointment to teaching committee.
		Honors or awards received for teaching.
		Exit interviews/ alumni testimonials regarding teaching.

Created by Jean E. L. Layne, Nancy J. Simpson, and Liz Miller, Center for Teaching Excellence, Texas A&M University. Reproduce only with appropriate attribution.

APPENDIX 3

Checklist for the Evaluation of Teaching Portfolios

✔ Does the portfolio include current information?

✔ Does the portfolio balance information from self, from others, and from products of student learning?

✔ Is there coherence among the various components of the portfolio, revealing demonstrated effectiveness in practice tied to an articulate philosophy?

✔ Does the portfolio demonstrate teaching consistent with departmental and institutional strategic priorities and missions?

✔ What constitutes valid documentation and evidence?

✔ Are multiple, selective sources of information included, offering a diverse and objective assessment of teaching?

✔ Does the portfolio adequately supplement narrative description, analysis, and goals with empirical evidence in the appendix?

✔ How clearly and specifically does the portfolio reveal the relevance of professional development, research, and scholarship to the teaching enterprise?

✔ Does the portfolio include a core of agreed-upon seminal statements with accompanying evidence? Are the core elements of the portfolio derived from disciplinary, departmental, and institutional standards?

✔ Do products or outcomes of student learning reveal successful teaching?

✔ Does the portfolio provide evidence of efforts to improve teaching? Is there evidence of improvement in methods, materials, evaluations, goals?

✔ Is the portfolio the *only* source of information on teaching effectiveness? Or is it complemented by additional materials and corroborative information about a professor's complex and varied roles?

✔ How does the portfolio profile individual style, achievements, discipline? Is a strong case made in both narrative and documentation in the appendix for the complexity and individuality of a professor's particular teaching effort in a particular discipline with a particular group of students?

✔ Does the portfolio meet established length requirements?

✔ Do evaluators understand and value how and why portfolios are used and know the strengths and limitations of portfolios?

John Zubizarreta
Columbia College

Part II

ELECTRONIC TEACHING PORTFOLIOS

6

Making Good Work Public Through Electronic Teaching Portfolios

Susan Kahn

Web-based electronic teaching portfolios are a logical step in the development of teaching portfolios. Electronic media can enhance the ability of teaching portfolios to provide rich representations of college teaching and learning and can fulfill several other important purposes:

- If teaching portfolios are intended, in part, to make teaching public—to open the classroom door—then placing them on the web makes them even more accessible to peers and others than paper-based portfolios.

- If teaching portfolios aim to capture the complexity of teaching and to bring greater transparency to it through the use of authentic work samples, then the capabilities of electronic technologies dramatically expand the range of authentic work available for inclusion. For example, the written work typically found in paper portfolios can be supplemented by audio, video, and graphical materials to provide an even clearer window into teaching and learning. In addition, online teaching and learning can be represented.

- The structure and capabilities of the web have the potential to support the formative aspects of teaching portfolios. As a portfolio developer creates hyperlinks, menus, and other navigational tools, as well as hierarchical arrangements of information and materials, the process, which is quite different from that of creating a linear paper document, can stimulate new thinking, perspectives, and insights. And the availability of multimedia—for example, video clips of a class session—provides a rich set of materials on which to base reflection.

I will discuss later the advantages—and pitfalls—of electronic teaching portfolios and strategies for developing them. But first, let me turn to a brief overview of current thinking on this relatively new genre of portfolios in higher education.

MAKING TEACHING PUBLIC FOR PEER REVIEW AND COLLECTIVE LEARNING

Any teaching portfolio stored on and accessed through electronic media, such as the Internet or a CD-ROM, qualifies as an electronic teaching portfolio. Many electronic portfolios consist simply of a set of documents, much like those that would be included in a paper portfolio, posted to the World Wide Web and organized around a table of contents whose items are hyperlinked to sets of relevant information and materials. While such portfolios do not fully exploit the capabilities of electronic technologies, they are relatively easy to develop and available to readers who may not have access to the latest hardware and software.

Most important, by placing a teaching portfolio on the web, a faculty member takes a crucial step toward making his or her work public and available for others to comment on and learn from. Lee Shulman (1993) has long argued that routinely making the work of teaching public—making teaching community property, susceptible to peer review—is crucial to elevating the status of teaching and gaining wider acceptance of teaching as a form of scholarship. In a recent essay on online course portfolios, Thomas Hatch (2000) notes that as more faculty make representations of their teaching publicly available via the web,

> *we will have increasing opportunities to look across the experiences of many different teachers working in many different disciplines and contexts, to generalize from those experiences, and to develop, explore, and challenge new ideas and theories about teaching and learning. (p. 10)*

Shulman and Hatch's comments speak to a paradigm shift in our thinking about the nature and process of faculty improvement. Dan Tompkins (2001) describes this shift as a movement toward "a new model . . . emphasizing peer collaboration and shared knowledge" (p. 94). For Tompkins, electronic teaching portfolios support this shift because their accessibility, interactivity, and transparency allow for dialogue and collective learning that ultimately lead to improved pedagogies: "Web-based work enables us to move from 'capturing and documenting' to 'sharing, collaborating, and benefiting,' from viewing to participating" (p. 104).

Indeed, some portfolio developers explicitly intend to make their work public so that other teachers can learn from it. Dennis Jacobs, a chemistry professor at the University of Notre Dame, created an online course portfolio partly for the purpose of helping other faculty members who might be interested in implementing the cooperative learning approach he uses in their own courses (Hatch, 2000). His portfolio is available at http://kml2.carnegiefoundation.org/gallery/djacobs/.

One current national project, Peer Review of Teaching, led by Dan Bernstein at the University of Nebraska–Lincoln, aims to advance the use of online teaching portfolios as vehicles for peer review and learning from others' experiences with teaching. Project participants have created online course portfolios that are accessible for purposes of peer review, and are intended, more broadly, to foster "a community of scholars who write about the intellectual work involved in their teaching and who share that writing with interested colleagues." The overall goal of the project is to "to help faculty become skilled as writers and readers of course portfolios, making these portfolios useful both to those who produce them and those whose teaching can benefit from reading them." More information on the Peer Review of Teaching project can be found at http://www.unl.edu/peerrev/.

Most of the portfolios in the Peer Review of Teaching project are technologically simple, consisting largely of written work and reflection. They are distinguished by their inclusion of generous samples of *assessed* student work to provide evidence of improvements in learning and teaching through successive iterations of a course over time. Bernstein's portfolio (http://www.unl.edu/peerrev/examples/bernstein/index.htm), for example, shows us an excellent example of a feedback loop in action: He describes a desired learning outcome for his psychology course, assesses for that outcome, makes changes based on the results of assessment, and continues to evaluate and refine based on the impact of those changes on student learning. Figures 6.1, 6.2, and 6.3 are sample pages from Dan Bernstein's online course portfolio. This is a technologically simple portfolio that relies on written media and clear organization to make its points.

USING THE WEB TO MAKE TEACHING TRANSPARENT

Portfolios that exploit the multimedia and linking capabilities of electronic environments can provide an especially full, authentic representation of teaching and learning and can generate new opportunities for learning

FIGURE 6.1

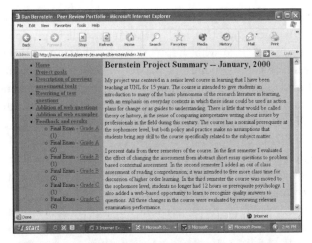

FIGURE 6.2

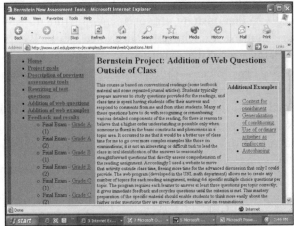

FIGURE 6.3

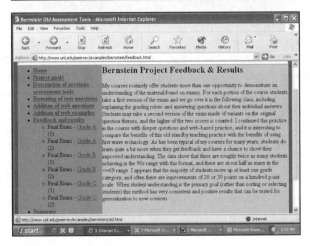

about teaching for both portfolio developers and readers. The use of video, audio, graphics, and other tools makes it possible to give portfolio reviewers a clear window into what happens in the classroom. Video clips tracing changes in a faculty member's classroom practices over time, for example, can directly display the evolution of those practices, supplying powerful evidence of improvement, especially in combination with authentic examples of syllabi, assignments, student work, displays of aggregated data, and reflection. William Cerbin, who developed one of the earliest online course portfolios, puts it this way: "It's just common sense that if you want people to understand a complex activity or performance, you *show* it to them" (personal communication, March 21, 2003).

Dennis Jacobs's course portfolio (http://kml2.carnegiefoundation.org/gallery/djacobs/), developed in conjunction with the Carnegie Foundation's Knowledge Media Laboratory, provides one example of the effective use of multimedia to demonstrate improvements in student learning in a general chemistry course at the University of Notre Dame. Poor performance and high attrition rates for the course, especially among students deemed at-risk, led Jacobs to experiment with implementing cooperative learning in his sections of the class. His portfolio includes segments on the rationale for the redesigned class, the implementation of the redesign, the impact of the changes on student learning and retention in the course and the major, and a site library. Within these sections are examples of assignments, video clips of students engaged in cooperative learning, and aggregated data that demonstrate improvement in student learning and retention. Figures 6.4, 6.5, and 6.6 are some sample pages from Dennis Jacobs's course portfolio. Notice how he presents specific examples of student learning (in the video clips), along with aggregated data on the outcomes of the course. The video clips are introduced with discussion of exactly what they are intended to illustrate.

A video introduction to the site shows Jacobs explaining and reflecting on the redesigned course and displays data that support his main points. In a written reflection, Jacobs notes that development of the portfolio, and, in particular, the use of videotapes of students at work, has "provided invaluable feedback on the types of assigned problems and questions that promote meaningful group discussion." As a result of Jacobs's experiment and his documentation of increased student success, Notre Dame's Department of Chemistry has now adopted his cooperative learning model for all sections of the general chemistry course.

FIGURE 6.4

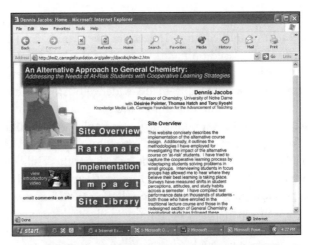

FIGURE 6.5

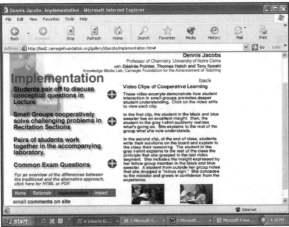

FIGURE 6.6

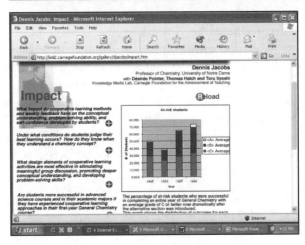

Another strength of electronic teaching portfolios is their ability to display online teaching and learning. Indeed, as Dan Tompkins (2001) has noted, course materials placed online can comprise the beginnings of an electronic course or teaching portfolio; similarly, student work completed online in various formats can supply ready-made evidence of student learning, provided that such work is organized and presented so that portfolio readers see clearly what ideas or outcomes it is intended to exemplify. A collection of course portfolios (or virtual posters) focused on technology-based and technology-enhanced courses can be found at the web site of the Visible Knowledge Project (VKP) at Georgetown University (http://crossroads.georgetown.edu/vkp/index.htm). Directed by Randy Bass of Georgetown University and Bret Eynon of LaGuardia Community College, the project aims to identify effective practices for integrating technology into teaching and learning. The VKP course portfolios bring together experiences with teaching and technology and related reflections of faculty members from colleges and universities across the country. Taken together, they supply a fount of good ideas for other professors involved in online teaching and learning.

USING THE WEB TO PROMPT NEW PERSPECTIVES ON TEACHING AND LEARNING

It is fascinating to consider whether the nonlinear, hyperlinked structure of the web can itself lead to new perspectives and insights for developers of online course portfolios. Comments from several faculty members who have created such portfolios suggest that representing their teaching and their students' learning on the web has indeed begun to prompt such new ways of thinking. For example, Elizabeth Barkley (2001), a professor of music at Foothill College, believes that developing a portfolio for the web presents both challenges and advantages to someone "accustomed to thinking in the linear mode of print media" (p. 112). Among the advantages she cites of constructing a web-based portfolio is that the process "forced me to think in the digital and visual ways that I believe dominate many of my students' ways of seeing and knowing. Narrowing the gap between us must certainly help clarify communication and enrich their learning" (p. 122).

Taking a somewhat different tack, Mills Kelly (2001), a history professor at George Mason University, argues that building a portfolio on the web deepened his thinking about teaching:

> *I had to make many decisions about look and feel, about navigation, about inclusion or exclusion of information, and about*

which media to use to make a certain point. As I worked my way through each question, I had to think much more deeply about my own discipline, about what the scholarship of teaching and learning is or is becoming, and about the multiple audiences for my work and how it might resonate with them. (p. 127)

But not all faculty members who create teaching portfolios for the web agree that the web aspect of their work in itself influenced their thinking about teaching and learning. It may be that we have not yet fully developed the tools, templates, and technological capacities for electronic teaching portfolios that enable the new perspectives that Barkley and Kelly report. I will come back to this topic later, but now I turn to some challenges and guidelines for creators of electronic teaching portfolios.

CHALLENGES FOR DEVELOPERS OF ELECTRONIC TEACHING PORTFOLIOS

This chapter has already had a great deal to say about the advantages and potential of electronic teaching portfolios to improve teaching and help others understand what occurs in the real or virtual classroom. But electronic teaching portfolios also have potential pitfalls and certainly present significant challenges to their creators. In this section, I discuss three major challenges and issues for developers of electronic teaching portfolios: information overload, technology, and copyright and privacy issues.

Information Overload

Perhaps the biggest challenge for creators of electronic teaching portfolios is the danger of overwhelming readers with excessive, badly organized, or uninterpreted information. Seldin (1997); Edgerton, Hutchings, and Quinlan (1991); and other writers on teaching portfolios have long emphasized the importance of careful selection and editing of materials included in a portfolio. Too many of us have found ourselves confronted with the task of evaluating teaching portfolios that include a mountain of repetitious, disorganized materials whose significance to the portfolio or to teaching and learning is never discussed.

The electronic environment, with its ability to store and link to vast quantities of information, magnifies this perennial challenge and adds the danger of poorly thought out navigation through materials. Dan Tompkins (2001) points out that "paper and electronic portfolios alike invite faculty to pile data on a problem" (p. 103), and advises portfolio developers that "careful editing . . . and careful development of pathways through information in electronic portfolios aid readers in making sense of information" (pp. 103–104). One might add that careful editing of information and development of electronic pathways aid the creators of portfolios as well. The deliberate selection of materials and the representation of relationships and linkages among those materials are part of what can make developing an electronic teaching portfolio a potentially powerful, even transformative, learning experience for the developer.

Elizabeth Barkley (2001) agrees on the importance of brevity in electronic teaching portfolios, but also wonders whether "this constant distilling for near 'sound bite' simplicity sacrifices significant depth, accuracy, and nuance" (p. 121). Ultimately, the portfolio developer must find the right balance for his or her purposes. Before making an electronic teaching portfolio public or submitting it to people whose evaluations will have important consequences for the portfolio developer, it is wise to familiarize oneself with principles of good practice in web design and to do some user testing of the portfolio with readers willing to comment frankly. Some resources on web design are listed at the end of this chapter, while the following section on "Getting Started" includes advice on selection of materials and information.

Technology

Many—perhaps most—faculty members have not yet had experience with developing materials in electronic formats. Fortunately, more and more colleges and universities are providing help to faculty in developing web sites related to their teaching, while web authoring programs are becoming increasingly simple to use. Your institution may even have created its own in-house web platform or customized a commercial platform, like Blackboard or WebCT, for faculty and students, so that you need very little knowledge of web programming to start an electronic portfolio web site. If you are new to creating materials for the web, try to take advantage of any available assistance on your campus and begin with a technologically simple portfolio built on a platform with the capacity to accommodate a variety of media as your expertise and available web tools continue to develop.

Copyright and Privacy Issues

Authentic examples of student work, properly contextualized, can provide the most compelling evidence for learning and effective teaching. Indeed, some experts argue that such examples are essential components of any teaching portfolio (see, for example, Cambridge, 2001; Tompkins, 2001). But publishing students' work on the web presents legal issues related to copyright and privacy concerns. A few institutions have even been known to insist on Institutional Review Board review for student work included in web portfolios.

Check with your institution's office of research compliance and its legal staff before placing student work on a portfolio web site open to the public. Chances are that they will ask you to have students sign a simple permission form agreeing to have their work posted to the web. Several institutions, including Indiana University–Purdue University Indianapolis and Portland State University, have developed models for such forms that can be easily adapted to the needs of other campuses.

Getting Started

Given all of the issues that might be addressed and types of materials that might be included in an electronic teaching portfolio, getting started can be a daunting task. It may be helpful, when beginning to plan an electronic teaching portfolio, to think of the choices of materials and strategies in the same way one would think about a paper portfolio. For example, as Tompkins (2001) points out, an electronic teaching portfolio generally includes materials from oneself, materials from others, and products of one's teaching, just as a paper portfolio would. Processes and strategies include collection, selection, and reflection, just as they would for a paper portfolio. The difference, of course, is that in an electronic portfolio, the choices of materials that might be included are much broader, especially for faculty members interested in using multimedia to represent their teaching and their students' learning. And the processes of collection, selection, and reflection may include developing video/audiotapes and gathering samples of other materials in nonwritten media.

Planning for an electronic teaching portfolio begins with several key questions:

- What are the purposes of the portfolio and who is the audience?

- Given these purposes and audience, what main themes or categories of information should the portfolio focus on?

- What contents best fit these purposes and communicates about these themes to the audience? How should this content be organized?

Audiences and Purposes

As is the case for paper-based teaching portfolios, the audience for and purpose of the portfolio will influence its themes, contents, and organization. A portfolio intended to document teaching for tenure and promotion or for a teaching award may be differently organized and present different materials than a portfolio aimed at exploring a teaching and learning dilemma or at informing peers about teaching practices. Succinctly defining the purpose of and audience for an electronic portfolio at the outset will provide a framework to guide all subsequent decisions about themes, content, and organization.

Themes

The themes of the portfolio should flow from its purposes. The selected themes will dictate not only the contents of the portfolio, but can provide an organizing framework for the portfolio web site, with sections of the site devoted to each major theme.

As with paper portfolios, themes can be conceptualized in any number of ways. Some of the course portfolios discussed in this chapter are organized, speaking very generally, around defining a teaching or learning issue or problem, describing and demonstrating an approach to the issue, describing and demonstrating the results or impact of the approach, and reflecting on or interpreting these outcomes. Another approach, often seen in electronic student portfolios as well, is to organize the portfolio around a set of goals and objectives, either for teaching or for student learning. Helen Barrett (2001) calls a portfolio based on learning outcomes a "standards-based" portfolio, and notes that such a portfolio "uses hypertext links to organize the materials, connecting artifacts to appropriate goals or standards" (p. 110).

With growing numbers of web-based teaching portfolios available for examination by anyone with Internet access, it makes sense to study existing examples for ideas about different organizing themes for one's own portfolio. A list of web sites that include collections of electronic teaching portfolios can be found at the end of this chapter. Figures 6.7, 6.8, and 6.9 are examples of the front pages of several online portfolios. Notice how these pages visually represent the organization and contents of the entire portfolio.

Contents and Organization of an Electronic Teaching Portfolio

As noted above, the contents of an electronic teaching portfolio fall into categories similar to those that characterize paper portfolios: materials from oneself, materials from others, and products of one's teaching. In an electronic portfolio, any of these categories might include multimedia materials that help portfolio readers to see authentic teaching and learning in action. Electronic portfolios on the web can also, of course, link to other relevant web sites—course web sites or other sites maintained by the developer of the portfolio, departmental or institutional sites with information that provides useful context for information in the portfolio itself, or sites related to the discipline or to teaching and learning issues raised in the portfolio.

FIGURE 6.7

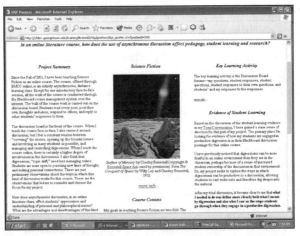

FIGURE 6.8

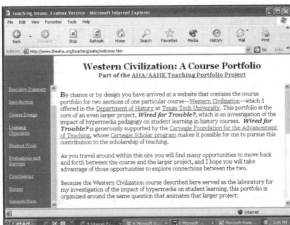

FIGURE 6.9

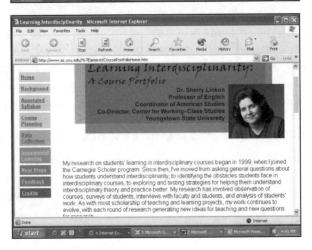

Here are some suggestions for selecting and organizing materials for an electronic teaching portfolio:

- Exercise rigorous selectivity when deciding on materials to include in the portfolio and use appropriate media. For example, video clips should be included *only* when they provide insights not available through other media.

- Web links to sites outside the portfolio should take readers directly to information that is truly relevant and illuminating.

- Be sure to include authentic examples and evidence of student learning; ultimately, it is only through impact on student learning that the effectiveness of teaching can be demonstrated and judged. Take advantage of the capacity of the electronic environment to include multiple examples that represent a range of work authentically, allowing readers to look across a series of activities so that readers can see achievement over a period of time (Cambridge, 2001).

- Explain the significance of each piece of authentic work that is presented, so that readers understand why it is there and what it is intended to tell or to demonstrate. Providing such context for portfolio items helps readers understand teaching and learning outcomes and the explanations for them, as well as the reasons for subsequent changes in teaching approaches (Cambridge, 2001).

- Use hyperlinks to connect desired outcomes with approaches used, assessment rubrics or criteria, relevant examples, and reflection.

- Early in the portfolio development process, create a table of contents, site map, or some other way of visually displaying the structure of the portfolio. A clear structure is of invaluable help to both the creator of an electronic portfolio and its readers. Mills Kelly (2001) comments that "because I spent a fair amount of time at the beginning of the project thinking carefully about what I expected the portfolio to look like, I think in the end it was easier to create than I had expected it to be" (p. 128).

THE FUTURE OF ELECTRONIC TEACHING PORTFOLIOS

The ubiquity of the web, the visibility of several current national projects using electronic teaching portfolios, and the proliferation of new types of electronic portfolios in higher education—student, program, and institutional electronic portfolios, for example—suggest that electronic teaching portfolios will be with us for some time to come. The challenge will be to realize the potential of these portfolios to be a force for improvement for their creators and readers and for higher education generally.

Several experts on electronic teaching portfolios have suggested ways that such portfolios and the electronic tools used to create them might lead to widespread improvement in teaching and learning. William Cerbin, for example, believes that multimedia, especially video, offer "great potential to explore the relationships between teaching and learning." He is especially intrigued by "the use of video to depict what and how students learn in the classroom—not just what the teacher does, but what students get from the experience" (personal communication, March 21, 2003).

Thomas Hatch (2000) of the Carnegie Foundation considers the implications of widespread development of online electronic teaching portfolios and suggests that if such portfolios become commonplace, "it would be possible to go to a college, school or department's Web site and find a wide variety of different views of the teaching and learning taking place there" (p. 4). One could imagine a department, program, or institution pulling information from electronic teaching portfolios into their own unit-level electronic portfolios to demonstrate and illustrate collective faculty efforts to improve teaching and learning and to display the outcomes of such efforts. Such unit-wide portfolios could provide compelling evidence to stakeholders of effective teaching and learning and could be a powerful tool for organizational learning and improvement as well.

Realizing these visions, though, will not be easy. It takes an act of courage for a faculty member to place a teaching portfolio online, open to anyone. Mills Kelly (2001) remarks that such an act "invites the entire world to pass judgment on [his] teaching" (p. 126), and observes that this level of disclosure "is not for everyone" (p. 126). Similarly, it may require a cultural change in the academy to reward those teachers who reveal even those experiments and attempts at improvement that are not initially successful.

Perhaps we need to broaden our notions of what constitutes excellent teaching to include a willingness to experiment with new approaches, to make a candid assessment of the impact of those approaches on student learning and success, and to change or refine accordingly. The growing popularity of electronic teaching portfolios suggests that such a transformation in our ideas about teaching may have already begun. As this change becomes widespread, we can expect to enjoy more and more opportunities to learn from one another's teaching successes and failures alike through online electronic teaching portfolios.

Acknowledgments

The excerpts from the portfolios of Daniel Bernstein, Dennis Jacobs, T. Mills Kelly (his Western Civilization course), and Sherry Lee Linkon are reprinted with permission from the authors and from the Knowledge Media Lab of the Carnegie Foundation for the Advancement of Teaching (http://www.carnegiefoundation.org/KML/).

The excerpt from Joseph Ugoretz's portfolio (the online science fiction course) is reprinted with permission from the author, the Carnegie Foundation Knowledge Media Lab, and Georgetown University's Center for New Designs in Learning and Scholarship (in conjunction with the Visible Knowledge Project at http://crossroads.Georgetown.edu/vkp).

Print Resources on Portfolios and Web Development

Batson, T. (2002, December). The electronic portfolio boom: What's it all about? *Syllabus, 16*(5), 14–18.

Gathercoal, P., Love, D., Bryde, B., & McKean, G. (2002). On implementing web-based electronic portfolios: A webfolio program lets instructors and students use the web to improve teaching and learning. *Educause Quarterly, 25*(2), 29–37.

Hutchings, P. (Ed.). (1998). *The course portfolio: How faculty can examine their teaching to advance practice and improve student learning.* Washington, DC: American Association for Higher Education.

Weinberger, D. (2002). *Small pieces loosely joined: A unified theory of the web.* Cambridge, MA: Perseus.

Electronic Resources on Portfolios and Web Development

American Association for Higher Education Portfolio Clearinghouse: http://www.aahe.org/teaching/portfolio_db.htm

Electronic Portfolio Virtual Community of Practice: http://www.educause.edu/vcop/eport/

The Alertbox: Current Issues in Web Usability by Jakob Nielsen: http://www.useit.com/alertbox/

National Learning Infrastructure Initiative: http://www.educause.edu/nlii/keythemes/eportfolios.asp

Part III

HOW PORTFOLIOS ARE USED
IN SEVEN INSTITUTIONS

Part III describes in detail how seven institutions—public and private, large and small—have implemented teaching portfolios.

The reports are arranged in alphabetical order by institution. Because each college or university is unique, the purposes and practices reported vary considerably. Some institutions use portfolios for personnel decisions, others for improvement, and still others for a combination of purposes. The full range of portfolio purposes and practices can best be understood and appreciated by reading all of the institutional reports.

7

The Teaching Portfolio Program at Drexel University

Teck-Kah Lim

GENESIS

Since the spring of 1999, more than 80 faculty members at Drexel University have participated in workshops to develop teaching portfolios. To fully understand how that came about and what stimulated the genesis of the Teaching Portfolio Program at this institution it is essential to recount the distressing sequence of events that befell this urban technological university in the decade preceding.

Founded in 1891, it began as the Drexel Institute of Art, Science, and Industry. By the early 1980s, at the end of the term of its longest serving president, it had progressed, if fitfully, from its simple foundations into a full-fledged university with aspirations to become a Carnegie I research university. Regrettably, the new management made some questionable moves in a period of challenging demographics: a declining high school population. These culminated in a revolving door of presidents; six made it to that office over a period of 12 years. The struggles in the top job were shadowed by a dismaying and precipitous drop in enrollment. Faculty hiring was frozen, and student retention rates plumbed depths never before seen.

Fortunately, after these missteps, the institution righted itself when the current president, a charismatic and dynamic former engineering dean came on board in 1995. By 1997, it was clear that the university's finances had stabilized, and undergraduate enrollment would return to earlier levels. The task turned from striving to survive to plotting the university's resumption of its climb to join the top-tier institutions.

Immediately, it became transparent that the institution was now saddled with a large corps of graying faculty who would have to be reinvigorated to shoulder the burden of teaching the once-again growing student body. Originally recruited for their research expertise during the expansionist 1970s, many were now less active in research and had undeveloped teaching skills. Thus, in 1998, the university decided to tackle head-on the faculty renewal imperative to avoid repeating history in what is still a "tuition-driven" institution and launched a post-tenure review (PTR) process that is both formative and developmental. It promulgated a new workload policy for all faculty so that those who are not research-active will be accorded more satisfactory evaluations and hence be eligible to receive larger raises if they willingly take on a heavier teaching responsibility and teach their courses well.

The university sought and found volunteers for a PTR pilot project that was funded in part by a grant from the American Association for Higher Education (AAHE). The first cohort of participants, according to the university's assessment of need, were mainly senior faculty interested in shifting workload emphasis from research to teaching, and were professedly open to learning about student learning styles and varied modes of instruction.

It was decided early on that the PTR team would attend AAHE's conference on Faculty Roles and Rewards, participating in selected workshops and interacting with peers from other institutions. A linchpin of the project's mandatory activities was to be campus workshops and training experiences organized by the Office of the Provost. These would be thrown open to all faculty so that those involved in the PTR process would not be stigmatized as the "deficients." Realizing that new faculty hires would benefit as well, and hoping to kill two birds with one stone, the associate provost and dean of undergraduate affairs decided she would cajole them into attending these events by stressing the increasing emphasis on teaching in the rewards system at Drexel.

During the first year, there was one workshop that involved the hands-on construction of teaching portfolios. Long used at other U.S. colleges, primarily teaching oriented, these had never before been considered at Drexel. Given the institution's present circumstances and the proven ability of teaching portfolios to advance faculty recognition of the value of teaching and improve the quality of teaching on campus, they seemed timely. Peter Seldin and his "A Team" were the consultant mentors, the exercise was a smashing success, and the rest, as they say, is history.

PURPOSES AND PRINCIPLES

Why did that workshop go so well? Beyond the fact that the mentoring crew was superb, it seems that the basic self-reflective nature of the teaching portfolio touched a resonant chord with our faculty. A common reaction among the participants is captured by this comment: "It gave me some good insight into things to consider to improve my teaching and helped me to understand why I do the things I do when teaching. It does document teaching better than anything else I can think of." Asked if teaching portfolios have a future here, all responded with a resounding yes.

Then, and at subsequent workshops using the same format, it was explained to participants that Drexel's idea of the teaching portfolio is that it is a record of a person's work as a teacher and that its style should be that of an adaptable template—the "stock portfolio"—that can be morphed into many final forms. By the administration's posture, it soon dawned on the involved faculty that this stock portfolio would be the private/formative teaching portfolio, one that is for the author's eyes only. It would be a written confessional, a reflective synopsis of one's teaching to be consulted every so often, perhaps never to be made public unless it is designed to be a legacy document. It could be used as a conversation piece with oneself and not an administrator or committee, a suitable reminder of the compact between teacher and student.

The private portfolio, however, can be tweaked when necessary for other purposes such as reviews for tenure, promotion, and awards. It then becomes the public/summative teaching portfolio, an organized documentation and a ready source of a person's accomplishments as a teacher wherein the author can cherrypick his best work and "toot his horn for the show." The public portfolio would then be the analog of the professional resume though less objective, less easily read in context, and without the built-in allowance for a person's length of career, but like it, reveals few, if any, blemishes. Sample portfolios dredged up through Internet searches and books hew toward the public style with nary a "bad" one represented. This had brought great discomfiture to our workshop participants who believed that there "was no way" they could produce "something like that." One said, "I find it difficult to be boastful; I don't see anyone with negatives though I suspect I would be reluctant to state any real negatives myself in a document used to evaluate me."

The acceptance of the private rather than the public portfolio as the product of the workshop encouraged and sustained our faculty through the process and remains a guiding principle. It alleviates distrust of the motives of the administration and most likely accounts for the widespread popularity of our workshops.

At all times it is stressed that the bedrock principle of the private teaching portfolio is that it is not a magic pill, a panacea for someone's ills in the classroom, and creating one does not automatically confer the mantle of a good teacher on its author. The act and the product can only allow the serious teacher to chart a roadmap to becoming one.

The administration also recognized that the subjective/reflective nature of every teaching portfolio mitigates against doing it alone—that is, working from a script—at least at the beginning. Most faculty rarely talk to each other about teaching and need someone to bounce their ideas off of. "My mentor helped me to understand my own teaching philosophy!" was the declaration of one of our participants. Besides, faculty, unless coerced, are not prepared to set aside substantial time for the process, and help from an expert, a consultant or mentor, would facilitate their efforts and seems essential for a good result.

But then, who should form our cadre of experts? There is something to be said for external mentors; they bring cachet to the exercise and they supply a national, not insular, baseline. On the other hand, because in-house mentors are more fully aware of institutional prerogatives and culture, they may be more sympathetic listeners. And if they are teachers who have used or are more open to the use of the full range of the resources available on campus they should be able to suggest teaching and learning techniques that can work locally. Finally, if they are esteemed individuals—who have "won everything"—they will be better placed to nurture increased collegiality, even a fleeting master teacher-disciple relationship, and challenge their peers to grow beyond the perceived notion of them as just one-dimensional research wonks. Be that as it may, it appears that the best arrangement is a mix of external and in-house counselors, if available. Finances permitting, Drexel will continue to subscribe to this principle.

Another principle is that the construction of portfolios should occur, whenever possible, within a workshop setting. The university has asked faculty to train other faculty one-on-one without benefit of the resources, the rigid timetable, and support structure of a workshop. The experience in each case has always been less than satisfactory for both mentor and advisee. Sandwiching portfolio activities within a regular schedule for both protagonists is difficult at best.

The exercise of compiling a teaching portfolio should be conducted in an organized gathering with an understanding director and a sympathetic team of mentors to ride herd since few faculty, left to their own devices, will commit the time to doing a good portfolio. Seeing others in the same boat, in a schedule blocked out and dedicated to one activity and knowing that the administration has marshaled its resources to support the get-together, does serve to motivate participants. The workshop can also become a social occasion to foster conversation about learning, improvement, assessment, and a strengthened understanding of the institution's special mission, roles, and accomplishments among people who would not normally come together.

STRATEGIES

So what do we actually do? Early each spring, applications are solicited for attendance at that year's teaching portfolio workshop. For the first cohort, all participants in the PTR program were automatically selected, while the remaining 20 slots were allocated to members of the university's teaching and learning committee and a few senior faculty. The associate provost used her office's clout to stock the class with respected professors, though never was anyone forced to attend. Indeed, there were some no-shows at every workshop but the official attitude was always only regret that the absent faculty had missed a good thing; nothing punitive happened.

In the following years, the pool became more diverse and included new faculty, those coming up for tenure, and others who believed themselves to be good teachers and thus were in the running for teaching awards—the associate provost having announced that the dossier submitted by any applicant for midterm tenure review and for these awards must include a teaching portfolio stirred the interest of these groups. The selection process always gave special preference to new hires and to senior faculty who spent more than half of their time teaching undergraduates. Unsuccessful applicants and the faculty who were interested but could not fit the workshops into their schedules were referred to Office of the Provost's in-house panel of experts.

It was stressed that the workshops would be free and would be run by outside experts. Some graduates of the original workshop were included in the mentoring teams in subsequent years to cut down on expenses and because their inclusion, as discussed previously, had merit.

Just prior to the workshops, which run in the holiday week between the spring and summer quarters in June so that teaching responsibilities would not interfere, reading materials were delivered to all designated attendees. These included Seldin's (1997) book, *The Teaching Portfolio,* and a questionnaire to be completed and brought to the first session. The questionnaire helps participants to start thinking about the workshop and provides the beginnings of their statements on teaching philosophy. Each participant was told that the minimum commitment to the workshop was three and a half full days, thought to be adequate for the work to be done but more probably matching the period that would not drive away interest altogether. Every announcement about the workshops and contacts with faculty on this project always were low-key and supportive, a constant reminder that the Office of the Provost is totally behind the project, an absolute prerequisite for faculty to put up their best. Two group meetings and three individual meetings with a designated mentor were scheduled for each participant with the end of the workshop marked by a celebration of the portfolios produced. The workshop is a one-off event, no participant can expect to be invited back to a second though this rule may be relaxed once the rush for places subsides.

IMPLEMENTATION

The first group session is a breakfast how-to-get-started/orientation meeting to kick off the workshop and to introduce participants and mentors to each other. The schedule is explained and the rules and regulations listed before the mentors disperse to various sites to meet their advisees in half-hour slots. Rooms are set aside for the workshop so that individual counseling can take place in peace and quiet. The initial group meeting is held in a room equipped with easy chairs and serving tables that will become the group's common room. It is always stocked with refreshments to encourage participants to use it as a home away from home, while the comfortable setting provides the ambience for socializing between work sessions. Participants, though discouraged to do so, usually retire to their own offices to do the homework that is assigned each day. In the second group gathering, held on the third day at a complimentary lunch and after each advisee has had three counseling sessions under his or her belt, the whole team puts their heads together to analyze what constitutes a good portfolio and to share experiences. The advisees have one more day to tidy up their portfolios before "graduation," when their completed portfolios are put on display and certificates awarded to successful participants. Particularly well-done portfolios, including those of teaching award winners, are exhibited on Teaching Awards Day.

WHAT WORKED AND WHAT DID NOT

Accurately measuring the overall success, or not, of the program at Drexel University is a difficult proposition. However, there is no such doubt from anecdotal data. If we break our assessments down into three categories—how faculty reacted to teaching portfolios, how they accepted the workshops, and the larger issue of whether teaching has improved university-wide—we can quote survey evidence on the first two and indirect data on the last.

Over the years, informal surveys of faculty opinion after the workshops show almost universal satisfaction with teaching portfolios, though a little less enthusiasm was exhibited for the rigorous workshops themselves. All respondents said writing the portfolio was not a waste of time, while most responded that their teaching portfolios allowed each to "gain insights that now inform (my) teaching activities." One said writing his teaching portfolio will give him sustenance in his "waning years on campus," and that he can be useful, even as a nonresearcher, and need no longer feel as if he is deadwood. Another, because he was impressed with the efforts expended by the administration to run the workshops, "discovered that scholarship of teaching is valued" and is an acceptable substitute for discipline-specific research. This made him determined to redouble his efforts in the classroom. Most relished the tips they received in the tête-à-tête with their mentors on how to improve their teaching techniques. They also appreciated being apprised of the appearance of new technologies that are making an impact in pedagogy. Everyone attested that the workshop's group sessions did facilitate discussions about teaching and about the resources in the Faculty Development Center, and contributed to a better understanding of the mission of the institution and the build-up of esprit de corps. A significant number became energized enough to work with colleagues on the construction of teaching materials and course revisions besides making major revisions in their own courses.

The negative notes struck were not against teaching portfolios as such but were directed at the organization of the workshops. Some faculty said they felt rushed to cobble together a satisfactory document during the workshop. It does appear as if thoughtful reflection is a challenge in such a short timeframe. Writing the first draft, especially the section on teaching philosophy, proved to be quite a hurdle for many. This was especially so if they did not gather evidence prior to the workshop or failed to clear their calendars so that they could completely devote themselves to preparation of their portfolios.

Has implementation of the teaching portfolio program led to improvement in the quality of teaching at Drexel? Anecdotal data suggest that participants feel they have improved in their performance in the classroom and it is certainly true that a number, using their portfolios no less, have received teaching awards. Quite a few have also reported that their scores in student evaluations have risen while the university has also seen student retention rates stabilizing and then increasing. Greater student satisfaction with academics at Drexel is also reflected in the drop in the number of complaints to the Office of the Provost and an increase in alumni giving. Of course these glittering results can be attributable to other factors. Indeed, the admissions office and the alumni office may have better claims to being responsible for the data's pleasing looks.

How can we keep faculty engaged in continually updating their portfolios, sharing their expertise and their portfolios, even proselytizing among their colleagues? At Drexel, we have created a panel of mentors who are available as consultants/coaches outside of the workshop setting to assist anyone who is interested in building a portfolio or refining an existing one. There is no formal structure to bring mentor and advisee together, but a December 1996 directive to all prospective tenure candidates to attend at least one promotion and tenure workshop prior to the beginning of their fifth year of probationary service has allowed the Office of the Provost to advertise teaching portfolios and the availability of mentors to provide guidance on assembling a dossier.

Faculty who have served on tenure review committees have commented that public/summative teaching portfolios, provided these follow a standardized format, have made the evaluation process much easier. The only questionable feature, they have noted, is the unverifiable evidence that crops up in some portfolios. Are letters from students solicited, and to what extent do their contents represent the true nature of the teacher-student relationship? How many instructors are gaming the system? Nevertheless, evaluation is still better now than before the emergence of portfolios.

FUTURE PLANS

Though Drexel has not written into the Faculty Handbook or professors' contracts, as yet, the requirement of summative portfolios in merit reviews and tenure and promotion exercises, graduates of our workshops have begun to submit them in their dossiers, and individual departments, noticing their usefulness for assessment, are asking for them. Having gained faculty acceptance, it is clear that teaching portfolios have taken root here. They are helping to make teaching more scholarly and public, and there is expectation that they will change the culture of teaching and learning at this institution. As Drexel strives to become a model student-centered research university, the Teaching Portfolio Program and its purposes and strategies will most likely undergo review and modification. If portfolios are to be made mandatory in personnel decisions—all signs seem to be pointed in that direction— the administration, working in close concert with the faculty who have already developed them, must carry the message far and wide that their primary purpose is to improve and reward teaching and that implementation of the policy will not be rushed and will not occur before everyone has attended a workshop and/or been counseled by a mentor. Professors would be advised to collect evidence of good teaching immediately and continuously. In the meantime, the administration and faculty must grapple with questions such as these:

- Should the construction of a portfolio be one where the onus is on the faculty to keep refreshing it or should there be a built-in, required "recertification" program with the university providing release time and resources?

- Should the portfolio program be workshop-oriented or can it be seminar-based?

- Who should be given preference to attend?

- Should there be a presession workshop/seminar?

- Must it involve one-on-one counseling?

- What style and contents must any portfolio have?

- What standardized format must there be? Can there be different requirements for different purposes and for different disciplines or must one insist on some degree of uniformity?

- Can the evidence in portfolios be made more verifiable or its sources stipulated?

- How should portfolios be judged or evaluated? What are the criteria?

- How do teaching portfolios really improve the quality of teaching and learning at a research university like Drexel?

The teaching portfolio is not without its detractors. But whatever its imperfections, it can play a key role in the teaching-learning enterprise at any school. At Drexel, a fair-minded assessment of the impact of our embrace of portfolios must admit that it has had beneficial effects, large or small, on the mindset of the faculty as they approach the task of teaching. Indeed, when all the data is in, we could conceivably realize then that the Teaching Portfolio Program began an enduring process to improve the education of our students.

8

Using Multiple Pathways to Foster Portfolio Development at Miami University of Ohio

Milton D. Cox

At Miami University of Ohio we have used multiple pathways to foster the development and use of teaching portfolios. These pathways have included a departmental focus involving faculty learning communities, a course mini-portfolio component within faculty learning communities, use of the portfolio as evidence for selecting recipients of teaching awards, a centralized three-day portfolio development workshop for the campus, and portfolios as a noteworthy focus of the scholarship of teaching and learning.

Founded in 1809, Miami University is a state-assisted research-intensive institution with approximately 21,500 undergraduates, 1,500 graduate students, and 980 full-time faculty on the Oxford campus, plus two regional, urban, commuter two-year campuses. There are 44 academic departments and six academic divisions. Miami has a history and tradition of valuing undergraduate education, which today creates a mindful tension between teaching and scholarship.

A FACULTY LEARNING COMMUNITY APPROACH

One venue for teaching portfolio development at Miami is the Faculty Learning Community (FLC) program. Faculty learning communities are cross-disciplinary communities of eight to ten faculty engaged in intensive, collaborative, yearlong curricula focused on enhancing and assessing learning with activities that promote development, scholarship of teaching, and community. Miami's FLC program outcomes include increased faculty retention, intellectual development, collaboration, active learning, civic responsibility, and interest in learning (Cox, 2001). To date, one-third of Miami faculty have participated in these FLCs, and over 100 faculty (over

10%) were engaged in 11 FLCs in 2002–2003. The course portfolio is a key part of the scholarship of teaching and learning component of some FLCs (Cox, 2003). For example, each junior faculty participant in Miami's Teaching Scholars FLC prepares a course portfolio for his or her focus course. These portfolios are called course mini-portfolios in order to emphasize that they contain succinct information that will fit into a report cover rather than require a three-ring binder. Appendix 8.1 indicates the format and items we recommend for the course mini-portfolio. FLC members participate in two or three portfolio seminars spaced monthly over the second semester of the FLC to generate drafts that lead to a completed course mini-portfolio.

A DEPARTMENTAL APPROACH INVOLVING FLCS

Miami's department-based teaching portfolio project was a faculty grassroots effort during 1993–1997 involving 20 departments and units designed by Teaching Effectiveness Programs, a two-person faculty teaching development "office" reporting to the provost, and the Committee for the Improvement of Instruction, a faculty and student committee of the university senate. Nationally, during the mid-1990s, most approaches to portfolio development were campus-wide, initiated by the visit of a national expert, and coordinated by the institution's teaching center or faculty development office. At Miami, we selected a department-based approach instead because "departments and disciplines have different cultures and are where faculty academic lives are lived and where faculty rewards are determined" (Cox, 1995, p. 118).

The organizational structure of the portfolio project involved a two-tiered FLC format. The first tier consisted of departmental FLCs in which each departmental team investigated, then prepared, portfolios. A second-tier university-wide FLC was made up of the departmental FLC facilitators, who met monthly over dinner to discuss their departments' portfolio plans and progress, share successes and failures, seek and offer support, examine portfolio drafts, and plan seminars to share results with the campus. Although new members joined the facilitators' FLC each semester, the group matured developmentally over three years. In the first year, sessions primarily involved seeking answers and reporting portfolio development progress. In the second year, portfolios constructed by first-year participants became available to read and discuss. In the third year, the FLC looked for portfolio patterns across departments, studied the evaluation of these portfolios, and discussed other teaching issues in higher education. Details about organizational aspects, disciplinary perspectives, and project outcomes are in Cox (1995, 1996).

In 1996, the Miami FLC facilitators provided final reports that led to the following recommendations for campuses considering a department-based approach to developing teaching portfolios:

- Make the initiative faculty-generated—a grassroots effort—with administrative endorsement at the central and departmental level.

- Keep participation by departments voluntary, thus avoiding department resentment and resistance when participation is required by central administrators attempting to change the teaching evaluation system.

- Reward departments that participate (each participating Miami department received $5,000).

- Use a university-wide project director *and* a department FLC team approach to defuse the "chosen expert" or "prophet in one's own land" effect that a lone faculty member might face in his or her department.

- Foster department- or discipline-specific approaches to developing portfolios, providing generic, across-the-discipline efforts as options or examples.

- Provide sufficient flexibility and time for departments to design their own approach, for example, investigating and choosing whether or not to use external consultants, take a formative or summative approach, begin with course or comprehensive portfolios, etc.

- Let the departmental FLC facilitator investigate and then select a portfolio development process that is directive or nondirective, suiting the facilitator's or department's style.

- Select department FLC facilitators who are respected in their departments, enthusiastic about teaching, and are former participants in campus-wide teaching programs.

- Secure strong support from the department chair, but allow flexibility in the chair's role in the portfolio project as dictated by the culture and comfort of the department.

- Provide support at two levels: at the first tier for each department FLC, and at the second tier for the campus-wide facilitators' FLC.

- Have the campus-wide portfolio FLC meet monthly to share experiences, establish networks across departments, and address issues of interest to the group.

- Accept the time inefficiency of a department-based portfolio approach. Some departments may seem to reinvent the wheel, but in most cases they will design an innovative approach that fits the culture of the department and discipline. Also, faculty are more excited and committed when, after investigating the literature, they can engage in a combination of the scholarship of discovery, application, and teaching.

- Accept the economic inefficiency of a department-based approach. For example, a department may bring in a national expert who does not have time to consult with other departments or the entire campus. A department values this special consultation and attention, especially questions and advice tailored to its culture and discipline. Invite all FLC facilitators to attend public presentations of interest in specific departments.

- Allow at least three years for completion or expansion of a department-based project.

- Provide incentives for continued participation each year. For example, some departments making progress in the Miami project used all of their grant dollars in the first or second year and needed additional funds.

- Be prepared for some departments to "stop out" for a year when undergoing chair searches, moving to temporary quarters while buildings are remodeled, etc. Encourage such departments to renew their portfolio development efforts the following year.

- Be alert for a possible change in the quality of leadership and department participation when a department FLC facilitator must step down before the project is completed. There must be frank and open discussion about project expectations between a new facilitator, the department chair, and the central faculty development person overseeing the department-based project.

- Provide portfolio progress reports to the campus at seminars presented by the FLC facilitators and in monthly newsletters.

- Continue a successful teaching development effort long-term to obtain a broad impact on the campus and to generate faculty leaders for other department-based projects.

- Engage multiple university-wide teaching portfolio development efforts in addition to the department approach. Some departments will not participate in the department project, some faculty within a department may not feel safe enough to reveal concerns to colleagues in the department, and some teaching methods initially may not be known or of interest to a department. However, the discussion about teaching with nonexperts (someone not in the discipline) may yield insights that were blocked by content issues in the discipline.

PORTFOLIOS AS EVIDENCE FOR TEACHING AWARDS

One outgrowth of Miami's department teaching portfolio project is the use of portfolios in determining the recipient of the university's most prestigious annual teaching recognition, the E. Phillips Knox Teaching Award. This opportunity arose when an alumnus endowed the award in 1995 (at $3,000, quite modest compared to the awards at some institutions) and the administration selected the Committee on the Improvement of Instruction to determine the recipient each year. Several department portfolio project facilitators who were on the committee designed an approach consisting of two rounds. For the first round, nominated faculty prepared a four-page teaching and learning summary, and then up to five finalists were selected to prepare teaching portfolios for the second round.

Since the inception of the Knox Award in 1995, eight worthy recipients have been selected using portfolios. The procedure has worked effectively but not efficiently. One outcome of concern was that all applicants, including the award recipient, had invested much time in preparation of their portfolios, filling enormous three-ring binders. As a result, the committee decided to reallocate some of its other funds to award $1,000 to each finalist who did not receive the principal award but who demonstrated teaching excellence via his or her portfolio. Expanding recognition and reward for excellent teaching was a positive outcome arising from this concern. A second concern was the great investment of a committee member's time required to read such lengthy portfolios carefully. After seven years, the committee reduced the page limit of the reflective statement from ten to six pages and the number of appendices from ten to six. However, the portfolios generated by the new guidelines were just as large, with applicants broadening the appendix categories to include the same volume (300–400 pages) of material. Next year, the number of pages in the appendices will be limited to 100 to ensure a more manageable portfolio.

One requirement of the Knox Award portfolio preparation that is always overlooked is the required cover sheet for each appendix item that clearly and briefly explains what claim in the reflective statement this appendix provides evidence for and where exactly the reader should look in the appendix to find it. For example, without such a cover sheet an appendix item containing the applicant's syllabi leaves the reader browsing the syllabi in general. An appropriate cover sheet could direct the reader to see the assignments about critical thinking to provide evidence that the applicant has specified the means to develop critical thinking and communicates this to students. Often applicants do not seem to grasp the meaning and application of this directive. Although those who take advantage of available portfolio preparation consultations do sometimes provide appendix cover sheets with this information, none does so consistently, thereby missing an opportunity to make reading the portfolio more efficient and focused.

LINKING PORTFOLIO DEVELOPMENT TO THE SCHOLARSHIP OF TEACHING

There has been debate as to whether the portfolio itself is an artifact that can be counted as scholarship or is just one part of the evaluation of teaching. Some argue that if the portfolio is peer reviewed and published for the community to see, then it is scholarship. Others claim that individual portfolios are too localized and broad to be scholarship, and that innovations and evidence included in portfolios should be prepared as articles and published in refereed journals. Miami has taken the latter perspective.

Miami's Teaching Effectiveness Programs office has endeavored to make the scholarship of teaching involving portfolios available to Miami faculty and, in fact, to faculty at all institutions. The national Lilly Conference on College Teaching, held annually at Miami, provides opportunities for faculty to attend sessions about teaching portfolios. For example, in 1993, as the department teaching portfolio project began at Miami, 11 national portfolio experts presented sessions at the conference, including a panel in which each provided his or her perspectives. The Miami FLCs using portfolios attended these sessions and then refined their portfolio approaches. Some used this opportunity to interview and select consultants to work with their departments. At the 1994 Lilly Conference, in addition to a similar panel and presentations, 13 Miami department FLC facilitators presented a panel workshop on the Miami department-based approach, thus contributing to the scholarship of teaching. Although initially the Lilly Conference articulates only the broad area of college teaching and learning, themes (topics that comprise a focus in at least five sessions) emerge from the many sessions offered. After 1993 and 1994, teaching portfolios did not appear as a theme at the conference, perhaps because they were no longer an innovation or curiosity, or they were rejected as difficult, impractical, or ineffective. However, in 2001 and 2002, portfolios again emerged as a conference theme, offering participants an opportunity to investigate the latest portfolio developments after almost ten years of use.

Miami also publishes a refereed journal to bring the latest scholarship of teaching to faculty. The *Journal on Excellence in College Teaching,* established in 1990, has grown into a national publication. In 1995, at the height of the Miami departmental portfolio development, we published an issue of the journal devoted entirely to the teaching portfolio.

EVIDENCE OF PORTFOLIO DEVELOPMENT EFFECTIVENESS AND IMPACT

Over the past ten years, Miami's efforts at developing portfolios have included several pathways, with the department teaching portfolio project and faculty learning community approach at the forefront. One legacy of this project is the university's broadened policy on the evaluation of teaching. Prior to 1995, departments and divisions provided disconnected local polices that relied primarily on student evaluation of teaching and its ubiquitous summary number for reporting the overall effectiveness of an instructor. Miami's Committee on the Improvement of Instruction, populated by teaching portfolio project facilitators, proposed a new university-wide policy that significantly broadened the evaluation of teaching. As a result, in 1995 the university senate passed a resolution requiring that departments develop teaching evaluation plans

> *that reflect the complexity of the teaching/learning process by including multiple sources of evaluation data, including both qualitative and quantitative assessment methods. . . . In addition to end-of-semester student evaluations, summative and formative activities could include, but are not limited to, ongoing classroom assessment, peer evaluations . . . teaching (faculty) portfolios, [and] classroom materials . . .*

The policy is not just rhetoric. Miami's current provost monitors these departmental policies, and at his request, in 2002–2003 the aforementioned committee, which has three of the former departmental portfolio project facilitators as members, completed a review of the year 2002 department teaching evaluation plans of Miami's 44 academic departments and wrote letters to each department noting both good practices and shortcomings. This review reveals that all but nine departments involve teaching portfolios, and two of those nine use documentation equivalent to portfolios. Only one of these nine departments was involved originally in the teaching portfolio project; thus, ten years after the project's inception, 19 of the 20 departments participating in the portfolio project are now involving portfolios in various ways in the evaluation of teaching. The degree and type of involvement is described in Table 8.1.

TABLE 8.1

Teaching Portfolio Use in Departmental Evaluation of Teaching in 2002 by the 44 Academic Departments at Miami University

Number	Portfolio Use
7	Not mentioned (not even an equivalent model)
6	Required every year in the summative process
4	Required in the summative process for both promotion and tenure, but not required every year
4	Required in the summative process for tenure, but not promotion
14	Optional for summative review for both promotion and tenure
4	Optional for summative review for tenure, but not optional or required for promotion
2	Optional for summative evidence for tenured faculty at all times, but not necessarily for promotion and tenure
3	Formative use but not included under any summative processes

A traditional approach to working with faculty to develop portfolios is the campus-wide three-day workshop, during which each participant constructs his or her initial portfolio. The following evidence indicates that at Miami this is an effective approach. In January 2002, 40 Miami faculty participated in such a workshop. A survey sent one year later to determine the effect of the workshop was returned by 16 participants. Individuals reported that as a result of the workshop and their portfolios, there was a moderate increase in their understanding of their teaching, and to a lesser extent, an increase in their teaching effectiveness. Over one-third reported that departmental usage of portfolios in the evaluation of teaching is attributable to the workshop. Over two-thirds attribute their use of portfolios in departmental evaluation of teaching to the workshop, and over half use portfolios for summative purposes. Over 80% update their portfolios at least once a year.

In conclusion, teaching portfolios at Miami have provided pathways to faculty development, the scholarship of teaching, the reform of teaching evaluation, and the recognition of teaching excellence. Thoughtful and innovative uses of teaching portfolios have played a key part in earning Miami a FIPSE grant and two Hesburgh recognitions for faculty development enhancing the learning of Miami students.

APPENDIX 8.1
Course Mini-Portfolio Guidelines and FAQs

What is a teaching portfolio?

A teaching portfolio is a document containing a text and an appended collection of materials organized in a scholarly way to describe, analyze, and provide evidence for the important aspects of and connections between your teaching and your students' learning. See Cerbin (1994) for more information.

What is the format?

Table of contents, text (overview, reflective statement, and analysis), and appendices (evidence).

Use a report cover and number pages.

What goes in it?

1) Table of contents with page numbers indicated

2) Teaching/reflective statement for this course with references to appendices

- The context (overview of the course, students, and how the course fits into the curriculum)

- Your learning objectives for the course

- Achieving the objectives: your teaching practices/processes in the course

- Innovations you tried in the course

- Challenges you discovered and how you addressed them

- Analysis of student learning

- Analysis of student feedback

- Summary

3) Appendices: artifacts, each with a cover page of explanation Evidence of your innovations, that you met your objectives, and that your students learned. For example:

- Syllabus

- Selection of student work

- Results of Small Group Instructional Diagnosis (SGID), Teaching Goals Inventory (TGI), and Classroom Assessment Techniques (CATs)

- Pre- and post-surveys/questionnaires and results

- Student evaluations: numbers and a content analysis of open-ended questions

How long should it be?
Not long. Think of the reader. All should fit into a report cover.

Who reads it?
Is it formative and/or summative? Share your teaching portfolio with your FLC colleagues as you develop it.

Cerbin, W. (1994). The course portfolio as a tool for continuous improvement of teaching and learning. *Journal on Excellence in College Teaching, 5*(1), 95–105.

9

Developing and Implementing the Teaching Portfolio at Oxford College of Emory University

Myra Frady

When you drive onto the Oxford College campus one of the first things you will see is a quote by one of our founding fathers, Atticus G. Haygood: "Let us stand by what is good and make it better if we can." Oxford has taken this motto and brought this commitment to deeper and broader levels. This small living-learning community understands that the good can be made better.

Since Oxford College has always defined itself by taking teaching seriously, Oxford faculty have long been in conversation about what works and what doesn't work in the classroom. They have learned, and wisely used the fact, that teaching effectiveness can always be improved and that the impact of any innovation can be extraordinarily powerful in a small place.

THE TEACHING PORTFOLIO PROJECT: A BRIEF HISTORY

It is impossible to know where new ideas will lead. As thinking began about teaching portfolios, no real direction was defined, just a strong commitment to teaching. Oxford is dedicated to addressing the student's learning needs—however that might change over time.

In 1993, the exchange of teaching ideas became more structured with a series of luncheons (that continue to this day) designed to provide an opportunity for faculty to meet together regularly, to bring a teaching or learning topic—a problem, a success—for feedback and sharing. In this context, the teaching portfolio was discussed here for the first time as a possible tool to aid faculty in evaluating the teaching and learning techniques they were using and discussing.

Oxford's Faculty Advisory Committee was keenly aware of the quality of teaching at Oxford but wondered how to gather tangible evidence to show that good teaching did exist. What were the guidelines and categories that faculty could use to document their work? How could Oxford claim excellence in teaching without appropriate evidence to show that the resulting learning lasts? Faculty wanted a way to document good teaching and to develop measures to evaluate student learning. To that end, the Faculty Advisory Committee sponsored the first Teaching Portfolio Workshop in September 1998.

This workshop gathered input from 45% of the faculty and generated a thoughtful discussion about how Oxford faculty teach. This discussion was fruitful and yielded some new ideas:

- There was a need to expand the notion of what was a teaching space to include laboratories—traditional and field—studios, the university community, and the community at large.

- Mentoring and advising students, peer teaching, and collaboration with colleagues provided rich teaching and learning opportunities for faculty and students alike.

But it was the teaching portfolio which sparked the greatest interest. Attention now centered on what should be included in the portfolio. Should every portfolio begin with a teaching statement or philosophy? And should other categories include teaching evaluations from students, peers, and administrators; course materials; research about teaching; service related to teaching; and activities to improve classroom teaching and learning? These categories were not imposed on the faculty, rather they arose organically as a product of this first workshop and the subsequent discussions centering on what teaching means at Oxford College.

Even though the workshop was valuable to those who attended, there was still no formal process in place or administrative push that encouraged faculty as a whole to consider creating a teaching portfolio. Alas, only one portfolio was generated as a result of this workshop.

In September 1997, Emory University's Commission on Teaching recommended that "each faculty member . . . document his or her development as a teacher, for both formative and assessment purposes." Given this recommendation and the desire of the faculty to gather evidence of good teaching, the teaching portfolio concept was explored for implementation at Oxford College.

In response to this university directive, faculty at Emory College sponsored a four-day Teaching Portfolio Workshop led by Peter Seldin on

Emory's Atlanta campus in the summer of 1999. Four Oxford faculty participated in this workshop, and as a result they became enthusiastic advocates of the value of teaching portfolios. Not only did they become mentors to other faculty, they read drafts and made suggestions for colleagues, and evangelized the portfolio as a tool to document good teaching. The only downside to the experience occurred because the Oxford faculty were not close to their offices. They worked in the library and did not have access to their files, evaluations, and course materials as they prepared the portfolio drafts each day to discuss with mentors. However, four teaching portfolios were created as a result of the workshop.

In 1999, Oxford's academic dean, Kent Linville, formed the Advisory Council on Teaching, Learning, and Professional Development (ACT) to create initiatives designed to strengthen Oxford's educational program by enhancing faculty and staff development and faculty-staff-student interaction. Concurrently, the provost and the President's Advisory Committee implemented the recommendations of the university's Commission on Teaching. Dean Linville saw Oxford's Advisory Council as a vehicle to support faculty in responding to the mandate that all substantive claims be documented. Under ACT's umbrella, the Task Force on the Scholarship of Teaching and Learning began the work that would result in an ongoing program of teaching excellence and scholarship.

In the fall of 2001, Oxford held its first yearlong series on Teaching Excellence and Scholarship. Each month nationally recognized leaders in teaching and learning initiatives presented a topic to support Oxford's goal of becoming a more intentional version of itself. One component of that series focused on the teaching portfolio, and Peter Seldin was invited to give an overview of the teaching portfolio development process. Michael Rogers, associate professor of mathematics, in the process of preparing a portfolio at that time said, "what was especially valuable was discussing examples of the various kinds of evidence that can be used." The session generated excitement and enough interest from the faculty to hold a four-day Teaching Portfolio Workshop on the Oxford campus in May 2002. Stephen W. Henderson, associate professor of geology, created a portfolio during that workshop and concluded that "I found out that by writing the portfolio, I really gained some insights into my teaching and got some good ideas for improvement, some of which I've already instituted" (his portfolio appears in Part V of this volume). Another participant, Steve Baker, associate professor of biology, remarked that

*once I got started, [preparing the teaching portfolio] was really
fun and allowed me to be creative. The workshop helped by
teaching the "how-tos," by providing deadlines to force performance, and by having a patient mentor to motivate and
offer on-the-spot advice.*

Patti Owen-Smith, professor of psychology, although unable to participate in a teaching portfolio workshop, recently completed her portfolio for
promotion with minimal internal mentoring. She reported that

*the portfolio construction process was one of the most interest-
ing and productive activities of my professional career. It
forced me to reflect intentionally on my teaching and my philosophy about teaching. At the completion of the process (and
it took about six months), I felt that I was in a much different
place in terms of ideological clarity than when I began.*

WHERE WE ARE NOW

Oxford's experience over time with the preparation of teaching portfolios
has been quite positive. The expectations for content are clear, the categories
for inclusion are well defined, and how the portfolios will be used in promotion and tenure decisions is gaining clarity. The workshops have been very
important in this evolution. To date, 48% of Oxford's full-time faculty have
completed a teaching portfolio. The Faculty Advisory Committee remains
involved, advising new faculty of institutional expectations with regard to
teaching portfolios. A group of faculty who have completed portfolios stand
ready to mentor others in the preparation process, and it should be noted
that a by-product of faculty collaboration tends to deepen relationships.

From an administrative perspective, Oxford's dean, Dana Greene,
remarked,

*Teaching portfolios will now be required for all forms of fac-
ulty evaluation, and the scholarship of teaching has been
added as a form of acceptable scholarship in the tenure and
promotion process. A good teaching portfolio is highly self-
reflective, integrated, and coherent. These qualities give evidence of the level of skill and extent of experience of the faculty
member. As such the teaching portfolio has been helpful in
evaluating teaching effectiveness, leading to both positive and
negative personnel decisions.*

Given the importance of the teaching portfolio in the tenure and promotion process, Oxford must ensure that the existing faculty and any new faculty have appropriate support and encouragement to update or complete a portfolio. Patti Owen-Smith shared that she was grateful that she "had saved a lot of materials through the years and that... for the most part, had done thoughtful annual reports each year for the deans. Those provided a framework from which to build my portfolio." Steve Baker supports this sentiment: "I was lucky that I saved many things through the years... this is a critical piece of information to tell any new faculty member."

With the exception of a grant from the University Teaching Fund that supported the Teaching Excellence and Scholarship program, funding for this entire process has been internal. Certainly, from an administrative point of view, it was a tough decision to redirect the funds necessary to support these teaching portfolio workshops. However, with the dedication of the Oxford faculty to this project and the university commitment to teaching portfolios, it is imperative that appropriate support for the preparation of teaching portfolios be provided. And, it is equally important that attention be paid to providing the rest of the permanent faculty and new faculty with appropriate opportunities and resources to either prepare or update a teaching portfolio.

WHAT REMAINS TO BE DONE

The faculty at Oxford have had several, varied opportunities to receive instruction in how to craft a teaching portfolio; however, the majority of the faculty who actually review the teaching portfolios have not received instruction in how to evaluate them. Presently, there is little overlap between the faculty who have prepared portfolios and the faculty who review portfolios. Certainly, this gap will close over time, but for now it is a concern. In this connection, Eloise Carter, professor of biology wonders "how you get to the heart of the portfolio." It is not possible to provide evidence of good teaching if, indeed, that evidence does not exist. However, the evaluator may be overwhelmed by the supporting documentation which may conceal the fact that it is not tied to an appropriate teaching statement and that it may not be evidence of good teaching.

NEXT STEPS

Work remains to be done at Oxford College to fully integrate the teaching portfolio into the culture of the institution. A college-wide discussion of what constitutes a good teaching portfolio will begin to address how teaching should be evaluated through a portfolio. To support this effort, teaching port-folios need to be shared more among faculty. Oxford needs to develop a plan to ensure that teaching portfolios are systematically updated. If the portfolio has been created for promotion and tenure decisions, value, then, needs to be placed on the portfolio as a tool for ongoing self-reflection and understand-ing the coherence of one's work. The portfolios could also be used to support institutional efforts to document the work of groups within the institution.

The creation of departmental portfolios, based on individual portfolios, could provide:

- Focus for the department.

- Support and guidance to new faculty.

- Support for ongoing improvement in teaching and collaboration at the institutional level.

Dean Greene concludes that the teaching portfolio

> *makes teaching public [and] can be the basis for mentoring, for collaboration, for evaluation. Whatever its uses, the prepa-ration and sharing of the teaching portfolio helps create a com-munity focused on the teaching process. In fact, the institution itself becomes a self-reflective organism. Faculty find commu-nity in their corporate efforts and they begin to analyze the structures and resources needed to support ongoing develop-ment of the institution's principal asset, that is the faculty's teaching effectiveness.*

Oxford will continue to incorporate teaching portfolios into its culture because Oxford is a teaching institution. Oxford will continue to use the teaching portfolio for reflection and evaluation and attention will be paid to the weaknesses that exist in the evaluative process. Oxford will become more intentional about providing support for all faculty with special attention to the needs of new faculty. As the preparation, evaluation, and institutional commitment to teaching portfolios takes shape, the individual teaching portfolios will collectively provide documentation for the central work of the institution. And Oxford will continue the evolution of being a "more intentional version of itself."

10

Teaching Portfolios at Pace University: A Culture in Transition

Linda Anstendig and Constance A. Knapp

INTRODUCTION

Pace University has been offering Teaching Portfolio Workshops annually since they were first organized in June 1999 by the Pforzheimer Center for Faculty Development. We have completed five workshops, with over 130 participants who have developed their portfolios for personal growth as well as promotion and tenure evaluation. Overall, these workshops have become a centerpiece of our faculty development efforts and we have learned a great deal about teaching and learning by being involved in the process.

PACE UNIVERSITY

Pace University is a private, multicampus university founded in 1906 as Pace Institute by the Pace brothers, Homer and Robert. In 1969, Pace became a university composed of six schools: Dyson College of the Arts and Sciences, the Lubin School of Business, the School of Computer Science and Information Systems, the Lienhard School of Nursing, the School of Education, and the School of Law. Besides the New York City campus, there are two campuses in Westchester County.

The student body is diverse across the campuses, representing many different economic, ethnic, and age groups. We attract students with many styles of learning who come to college with varying levels of preparation and life experiences. Quite a large percentage of part-time students work during the day and attend classes in the evenings. Many of our students are the first in their families to complete college; some are the first in their families to attend school in the United States. Teaching this cross-section of students is challenging and exciting.

The faculty of the university also reflect the diversity of locations and disciplines. Each school shares a commitment to excellent teaching, but it has not always been easy to get faculty from the different schools together to share pedagogical concerns and successes. Like many other institutions, Pace wasn't sure how to document excellent teaching. We found ourselves asking, how do we know what excellent teaching is?

TEACHING PORTFOLIOS AT PACE

In June 1999, the then codirectors of the Pforzheimer Center for Faculty Development, Sandra Flank and James Hall, held the inaugural Teaching Portfolio Workshop. Jim and Sandy were looking for a faculty development effort that would have a greater impact than the one-on-one activities that the Pforzheimer Center had been doing. As Jim put it, they were looking to find "the thing that could make a difference" in faculty development at Pace. The center's advisory council, along with the two codirectors and Marilyn Jaffe-Ruiz, the provost, was looking for "different approaches to improving pedagogy." They believed that portfolio development was "in keeping with what we wanted to happen as a more reflective practice with regard to teaching." Marilyn believed that having faculty members develop their own portfolios was "much more organic, more developmental" than attending one workshop. According to Sandy Flank, the directors were looking for something they could "do that would be introspective." The idea was to develop portfolios for faculty development, not necessarily for promotion and tenure purposes.

Jim knew Peter Seldin, both as a colleague in the Lubin School and as the national leader of the teaching portfolio movement, and Sandy, as a professor of education, was familiar with the concept of portfolio development. However, the two codirectors of the faculty development center realized that without support from the deans of the six schools the effort of developing portfolios might not have the impact that they wanted. To ensure that the deans would support faculty who developed portfolios, Jim and Sandy made a presentation at dean's council arguing that the teaching portfolio was a significant faculty development tool to provide individuals with the opportunity to reflect on their teaching, set goals, and evaluate whether those goals were attained. At the same time faculty leaders and administrators realized portfolios might be used in an evaluative way. If the deans could be made comfortable with portfolios, both as a developmental and an evaluative tool, faculty members would be willing to participate. The deans endorsed this effort and gave it their support. The provost believed that the idea would "take off" and especially liked that the responsibility for developing a portfolio was placed in the hands of the professor, "where it belongs."

Twenty-six faculty members from every school in the university attended the first four-day workshop. Peter Seldin facilitated the workshop along with four outside mentors. Each participant was provided with a copy of the book *The Teaching Portfolio* (Seldin, 1997), and was sent other getting-started materials and the four-day schedule. We didn't realize it then, but we were on the road to changing the way that Pace faculty thought about presenting their teaching. We were becoming an institution where faculty statements about their teaching would become much more grounded in evidence.

The president gave the welcome at the first session and the provost spoke at the "graduation," showing that this enterprise was important for the university. The intensity and excitement of that first venture was palpable, and the closing ceremony ended with a 99% completion rate. We all celebrated with champagne, chocolate-covered strawberries, and certificates of completion.

At least one of the participants decided to apply for promotion to full professor, based on her participation in this workshop. Others also used their teaching portfolios to build dossiers for tenure and/or promotion that academic year. Some were full professors who participated for the opportunity to reflect on their teaching. Junior faculty, who were interested in improving their teaching methods or documenting their approaches, attended, as did a number of adjuncts who wanted to develop teaching portfolios to enhance their marketability.

An outside facilitator along with a combination of outside and internal mentors also led the second workshop in January 2000. Twenty-three faculty members participated. Mentors were chosen from the pool of faculty members who had already completed their own teaching portfolios. Jim and Sandy looked for faculty members who were enthusiastic about the development of teaching portfolios, who would relate well to their peers and be respected, and who might represent more than one of the schools that make up Pace University. The "mentors in training" met with fewer faculty members than the more experienced mentors. Each internal mentor was paired with an experienced, external mentor to whom the internal mentor could turn for advice during the workshop. The internal mentors found the experience challenging but rewarding. By the time of the third workshop in

August 2000 we were ready to use all internal mentors. The two new mentors and the two veteran mentors spent a few hours together in hands-on training, going over what we had learned from the consultant and the experienced outside mentors, and sharing our own experiences as participants.

We all agreed on the following guidelines:

- To act as a colleague in discussing teaching and learning.

- To be "a second set of eyes" in looking at the participants' writing.

- To provide guidance on the nuts and bolts of portfolio creation.

- To help participants focus on gathering evidence to document their teaching narrative.

One of the most helpful guidelines was to follow the "rule of two": As mentors we would make a suggestion twice, or "nudge" two times. If the mentee did not respond, we would drop it.

We also revised the "Getting Started" worksheet to make it conform more to the table of contents of the portfolio. Each of the seven questions asked faculty to describe an aspect of teaching: responsibilities, methods, course projects, and evaluation.

The president and provost came again to welcome the 22 participants. By now these workshops had achieved a certain cachet. The deans recommended that those professors who were seeking tenure or promotion should attend. Other professors had heard positive feedback from colleagues. At the final luncheon, we asked participants to evaluate their experiences, in terms of what worked well and what suggestions they had. The following comments are illustrative:

> *"I found I need to spend more time on student learning outcomes—not just on exams and papers."*

> *"I found it valuable to have a chance to focus on teaching and to learn that my challenges aren't unique, that we have much in common."*

> *"The workshop gave me a chance to think about the "progression" of teaching approaches I'd been through. I've moved from lecturing to experiential approaches that are hands on and have learned how to make things work better as I went along."*

Helpful suggestions such as adding more organized group work and portfolio samples, providing a reading list on pedagogy, and a more flexible workshop schedule were also offered.

Although the fourth workshop followed the same format, the fifth workshop, offered in the summer of 2002, took a nontraditional turn. Some of the suggestions we received after earlier workshops spoke to a faculty need for a more flexible schedule and the desire to incorporate the very technology that we are using to enhance our classroom teaching. Moreover, we wanted to make the workshop accessible to the greatest number of faculty members. Since Pace had adopted Blackboard as our university course management system, and many faculty were using it for their courses, we decided we could use it to spread the workshop out over a longer time period to meet faculty demands.

We decided to hold the first session on the last day of our first Summer Institute for Faculty Development, a three-day intensive retreat, with keynote speakers and workshops. Responding to the requests of faculty who wanted more time to prepare their portfolios, we decided to pursue a combination of face-to-face and online mentoring. We posted materials online and created online discussion forums. During the first session of the workshop, participants and mentors met as a large group, and then mentors met individually or in small groups with their mentees. The next scheduled face-to-face meeting would be four weeks away, when we would have our final luncheon, discussion, and portfolio and certificate presentation. In the meantime, participants wrote their narratives and gathered their materials, either emailing their mentors, meeting in person with them, or a combination of both.

This format provided extreme flexibility, but the result was a much lower completion rate within the four-week period. Whereas in the past four workshops over 90% of participants attended the final luncheon with their completed portfolios, this time only 35%–40% completed their portfolios by the time of the final luncheon. Some did, however, complete portfolios after that date.

Because individuals had more time, they had difficulty making it a priority. Faculty members lost the collegiality of a tight four-day program, where everyone is working together and where chance encounters over the refreshments can lead to new insights.

In addition to conducting workshops and training mentors, we published a compilation of Teaching Philosophies. Developed by 14 faculty members who participated in the first Teaching Portfolio Workshop, these teaching philosophies have served as models for new participants. This collection reinforces the notion that there are many "right" ways of developing a statement of teaching philosophy, putting together a teaching portfolio, and of approaching pedagogical challenges.

INSTITUTIONALIZING PORTFOLIOS: THE CHANGING CULTURE

Dossiers for promotion and tenure at Pace University, as at many institutions, must conform to published guidelines and standards. Each year the provost publishes a detailed description of the dossier that now refers specifically to a candidate's teaching portfolio. The provost can assume that all faculty know what a teaching portfolio is and that many faculty in each of the six schools have either completed a portfolio for themselves or know of a colleague who has. Faculty members have been eager to display the results of their efforts, and portfolios have been circulated in at least one school to illustrate exactly what constitutes evidence of teaching.

While we might not yet have institutionalized the development of teaching portfolios, Marilyn Jaffe-Ruiz, our provost, believes that teaching portfolios have "become part of the common parlance."

One of the unanticipated results of using teaching portfolios is the impact that they have had on tenure and promotion discussions. All candidates for tenure and promotion present their dossiers to the Council of Deans and Faculty on Tenure and Promotion. Candidates who have invested the time in developing good teaching portfolios have much stronger dossiers, and represent themselves as effective teachers with supporting evidence. One of the deans commented that dossiers containing material from teaching portfolios completed during the workshop "jumped out of the pile" for their quality and thoroughness. The provost agrees that these dossiers are much improved. Comments like these have encouraged faculty members who are facing tenure and promotion to complete a Teaching Portfolio Workshop.

CONCLUSION

For those who participate in the Teaching Portfolio Workshop, or for those who consult with former participants, teaching portfolios are now the standard for the teaching section of the dossier.

School-based tenure and promotion committees expect to see parts of the portfolio included in the dossiers. Many committees look for evidence in the forms of products of teaching, or materials from others, where before materials from the professor alone would have sufficed. The expectation is that, just as a faculty member includes evidence of research, he or she should provide evidence of teaching. These expectations have "raised the bar," as the provost puts it. As a university we are moving toward the time when the philosophy underlying teaching portfolios becomes a part of the culture, and more faculty will be encouraged to share their teaching narratives. The faculty development leaders and the provost agree that faculty members who have participated have valued the experience. Marilyn Jaffe-Ruiz added that "the commitment to academic excellence is our commitment to high quality teaching" and the reflective practice of portfolio development fosters this. She describes the teaching portfolio as an important assessment tool: "The process of developing it is formative, and the product is summative." Sandy Flank suggests that this initiative at Pace University is all the more powerful because it "came from the faculty but was supported by the administration." As the current directors of the Pforzheimer Faculty Development Center, we intend to continue the transformative work of teaching portfolios at Pace University.

11

The Teaching Portfolio at Rutgers University

Monica A. Devanas

THE TEACHING EXCELLENCE CENTER AND THE TEACHING PORTFOLIO

The Teaching Excellence Center at Rutgers University was founded in July 1992 after many years of discussion by faculty and administration. Our original charge was the promotion and support of excellence in teaching, while at the same time being responsible for the university-wide Student Instructional Rating Survey process. This dual role of support and assessment was a unique challenge. Early on it was clear to us that the one indispensable tool to help us meet our charge was the teaching portfolio.

With the initiation of the university's Student Instructional Rating Survey, faculty were being asked to involve their students in a very standardized questionnaire format, one that was useful for most traditional lecture courses, but limited in capturing the unique aspects of the course or the impact of the instructor, especially in the case of seminars or more experiential student-centered courses. The teaching portfolio alleviated faculty concerns about limitations of a standardized assessment instrument. It allowed faculty to showcase their teaching contributions beyond the summative survey statistical data.

The benefits of preparing a teaching portfolio are numerous in areas of reflective practice, teaching improvement, curriculum design, formative and summative assessment, and personnel decisions. The drawbacks, likewise, are important: The process of preparing a teaching portfolio takes time. Faculty are extraordinarily busy people—they will not spend time on any activity without seeing a successful and useful outcome. Faculty are also extraordinarily rational—they quickly see the merits of a process that can improve the quality of their academic life.

We decided that there would be no use in "bullying" the faculty into using the teaching portfolio as an end in itself, but as preparation for personnel decisions, numerous teaching awards and fellowships, and grants. We believed that the teaching portfolio would stand on its merits as a multidimensional assessment instrument and that faculty would find its preparation very rewarding. Toward that end, we decided to prepare an easy guide to the basic structure of the teaching portfolio that follows the structure of the university guide for promotion and tenure. First we distributed the outline in a newsletter, but now it is available to everyone, all the time, on our Teaching Excellence Center web site (http://TeachX.rutgers.edu).

RESEARCH FACULTY AND FACULTY ATTITUDES

Research faculty are committed to their disciplines, and their lives are committed to expanding and developing that discipline. Teaching allows faculty to engage students with their own love and knowledge of their discipline. Teaching is not an end in itself, but an exciting journey of discovery with a group of bright and motivated students. Tasks for activities that take the faculty member away from these efforts are distractions. The reason that faculty have enthusiastically participated in the creation of teaching portfolios is because the experience is transformative and enduring. Faculty begin to examine and reflect upon their own teaching and its significance in their own academic life and the lives of their students. Therefore, the teaching portfolio allows faculty to address teaching and its importance in the same way that they daily address research and its value in their discipline. Faculty who have prepared a teaching portfolio do not follow the easy path of using last year's notes or pay only lip service to teaching.

The creation of teaching portfolios has had specific results at Rutgers. In New Brunswick, the largest of Rutgers' three regional campuses, we have seen these results in the ways in that faculty mentor junior faculty, a change in attitudes of faculty and administrators toward the scholarship of teaching, and a change in personnel decisions.

Faculty Mentoring Junior Faculty

Some of the faculty who were in the initial group of faculty recruited to work with Peter Seldin and his team of teaching portfolio consultants in 1994 have since gotten tenure, risen through the ranks, and now hold positions in administration as deans, department chairs, directors of centers, and chairs of the university senate. They have served as successful models and encouraged many colleagues to follow their lead in creating teaching portfolios. In some cases chairpersons have recommended the process, and in others faculty governing bodies have gone so far as to require teaching portfolios for all personnel decisions.

Senior faculty have been key in assisting junior faculty, always guiding the process of creation to parallel the structure required by the university for tenure and promotion. It is imperative to use this strategy since time is such a critical issue for all faculty, especially junior faculty.

Faculty Attitudes Toward the Scholarship of Teaching

Once faculty prepare a teaching portfolio, teaching is no longer just showing up for class but is a body of knowledge about their discipline that they bring to their students. When faculty know the value of preparing a teaching portfolio, they realize that teaching is scholarship and they want to disseminate this model in a fashion similar to and with the same enthusiasm that they disseminate their research findings. And so some bodies of faculty have decided to make teaching portfolios required for themselves and all of their peers. For example, at Cook College of Rutgers University, the Academic Forum recommended that teaching portfolios be required for all personnel decisions, reappointment, tenure, promotion, merit pay, and for college teaching awards. One might be surprised that so many overworked and overcommitted faculty would add to their administrative burdens, but the teaching portfolio provides them with the opportunity to place on the record the innovations and initiatives and the intellectual energy that they have expended through their teaching. Faculty are proud to have a document that shows their thinking, their efforts, and their accomplishments as teachers.

Administration's Attitude Toward the Scholarship of Teaching

Any university administration is constantly dealing with a large volume of paper for any promotion, tenure process, or post tenure review. The creation of the teaching portfolio gives the administration a clear picture of the depth and breath of any candidate's teaching life. The teaching portfolio makes the case for the quality and scholarship of teaching to the administration that cannot be ignored. This effects the administration's attitudes about an individual's teaching and about the place and value of teaching in the institution itself.

One area in which the teaching portfolio has been incredibly valuable is in the documentation of the impact of implementing new instructional technologies. The comprehensive overview of success and failure of innovation presented in teaching portfolios provides the administration with hard evidence on which projects are successful and should be invested in and which should not.

Personnel Decisions

Typically, promotion and tenure committees handle boxes of support material so large that teaching portfolios may not even be useful beyond the departmental review level because there is just too much to read. So pressed are these upper-level committees that the actual teaching portfolio may be examined only if there are specifics about teaching that come into question. Therefore, faculty would be well advised to have succinct, well-structured teaching portfolios with considerable evidence beyond self-reported observations. Voluminous compendia, with every iteration of syllabus and exam and great quantities of self-reported content, have little power to prove the case of successful, effective teaching. Brief executive summaries of two to four pages that are included with the traditional teaching statement are most useful to promotion and tenure committees as the materials move to upper-level review committees.

At Rutgers, the Student Instructional Rating Survey provided reliable, valid, and useful information about teaching. The reappointment and tenure process was changed to include comprehensive descriptions of teaching. The basic format of the teaching portfolio was acknowledged and accepted as a structure for supplemental information about the individual teaching activities of faculty. The teaching portfolio structure became a guide for writing the teaching statements required for reappointment, tenure, and promotion decisions. With the increased use of informed teaching statements, that is, teaching portfolios, the administration requests more qualitative information about teaching. So, now included in promotion and tenure materials are questions typically addressed in teaching portfolios, such as faculty development initiatives, workshops attended, curricular innovations, and evidence of the scholarship of teaching.

A post-tenure review process was instituted at Rutgers in 1993. These are collegial discussions of a professor's academic contributions over the last five years. The teaching portfolio lays out the scholarship of teaching in a very practical and useful way for these discussions.

EXTENSION OF THE PORTFOLIO CONCEPT AT RUTGERS

Administrative Reviews

With interest in assessing teaching at the university, faculty began to ask for a review process for administrative personnel. The university Senate Faculty

Affairs and Personnel Committee issued recommendations that have been implemented by the president—to have the deans of all units reviewed by their faculty every five years. The Teaching Excellence Center is charged with assisting in this process. Once again the principles of the teaching portfolio (what do you do? why do you do it? how effective are you?) have proved incredibly useful. We have assisted deans in the creation of their own administrative portfolios. These portfolios are submitted to a committee of faculty who review them. Six of the 12 deans in New Brunswick have already created some form of an administrative portfolio for the dean's review process.

The Clinical Teaching Portfolio

In the past year, the deans of the University of Medicine and Dentistry of New Jersey have required all staff members, teaching faculty as well as clinical physicians, to document their teaching effectiveness. The Teaching Excellence Center was requested to assist its sister institution with these issues. The notion of the teaching portfolio was modified for the medical school and clinical faculty with input from the chairs and deans. The outcome was a clinical teaching portfolio model with a streamlined template outline for a guide (see Appendix 11.1). Just as faculty at Rutgers are busy, the medical school and clinical staff are busy researchers and clinicians. They have found the process rewarding, despite the time needed to prepare and collect the materials and supporting evidence of effectiveness. The administration reports from the personnel review committees have been very positive for this new structure of clinical teaching portfolios.

Specialized Teaching Environments

Teaching portfolios are also seen as a tool for research faculty who have limited teaching roles in the traditional venues, that is, classrooms. There are many scholars who are directors of centers and institutes—faculty whose main role is one of research and the teaching of research associates, postdoctoral fellows, graduate students, and technicians. These faculty teach in ways that are more difficult to capture and thus more difficult to document. The teaching portfolio is profoundly adaptable for these out of the ordinary teaching situations, provided that there is some way to document effectiveness beyond the limitations of self-reporting.

INSTITUTIONALIZING THE TEACHING PORTFOLIO AND ITS OTHER APPLICATIONS

The teaching portfolio has clearly been a process for change in higher education. But to have it endure as a well-established structure in the institution, several needs must be met.

First, faculty must buy in to the process with no bullying. At Rutgers University, the Senate Faculty Affairs and Personnel Committee spent a year studying the issues of assessment and evaluation of teaching. Following its research and testimony from many faculty, in spring 2002 the committee issued seven recommendations as "Best Practice in Evaluation of Teaching." At the top of the list was the suggestion that all faculty prepare a teaching portfolio. The other recommendations include mentoring of junior faculty, systematic peer review, and careful attention to the data from the Student Instructional Rating Survey with special analyses within departments. The teaching portfolio concept has proved its worth and is now part of the institution.

Second, there must be administrative support for the teaching portfolio process in the form of availability of information. The faculty and departments need to have access to information on teaching and the teaching records of faculty, lists of courses, enrollments, and descriptions of students as well as data from student surveys. The Teaching Excellence Center has made efforts to provide some of these data to departments and faculty through access to online resources and data as well as personal guidance to assist faculty members in creating teaching portfolios.

Third, academic departments must contribute to the development of environments where the scholarship of teaching is part of the culture of the department. This requires leadership among the departmental officers and senior faculty. Departments at Rutgers that have achieved this level of responsibility for scholarship, teaching, and the scholarship of teaching are those who are leaders both in Rutgers and in higher education.

Fourth, the administration needs to be committed to its use of information on teaching in the tenure and promotion processes. The balance of research, teaching, and service must be real and not merely lip service for these principles to emerge as core to the mission of the research university.

Once these conditions are met, then and only then can the scholarship of teaching as documented by the teaching portfolio be meaningful, not only in promotion processes and just for an individual faculty member's case, but for the institution at large and for all of higher education.

Appendix **11.1**

University of Medicine and Dentistry of New Jersey
Robert Wood Johnson Medical School
Template for Teaching Portfolio

A teaching portfolio is an executive summary of the staff member as an educator. Typically this summary is four to five pages with supporting materials collected into appendices. The teaching portfolio should be concise and selective, but with sufficient description and documentation to provide a record of teaching activities, a personal statement or philosophy of teaching, and evidence of teaching effectiveness.

Part ONE: Teaching Responsibilities

List and describe all teaching-related activities in as complete a context as possible, that is, the names of courses or presentations, the level of involvement or frequency, the number and types of students, the teaching materials that may have been produced, or the role of the staff member in other teaching-related activities (supervisor, advisor, mentor). Provide material were applicable.

1) Teaching activities

   A) Teaching

      a) Undergraduate

         • Basic Science

         • Clinical

      b) Graduate

      c) House staff and fellows

   B) Presentations/lectures

   C) Grand rounds

   D) One-on-one teaching

   E) Laboratory teaching

   F) Seminar teaching

2) Curriculum development

   A) Courses

   B) Clerkships

   C) Residency programs

   D) Fellowship programs

3) Mentoring/advising

4) Continuing medical education programs

5) Programs for public education

6) Administrative educational experience (i.e., course or program directors)

Part TWO: Evidence of Teaching Effectiveness
A brief description of these types of materials is included in this section, while the actual documents, evaluations, letters, etc., are included in the appendices. As each area of evidence is described, it is very important to cite the place in the appendices where each item can be found.

1) Course materials

2) Student and resident evaluations

3) Peer review

4) Professional recognition

5) Participation in professional development

Part THREE: Teaching Philosophy (optional)
The teaching philosophy is a narrative personal statement that includes a discussion of what the staff member believes is important in teaching and how these beliefs are applied and practiced. This statement may include discussions of the following:

1) Describe strategies and methods used in different teaching situations.

2) Explain the rationale for using these methods and strategies.

3) Why are these rationales important to you for the training of medical students, graduate students, post-doctoral students, residents, and staff?

Appendices
In this section, representative materials used or developed for teaching are presented, having been described in Part Two above.

12

Teaching Portfolios at Texas A&M University: Reflections on a Decade of Practice

Nancy J. Simpson and Jean E. L. Layne

Teaching Portfolios were introduced to Texas A&M University (TAMU) by the university's Center for Teaching Excellence (CTE) in the spring of 1992. At that time, the CTE's Visiting Scholar Program brought to campus Dr. Peter Seldin of Pace University, and his associates Dr. Ray Shackelford and Dr. Linda Annis of Ball State University. These three consultants led a group of ten TAMU faculty and one upper-level administrator through the process of constructing their teaching portfolios. One year later, in the spring of 1993, Dr. Liz Miller, associate director of the CTE, chaired a national symposium focused on the teaching portfolio as a vehicle for improving and assessing teaching quality. The symposium brought together faculty and administrators from across the country interested in exploring the potential of the teaching portfolio for both improving and assessing the quality of teaching on our campuses. Since the initial introduction of the teaching portfolio to our campus, well over 500 faculty at TAMU have reflected on their teaching practice and documented their teaching accomplishments by creating a teaching portfolio.

While the process that the CTE uses to help faculty with their teaching portfolios has evolved over the past decade, key principles learned during that first week, and supported by the literature on teaching portfolios, have remained foundational to this work. First, the teaching portfolio is valuable both as a process (Edgerton, Hutchings, & Quinlan, 1991) and as a product (Seldin, 1993). Second, for optimal results, writing a teaching portfolio involves interaction with colleagues (Seldin, 1997). Third, a teaching portfolio makes use of multiple sources of evidence (Edgerton, Hutchings, & Quinlan, 1991). And fourth, a teaching portfolio serves faculty best when it is a choice, not a mandate (Seldin, 1993). We begin this chapter by discussing these principles.

KEY PRINCIPLES

Teaching Portfolio as Process and Product

The teaching portfolio is valuable both as a *process* for reflecting on and improving one's teaching practice and as a *product* for documenting one's teaching accomplishments. We tell our faculty that the process involves self-examination, self-discovery, and self-disclosure, and that the product will consist of a narrative that they write plus documentation that they will select and compile. We have chosen not to emphasize one over the other, but rather ask the faculty with whom we work to consider their purpose and their audience as they write. In our experience, most faculty who undertake the creation of a teaching portfolio do so both for the purpose of improving their teaching and for the purpose of producing a document that may be used for promotion and tenure purposes, job prospecting, or teaching award competitions. In some cases, the product is the primary purpose, and the faculty member reports being pleasantly surprised that the process itself was useful for teaching improvement. In other cases, the faculty member begins the teaching portfolio work primarily for the purpose of teaching improvement or course planning, and ends up with a document that is later adapted for summative evaluation purposes.

Teaching Portfolios and Interaction

We learned early that both the process and product of the teaching portfolio are enhanced through interaction with peers and/or with teaching consultants. While it is certainly possible for a faculty member to construct a teaching portfolio in isolation, we do not recommend it. When faculty members discuss—even argue about—learning and teaching, their own thinking is sharpened and they are better able to articulate the beliefs that drive their practice. When faculty describe their teaching methodologies to each other, they gain ideas of new strategies to try with their own students, as well as insight into why some elements of their teaching might not be accomplishing what they intend. Faculty can also help each other determine what kinds of documentation would best serve to give evidence of the teaching portfolio author's effectiveness as a teacher. When CTE teaching consultants work with teaching portfolio writers, they raise questions that have not yet been considered or addressed in the teaching portfolio, push faculty to think deeply about *why* they do what they do in the classroom, help faculty see how their teaching strategies are (or are not) supported by teaching and learning research, and point out consistency as well as inconsistency between teaching philosophy and practice described in the portfolio.

Teaching Portfolios and Multiple Sources of Evidence

Both the product and the process of the teaching portfolio are enhanced when the faculty member considers and presents multiple sources of evidence. By honestly seeking evidence to answer many questions—beginning with "what do I believe about teaching and learning?" and continuing through "what do my students, peers, department head, and teaching consultant say about my teaching?" to "what and how well are my students learning?"—faculty are able to gather a rich collection of information that enables them to both improve and document their teaching. While it demands more of faculty, and of those who evaluate faculty, the teaching portfolio as a source of information to improve and evaluate teaching is much more satisfying to most faculty than student ratings of teaching data used by itself.

The Teaching Portfolio as a Faculty Choice

A key decision, made early in the process, was that the teaching portfolio would *not* be mandated at the university level. This decision does not mean that teaching portfolios are not supported by the administration or that they are not useful to faculty for the tenure and promotion process. On the contrary, the university's tenure and promotion guidelines for evidence of teaching accomplishment include many of the items typically found in a teaching portfolio. So, while the full teaching portfolio does not generally go past the department-level promotion and tenure committee, pieces of the portfolio are often found in the promotion and tenure dossier. Further, department heads are able to write much more substantive letters about the candidate's teaching. While not mandated to do so, faculty are encouraged to create teaching portfolios. That is, there is a strong message that teaching portfolios are a "good thing to do." But by leaving the decision about whether or not to invest time in creating a teaching portfolio in faculty hands, the value of the *process* has been protected. As one faculty participant at a recent teaching portfolio retreat commented, "one of the best parts of the weekend is that everyone here chose to come and is motivated to do this work."

Evolution of the Teaching Portfolio Project at Texas A&M University

As indicated earlier, we introduced teaching portfolios to our campus in 1992 with a weeklong workshop. Ten award-winning teachers as well as an associate provost were invited to participate. The week began with an introductory session for the whole group, continued with individual mentoring sessions, and concluded with a social event to celebrate and "show off" the teaching portfolios of these 11 participants. To prepare ourselves to continue this teaching portfolio work, the CTE assistant director and two instructional consultants observed the mentoring sessions during which our outside consultants gave faculty participants feedback on drafts of their portfolios. Those first faculty participants were uniformly positive about the value of the teaching portfolio, and we were strongly encouraged to make the opportunity available to other faculty.

With this encouragement, the CTE began offering teaching portfolio workshops one or two times per semester. In the beginning, we retained the one-week model that our consultants had used. Later, to give faculty more time to work on their portfolio drafts, and to ease the intensity of the work for CTE staff, we experimented with a model that stretched the work over one month. When we found that it was difficult to sustain the energy and enthusiasm for the project for an entire month, we went to a two-week model; this proved to be the right amount of time. In all cases, we met with the whole group on three different occasions—at the beginning to introduce the project; in the middle to share insights, challenges, and questions; and at the end to celebrate completion of portfolios. CTE staff met with faculty participants individually two to three times to provide feedback and mentoring during the process.

The materials that we provide faculty to guide their teaching portfolio work have also evolved over time. Initially, we adapted materials used by Drs. Seldin, Shackelford, and Annis, and made available copies of Seldin's *The Teaching Portfolio: A Practical Guide to Improved Performance and Promotion/Tenure Decisions* (first edition 1991) and, after it came out in 1993, Seldin and Associates' *Successful Use of Teaching Portfolios*. As our collection of completed teaching portfolios grew, we were able to provide faculty with an array of sample teaching portfolios from different disciplines. The most significant leap forward in this regard came in 1996 when Jean Layne, then a CTE instructional consultant, synthesized our collective thinking and experience about the teaching portfolio into a "Teaching Portfolio Reflection Process Guide" that appears in Part I of this volume. This matrix has since undergone several revisions, and continues to be the centerpiece of the guidance we provide faculty as they create their portfolio.

After several years of offering three to four teaching portfolio workshops per year, we learned of a different model for assisting faculty with teaching portfolios: the teaching portfolio retreat. At a Professional and Organizational Development (POD) Network conference, Dr. Jim Groccia and his colleagues at the Program for Excellence in Teaching at the University of Missouri–Columbia shared their experience with this approach. We were intrigued, and decided to see if such a retreat would work well with our faculty. In 1998, we hosted our first teaching portfolio weekend. The weekend, described in more detail below, was so well received that we have made it an annual event, and beginning in 2003 offered such weekends semiannually.

THE TEACHING PORTFOLIO WEEKEND

The teaching portfolio weekend provides faculty a day and a half to focus on nothing but their teaching portfolio. We take our faculty participants—with their laptops—away from campus and away from phones, email, and all of the demands and distractions of the office. They come ready to think and write about their teaching. We provide a structure that allows them to leave with a good draft of their teaching philosophy, an outline of their teaching strategies, and a plan for collecting evidence to document their teaching accomplishments. The weekend consists of a combination of short presentations by CTE staff, whole-group brainstorming and discussion sessions, individual writing time, and time for peer feedback. We bring a variety of books about teaching and learning as well as sample portfolios as resources to which faculty refer throughout the weekend. Faculty participants are energized and challenged by the dialogue about teaching and learning and are focused and ready to write during the time provided. A typical weekend agenda, along with the materials we use as catalysts for discussion, are found in Appendix 12.1.

Since their introduction to our campus in 1992, teaching portfolios have played a central role in our faculty development work. Working on a teaching portfolio is often the initial point of entry for faculty who become engaged in the programs of the CTE. They may choose to attend other workshops to learn more about teaching strategies that have been introduced at the teaching portfolio retreat. Or they may choose to participate in one of our teaching conferences or in faculty learning communities, in order to continue the conversation with colleagues about teaching and learning. Additionally, involving CTE teaching consultants in the assessment of their teaching is often a part of the teaching evaluation plan faculty develop during the retreat. The teaching portfolio work has benefited all of us at the CTE as well. When we work with faculty on their teaching portfolios, we hear about the challenges they face in the classroom as well as the many creative strategies they have developed to meet these challenges. This depth of interaction with our faculty has enriched and strengthened our work, both broadening and deepening our understanding of teaching and learning in the college classroom.

FUTURE THOUGHTS

Literature about the teaching portfolio began appearing shortly before Boyer's (1990) influential work on scholarship and the professoriate. As teaching portfolios have become more widely used, the concept of the scholarship of teaching has become more refined. Practical aspects of this ongoing connection can be seen in the adoption of the course portfolio as a major component of the Pew-funded Peer Review of Teaching Project (in which TAMU is a participant institution) and the adaptation of the model for production of portfolios by faculty development professionals.

As we examine the extension of Boyer's work on the assessment of scholarship (Glassick, Huber, & Maeroff, 1997) we believe that teaching portfolios will continue to play an important role on our campus. It is an ideal tool for faculty to use as they plan and monitor their professional growth from effective teachers to contributors to the emerging scholarship of teaching.

APPENDIX 12.1

I. Sample Teaching Portfolio Retreat Agenda

Friday

11:00	Introductions
12:00	Lunch
1:00	Teaching philosophy—focused freewrites #1, 2, 3, and 4
2:30	Individual writing time
4:30	Teaching a diverse population
6:00	Dinner
7:00	Time for writing, reflection, collaboration

Saturday

8:15	Breakfast
9:00	Teaching strategies overview—worksheet #1
10:00	Individual writing time and peer feedback
12:00	Lunch

1:00   Methods and sources for evaluation of teaching—worksheet #2
2:00   Work in pairs to develop a plan for evaluating teaching
3:00   Final questions; next steps

II. Focused Freewrites

These are used to "prime the pump"—to get faculty participants thinking and talking about learning and teaching and to prepare them to write a draft of their teaching philosophy.

Focused Freewrite #1
Characteristics and Practices of Best/Worst Teachers

Consider your entire educational experience. Who was your best teacher? What made him or her the best?

Who was your worst teacher? What made him or her the worst?

Focused Freewrite #2
Learning

What is learning? How does it happen? What does it look like? What does it feel like?

What metaphors for learning capture what you believe about learning? Try completing the following sentences:

Learning is . . .

or

Learning is like . . .

Try drawing a picture that illustrates what you believe about learning.

What are the qualities of a good learner?

Focused Freewrite #3
Teaching

What is teaching? How does it happen? What does it look like? What does it feel like?

What metaphors for learning capture what you believe about teaching? Try completing the following sentences:

Teaching is . . .

or

Teaching is like . . .

Try drawing a picture that illustrates what you believe about teaching.

Focused Freewrite #4
Teaching and Learning
Reflect on the images and metaphors that you used for learning and for teaching. Are they compatible? How do they fit together?

Complete the following analogy in as many ways as you can:

Teaching is to learning as _____ is to _____.

What is the role of the learner in the learning process? What is your role as the teacher in the learning process?

III. Worksheets
These are used to guide faculty thinking about teaching strategies and teaching evaluation

Worksheet #1
Teaching Strategies
For each course, you make choices about how your students will be exposed to new information and new skills, how they will work with new information and practice new skills, and how you will assess and give feedback regarding their mastery of new information and skills. It is important that the teaching strategies section of your teaching portfolio clearly communicate the connections among your teaching philosophy, your learning goals for your students, and your choice of teaching strategies. This worksheet is intended to facilitate this communication.

I. Learning goals
When my students leave my course . . .
- What do I want them to know?
- What do I want them to be able to do with what they know?
- How do I want them to have developed intellectually, socially, culturally, globally, attitudinally, ethically, etc.?

II. Assessment strategies
How do I know that these learning goals have been accomplished?

III. How do I facilitate the achievement of these learning goals?
How do I expose my students to new information, ideas, concepts, and skills?

How do I help my students learn to integrate new information, ideas, and concepts into what they already know?
- How do I help them learn to apply new information, ideas, and concepts to a variety of situations and problems?
- What opportunities do I provide for practicing new skills?
- How do I assess my students' learning and provide feedback in between the "major" assessments?

IV. What do I do to create an environment that is conducive to learning for a diverse population of learners? What do I do to influence student motivation to learn in my class?

Worksheet #2
Evaluation of Teaching

You may be constructing your teaching portfolio to help you reflect on and improve your teaching. Or, your purpose may be to provide evidence of your teaching effectiveness and accomplishments. In either case, you will need a plan for evaluating your teaching. This worksheet is intended to help you develop such a plan.

I. Information/evidence from students about me as a teacher

   For what aspects of my teaching are students an appropriate source of information?

   How will I collect this information?

II. Information/evidence from my peers about me as a teacher

   For what aspects of my teaching are my peers an appropriate source of information?

   How will I collect this information?

III. Information/evidence from other sources (e.g., administrators, faculty development consultants)

   For what aspects of my teaching are other sources an appropriate source of information?

   How will I collect this information?

IV. Information/evidence from myself

   What information do I need to provide?

   What samples of my work should I include?

V. Evidence of student learning

   What evidence of my students' learning can I provide?

   How can this evidence best be presented?

13

Teaching Portfolios at the University of Evansville

Tamara L. Wandel

Teaching portfolios can be viewed as a renewed emphasis for universities to get back to the basics; a higher level of accountability expected of faculty; or a long-term need by deans and vice presidents for a more equitable, consistent approach to determining a faculty member's effectiveness as a teacher. Members of the University of Evansville (UE) community have embraced teaching portfolios for these different reasons, yet all involved agree that the burgeoning prominence of portfolios indicate that postsecondary education is moving in the right direction. The teaching portfolio process is a movement in that it showcases and documents a faculty member's effectiveness over time.

The *American Heritage Dictionary* defines movement, in relation to poetry, as the rhythmical or metrical structure of a poetic composition. In literature, it is described as the progression of events in the development of the plot. Perhaps in teaching we could say movement is like a delicate dance in which you are the lead, starting the semester off in tandem, teaching the necessary steps—sometimes basic, sometimes complex. It is a duet that, ideally, ends as a solo with your student as the star. Effective teaching can help a student to demonstrate all the nuances, possess all the talent, and demonstrate all the right moves of his or her discipline. He or she can think *critically*.

If only it were that easy. Many times the student painfully dances on our toes. Moreover, as much as it may be unpleasant to admit, faculty members do not always choose the right moves to make sweet music. Faculty members have been taught to be experts in their disciplines, yet have limited information on how to effectively *teach* their disciplines. It is a remarkable and rare occasion when students easily fit into the stereotypically stunning before-and-after makeover category. Even on those atypical occasions it is extremely difficult to determine just how much influence—even assuming the influence is positive—that faculty members have had on an individual.

It was this struggle that first brought teaching portfolios to the University of Evansville in 1997, through an invitation extended to Peter Seldin to serve as the keynote speaker for the Fall Faculty Conference. Academicians are students at heart, craving the challenge of mastering subject matter. Remember how exciting the first day of class was back in elementary school? Most academicians never lose the feeling of excitement that the first day delivers. It is a day when the slate is wiped clean and everyone plans to be the perfect student... or perfect professor. It was also the perfect time to introduce a concept that would offer a systematic approach, a form of movement from one step to the next, for determining teaching effectiveness.

While the systematic, structured approach to documenting effectiveness was appreciated, at the same time faculty were impressed that the portfolio process places a heavy value on freedom. Much in the same way academic freedom is valued, the portfolio process does not compromise freedom in defining teaching philosophies, teaching styles, and what is considered success. Perhaps most importantly, it was crystal clear that another freedom existed—determining at what career stage the teaching portfolio is put together. For some it was as a relatively inexperienced faculty member struggling to adjust to harsh teaching evaluations and for others it was as a teaching veteran who wants to significantly revise a course that has become stale over time.

Winning respect upfront for the goals and processes of teaching portfolios was a crucial step. Having the "guru" of teaching portfolios present made a significant difference. It was not top administration selling the process but another faculty member with great expertise in the area discussing its benefits. The end result of the teaching portfolios discussion at the Fall Faculty Conference was to offer a workshop for the next semester, January 1998, and limit the number of participants using a first-come, first-serve approach.

Since that date, 75 of 179 faculty members have participated in the teaching portfolio workshop. Over a five-year period, 42% of the University of Evansville full-time faculty members have produced a portfolio, which in turn means that over 40% of faculty members have made a concerted, focused effort to improve their teaching. It is possible that what makes teaching portfolios successful is distinctive for every participating institution. Luckily, answering the question, "What makes teaching portfolios successful at a private, Midwestern university?" has a more definitive answer than, "Why is there no 'J' street in Washington DC, even though all Washington, DC streets are named alphabetically?" Some questions may remain elusive, but at the University of Evansville, what makes teaching portfolios work is F-A-C-U-L-T-Y.

Faculty-Driven

Having outside teaching portfolio consultants lead the initial workshop is ideal. The first year it is imperative, the second year it is extremely helpful, but after that it becomes a luxury. For most universities it is simply not financially feasible to pay consulting and traveling fees year after year. Therefore, it is critical during the first few years that a foundation is laid for several faculty members to become in-house teaching portfolio mentors. UE handled this by having four faculty members, who were participants in UE's inaugural workshop, serve as mentors during the second year. What aided this in its success was that former outside counsel was in attendance at many of the sessions in an observation capacity. The in-house mentors and outside counsel would then meet for constructive feedback, participating in discussions on how the mentors could employ different methods to be more effective. The steps toward faculty ownership of the project were well on its way, but with a soft security blanket to ease any bumps or falls. By the third year, faculty members were empowered. UE's teaching portfolio process had become entirely faculty-driven.

Michael Cullen, department chair and professor in the biology department, has served as a mentor for several years.

> *As a mentor, I enjoy seeing others come to the realization that teaching assessment, teaching planning, and formal documentation are of benefit in their career development. Personally, I gain a great deal in working with faculty in disciplines other than mine. I learn about issues either unique or prominent in their disciplines. It is also exciting to talk about different teaching strategies and learn from each other.*

Administrative Coordinator

An administrator serving as the teaching portfolio coordinator was assigned to handle tasks ranging from recruitment of participants to budgeting issues. Without an individual to be held accountable for assigning the one-on-one meeting times of mentors and participants, ordering books and supplies for the participants, and arranging room locations for the meetings, the program may not have survived past its first year. Having specifically designated rooms for the mentors and participants to meet, for example, may sound like a small, unnecessary step. The alternative is to have meetings take place in a location such as the mentor's office where distractions are at a premium. Participants and mentors need to focus during the 45-minute meetings. Phones ringing, people strolling in to say hello, and beeps announcing a new email message arrival are simply disruptive.

The coordinator also has the dubious honor of assigning homework to the participants. Eight weeks before the workshop, the coordinator sends a list of nine questions to each portfolio participant. The participants are asked to bring their written responses to the first workshop meeting. This allows the workshop to have a solid opening, ensuring that it gets underway in a quick, effective manner. The nine items that participants are asked to address follow:

1) What is your job description? List your various teaching responsibilities and the percentage of time you feel you spend on each item. Does the allocated time seem appropriate? If not, what would you like to change?

2) Describe your teaching methods and explain why you teach as you do. Offer specific examples. When are you most comfortable teaching? When do you feel you are at your best? Which method(s) do you use that you feel are most helpful to your students?

3) What course projects, class assignments, or other activities help you integrate your subject matter with your students' outside experience. Do you help students bridge the gap between the real world and what they are being taught in your classes? If so, how?

4) What mechanisms do you utilize to encourage and motivate your students?

5) Describe your efforts to develop your teaching effectiveness.

   • Teaching workshops attended

   • Informal research conducted on your own teaching

   • Seminars, presentations, or publications on teaching

   • Peer observations

6) How do you stay current in your discipline? How do you translate this knowledge into your classes? What more could you be doing to stay current in your discipline?

7) What is your greatest strength as a teacher? How do you know this?

8) What is your greatest weakness as a teacher? What are you doing, besides getting ready to participate in the teaching portfolios workshop, to improve upon this?

9) What mechanisms do you utilize to assess your teaching effectiveness?

Finally, the administrative coordinator is also responsible for arranging roundtable discussions at the kickoff breakfast as well as for conducting assessment of the portfolio process. The assessment aspect will be touched upon later, but the roundtable discussions are a way to introduce participants to each other, create an environment where sharing successes and failures is encouraged, and focus on the common teaching-learning problems and patterns that are seen in numerous disciplines. The key is that there is one individual charged with handling the logistical details and who serves as the point person on portfolio issues.

Communication Among Disciplines

The interdisciplinary aspect has been a positive byproduct of the way the workshop is structured. Time and again faculty have commented on how they enjoy talking with (and in some cases meeting for the first time!) faculty from other disciplines and departments. This interdisciplinary mingling and collaboration helps alleviate certain fears of asking for help, acknowledging weaknesses, sharing what at times can feel like horrendous teaching evaluations, or critiquing a colleague's teaching portfolio when he or she may wind up as your department chair in two years.

The other unexpected benefit to the interdisciplinary aspect of the teaching portfolio workshop is that it forces participants to focus on teaching as opposed to getting lost in the minutia of a research area, a particular detail of a class, or nitpicking over a microscopic issue that only a certain discipline may experience. In other words, it would be easy for two communication professors (or two biology professors, two engineering professors, etc.) to focus more on a technical or specialized issue during the workshop instead of emphasizing effective teaching. By offering an interdisciplinary workshop, many of these obstacles and barriers are naturally removed. Finally, it is a superb excuse to bring together bright minds to discuss an important topic in an intellectually charged environment.

Unequivocal Top-Down Support

It is certainly desirable for faculty members to feel they get noticed for participating in the workshop and for setting aside time to focus on teaching improvements. When this is done correctly in a relaxed atmosphere, it is all the more enjoyable and beneficial. The University of Evansville supports this in two ways. First, the workshop begins with a kickoff breakfast that each of the four academic deans attend. At the breakfast meeting each of the deans has an opportunity to talk about the importance of the portfolio process as well as to congratulate their specific faculty members for their dedication and commitment to teaching excellence. It is a small but important step.

On those same lines exist the workshop-ending dinner. The president of the university attends, socializes with participants, and hands out certificates (that the administrative coordinator designed and printed) to those individuals who successfully completed the workshop. This is not a solemn, stuffy affair. It is a time for celebration, good food, and for perusing each other's portfolios. In addition, past workshop participants are invited to attend the dinner, bring their portfolios, and discuss how they continue to update and utilize their portfolios. This allows for a positive, elite group to form a bond that helps them encourage each other to continue to keep up their portfolios and their goals of excellence in teaching.

Whether it be in the form of a kickoff breakfast or a workshop-ending celebration, having high visibility with top administrators and academic officers is appropriate for this type of professional development. Many participants take part in the workshop for promotion and tenure reasons. It is a substantial motivator to feel that the creation of the portfolio and the energy put into the portfolio workshop is noted by those who help in making promotion and tenure decisions.

Limited Participation and Limited Timeline

The teaching portfolios process is like exercise. Nobody feels they have time for it, yet by participating you actually save yourself time in the long run (you can save *years* with both!). At UE, the workshop is scheduled over a four-day period during the holiday break. This allows for minimal disruption in the lives of participants and mentors. Do faculty members complain about the timing, stating that they are busy with holiday plans and prepping for the spring semester? Yes. However, when offered other times (summer, spring break, fall break, etc.), the week in January before classes start is always the hands-down favorite. Do faculty members complain about the intensity of the workshop? Yes. But many comments, such as these two taken from different surveys, provide valuable reflection on the experience:

> *The process was highly structured and full of deadlines and assignments—not at all the way I work if I'm left to my own devices. It was also exceptionally productive and thought-pro-*

voking and at the end of it I had a complete portfolio and a system for keeping track of materials to keep it up to date. When I have occasion to talk to someone who has worked on a portfolio in less structured settings they almost invariably ended up without completing it. The pressures of everyday teaching life intervene, and you rarely have time and/or motivation to work on it independently.

Very intense! It helped me organize my thoughts relative to teaching. The workshop provided the opportunity for guided reflective thought on what I believe is important in teaching and how I try to achieve my goals in teaching.

In addition, only offering limited participation in the workshop has worked well. Time is not wasted on selling the portfolio concept to those not interested in hearing its benefits. The focus remains on those individuals who feel they can grow as faculty members by producing a portfolio. Moreover, and most important to the concept of limited participation, is the desire to not outgrow the tailored, customized approach offered to past participants. One-on-one interaction between mentors and participants, as well as provocative discussions and engagement with small, interdisciplinary groups, have been the staples to making the program successful and unique. Compromising this in order to obtain greater faculty participation would be a short-term benefit with long-term negative implications.

Tracking

Central to the teaching portfolio is documentation of the effectiveness or even ineffectiveness of teaching. Given this emphasis, it is imperative that the portfolio workshop itself is evaluated regularly. The administrative coordinator designed a brief survey and solicits anonymous feedback after each workshop.

The feedback from these surveys is used to make necessary changes from year to year. For instance, it was suggested on several surveys to " . . . add extended social time during the workshop to allow for more exchange between faculty members..." That led to a positive change to increase the interdisciplinary discussions. Now, a structured but light two-hour afternoon session, complete with snacks and drinks, and is one of the highlights during the otherwise intensive workshop.

An example of the survey follows:

Teaching Portfolios Workshop

Please take a few minutes to answer the following questions. Your feedback is essential in assessing the value and practicality of utilizing the concept of teaching portfolios at the University of Evansville. A return envelope has been provided for your convenience. Thank you!

1. How was participating in the Teaching Portfolios Workshop beneficial to you?

2. What do you believe could have been improved?

3. Would you recommend producing a teaching portfolio to other faculty?
   ❒ Yes ❒ No ❒ I Don't Know

4. Circle the response which best fits your overall satisfaction with the Workshop.

   Very Satisfied Satisfied Neutral Somewhat Satisfied Not Satisfied

5. Other comments regarding the workshop:

6. Please circle the name of your mentor:
   Mentor A Mentor B Mentor C Mentor D

7. Circle the response that best fits your overall satisfaction with your mentor.

   Very Satisfied Satisfied Neutral Somewhat Satisfied Not Satisfied

Please feel free to elaborate on your experience with your mentor, what worked well, or what would have worked more effectively.

Another change that will take place in the future due to survey results is a greater time allocation to the discussion and development of the teaching philosophy. Faculty members have stated this aspect as being one of the most beneficial to the teaching portfolio process. The following are comments taken from surveys:

> *I think the most useful aspect of the workshop was that it forced me to really think my teaching philosophy through, something I had not done in years. I have been on autopilot for practically as long as I can remember.*

> *The workshop helped me to reassess what I was doing in two of the courses I teach. It was extremely beneficial to describe my teaching philosophy and evaluate whether I was using the*

> *best methods to get points across to the students. I have bene-*
> *fited greatly from the experience and so have my students.*

> *I detailed some valid weaknesses in my teaching style and*
> *process. I found that my teaching did not always match up*
> *with my teaching philosophy. I now have concrete concepts*
> *that will improve my teaching.*

The survey also ensures that participants are finding worth in allocating four days to the workshop, that mentors are serving the role that participants need, and that improvements can be made as needed. Over a five-year period, 100% of faculty members have stated "yes" they would recommend producing a teaching portfolio to other faculty. Ninety-five percent have stated they were "very satisfied" with the workshop and five percent were "satisfied."

You

Unique. Voluntary. Tailored. Specific to your needs. The bottom line is that *you* are at the heart of your teaching portfolio. The teaching portfolio is an individual element to be used by faculty as they see fit. Each faculty member decides when to share it or not share it, what to focus on, and what pieces or components to use. There is a constant striving to ensure that the workshop and the entire portfolio process remain customized to the individual needs of each participant.

For many, the hope of successfully aiding the tenure process is reason enough to develop a portfolio. Annette Parks, a faculty member in the history department who received tenure in spring 2003, said:

> *The portfolio was invaluable in negotiating the tenure process.*
> *It provided an organizational framework for the material; the*
> *narratives from the portfolio helped me to shape the larger*
> *narrative for the tenure letter; and the portfolio itself was a*
> *wonderful repository for materials I needed to include in the*
> *tenure portfolio including some assignments and materials*
> *that I'd not saved elsewhere. Also, the regular process of evalu-*
> *ating the portfolio materials helped me to think through the*
> *process of self-evaluation for the tenure narrative. For someone*
> *uncomfortable with the process of "selling yourself" the portfo-*
> *lio was an objective source of information about successes and*
> *failures and gave me a way of talking about how I could (or*
> *had) used both to become a better teacher.*

Another participant also stated that his original intent for signing up to be a workshop participant was to produce a document to be used toward promotion and tenure decisions. Upon reflection, however, the workshop was one of the most important steps the individual ever took toward improving his teaching.

> *In constructing my portfolio, I was forced to think very care-fully about what I do in the classroom, why I do it and how effective I have been. I know of no better tool for evaluating one's effectiveness as a teacher, and learning where and how to improve. As for promotion and tenure decisions, the portfolio goes far beyond student evaluations in providing a comprehensive picture on oneself as a teacher. Quite simply, no professor committed to teaching should be without one.*

Personally, I have a specialized teaching portfolio for classes I have taught on organizational communication. Now, however, I recognize a need to extend the portfolio to include elements from the public relations and strategic writing courses I am teaching at the University of Southern Indiana. I plan to incorporate information on the service learning aspect of the courses, information on the effectiveness of my role as an advisor with the University of Southern Indiana Public Relations Student Society of America chapter, and actual examples of writing and design that my students have created. As I stated earlier, I believe academicians are students at heart. My portfolio changes shape as I grow and learn more about effective teaching and what instills the greatest learning in my students. The teaching portfolio movement continues.

Part IV

KEEPING THE PORTFOLIO CURRENT

14

Strategies for Updating and Improving the Teaching Portfolio

John Zubizarreta

The teaching portfolio is one of the most powerful tools for improving, assessing, and evaluating teaching performance, but as with any method of capturing the complexity of teaching and its influence on students' academic and personal development, the portfolio must be a vital, ongoing process involving continually recorded reflection, conscientious mentoring and collaboration, and vigilant documentation of judiciously selected evidence. The portfolio must be revised and updated regularly if we want to take advantage of its agency in strengthening our work as teachers and documenting our impact on student learning. The importance of ensuring that when we analyze or evaluate teaching we include a variety of approaches and multiple sources of information is well established, and portfolios should therefore not be the only source for determining teaching effectiveness. But when used as part of a strong faculty development program and comprehensive system of evaluation, portfolios must be current and well supported, providing a reflectively rich, diverse, and collaboratively mentored profile: It must be a living process.

Developing a teaching portfolio, in other words, is hard but gratifying work. Rooted in the notion of reflective practice as articulated by Donald Schön (1983), portfolios demonstrate that good teaching is constantly in flux, challenging us to reexamine *what* and *how* we teach, but more importantly, *why* we teach. Portfolios provide a means to question the assumptions, methods, materials, and goals of our teaching in order to test continually the extent of their influence on student learning. Successful teachers recognize the process nature of their craft and seek regularly to strengthen their impact on learning by engaging in meticulous, intentional research about their labor in the classroom, what Ernest Boyer (1990) calls the scholarship of teaching. They take seriously the call to improve practice through reflection, peer collaboration, recorded action, and documented outcomes.

The teaching portfolio offers a process document that promotes continual improvement of the teaching enterprise if it is revised conscientiously and regularly. The portfolio provides a vehicle for recorded evidence of performance and, more importantly, for analysis and detailed goal setting, indispensable steps in a process of teaching enhancement. Revisions of a portfolio should go beyond routine replacement of evidential materials in a file folder, a simple act that reduces the portfolio to not much more than an elaborate, time-consuming filing system. *Instead, revisions should stress current, concise, written review of the relationship of teaching performance to student learning measured and recorded over time.* Such work, especially when peer mentored and reviewed, is consistent with the scholarship of teaching and provides the groundwork for maintaining and updating a meaningful and valid portfolio project.

TWO PREREQUISITES FOR SUCCESS

Mentor Support

One of the keys to the conciseness and efficacy of a successful process of portfolio revision is the involvement of a knowledgeable, supportive mentor who serves as formative coach and peer reviewer in prompting useful and creative strategies for revision without the high stakes of summative evaluation. Collaboration offers significant opportunities for strengthening the quality of teaching and learning by engaging professors in open discourse on pedagogical substance, making teaching a more public and peer-reviewed activity. When collaboration involves a colleague from another discipline or from outside the instructor's institution, the focus of portfolio development is more readily kept on teaching enhancement through meticulous, objective inspection of evidence.

Institutional Support

Institutional support is also crucial to the process of developing and updating portfolios, and faculty are more willing to maintain momentum and continue to use the portfolio as a living document and a tool for improvement when they know that such teaching development activities are valued and rewarded. Faculty need the encouragement and support of a formal institutional commitment to instructional development and must trust administrators' recognition of the scholarship of teaching as exemplified by rigorous revisions of portfolios. Four or five days devoted to concentrated writing and collaboration with a mentor provide the optimum occasion for development of an initial portfolio draft, and institutions should provide the resources needed to allow faculty to continue the process successfully and revise portfolios not only for periodic personnel decisions but for continual improvement.

HOW MY OWN PORTFOLIO HAS EVOLVED: AN UPDATED CASE

In the earlier version of this chapter (Zubizarreta, 1997), I elaborated on two examples of how updating my portfolio with the guidance of a peer mentor helped me improve my teaching. In reviewing, reusing, and revising parts of the chapter, I am struck by how my portfolio has changed over time but also by how the key principles of portfolio development and revision have remained steadfastly relevant and practical. Shifting through phases of using the portfolio for faculty development, for teaching assessment and evaluation, for connecting teaching to scholarship and service, for distinguished awards, for merit review, and for administrative improvement and evaluation as a program director and dean, I have successfully borne out the principles I myself advocated earlier.

The following chapter contains a copy of one of my updated portfolio drafts, an effort to use portfolio strategies to represent not only my teaching but also my scholarly work and engagement in service, an effort to capture the full scope and achievement of a year's dedication to academic citizenship through reflective narrative and selective evidence. The update was prompted by the introduction of merit review and rewards at the college, a yearly process requiring faculty to document accomplishments in teaching, scholarship, and service using a prescribed institutional form and inviting additional narrative and evidence. The portfolio has allowed me to go a step further in recording what I have valued in my work and how and why I have integrated the often disparate dimensions of the professoriate. The draft is accompanied by keyed items that suggest the ways in which I revised and updated the portfolio for improvement and clearer assessment of my work as teacher-scholar for comprehensive merit review and evaluation.

In the final analysis, however, the most powerful lesson in the continual attention to revising a portfolio is that the reflective and collaborative process, not the product, is the most valuable piece of portfolio development, the piece that most improves, reaffirms, and rewards our work. My first effort was a teaching portfolio fashioned after Seldin's (1993) model and developed collaboratively with his mentoring. Later, I devised a course portfolio (Zubizarreta, 1995), a concept developed concurrently in Cerbin

(1994) and later in Hutchings (1998), articulating the power of such tools for improving individual courses. Then I found the portfolio useful in merit review. Soon, as I accepted multiple administrative roles and responsibilities, I found portfolio strategies useful in enhancing and documenting administrative philosophy, duties, methods, accomplishments, and goals (see Seldin & Higgerson, 2002, pp. 110–120). Now back to teaching, scholarly work, and serving as an academic program leader, I continue to use the portfolio as a vehicle for reflection, documentation, and future planning. Through all the successive drafts of my portfolio, the underlying, pervasive, and connecting motivation for maintaining a carefully and thoughtfully updated portfolio is that the process has made me a better teacher, better scholar, and better academic leader.

TIPS ON MAINTAINING PORTFOLIO REVISIONS

Keeping up the momentum of improvement begun by the initial act of writing a teaching portfolio is not as easy as it seems, especially once the consuming duties of the semester take over. Yet, conscientious teachers can and do make time for crucial development activities as part of their commitment to exemplary teaching and their responsibility to student learning. Here are some suggestions that may make the important step of regular and timely revisions of a portfolio more manageable and productive.

- Use the appendix as a convenient, self-defined filing system for hard-copy information and documentation. For example, the portfolio should have an appendix for materials such as examinations or handouts. As new materials are developed for the purpose of trying to improve student learning, pitch them into the appropriate appendix for future assessment. As evaluations come in at midterm or at the end of the course, store them in the corresponding appendix, where they can later be analyzed for patterns of improvement or areas of concern.

- Don't reinvent the wheel. If year-end self-reports are part of one's evaluation of teaching system, then combine the narrative revision of the portfolio and its assessment of quantitative information in the appendix with the required report. Find ways of making required assessment and evaluation activities integral dimensions of portfolio revisions which, unlike most forms and data-driven reports, prompt genuine growth and intellectual engagement because of the power of reflective writing combined with the benefits of rigorous documentation.

- Focus on selected areas for enhancement. Narrow the scope of improvement efforts and the amount of information analyzed in a revision. Identify, for instance, one particular assignment in one course and the role of the teacher's periodic, written feedback on the work of three students of varying abilities.

- Keep revisions detailed and specific. Conceiving of revision as a complete reshaping of all the fundamental components of a portfolio is intimidating and unnecessary. Rarely do we undergo such dramatic revelations about philosophy and practice that the entire portfolio must be recast. Remember that the portfolio is a *process of continual analysis and improvement.* Revise deliberately, a step at a time, for clearer evidence of steady, systematic renewal.

- Take advantage of faculty development staff to help identify areas for improvement and suggest specific revisions of portions of the portfolio. Trained in implementing videotapes of teaching, peer review systems, teaching and learning styles inventories, classroom assessment techniques, and other strategies for improvement, faculty developers can introduce new modes of research into teaching that may prompt ideas for further revisions.

- Entrust a mentor to help guide the development of a portfolio through its various revisions. While collaboration with an experienced colleague outside one's institution is often best in the initial stage of writing a draft of a portfolio, teaming with a colleague within or outside the department or with a department chair can help create a useful perspective on the portfolio that stimulates worthwhile revision. The allied benefit of such collaboration is that teaching begins to grow in value across disciplines because of the cross-fertilization of serious commitment to ongoing improvement.

The final tip provides a practical, instructive venue for collaboration on several important issues that should be addressed in evaluating the content, format, and evidence of a teaching portfolio. A mentor and a professor should discuss such issues throughout the process of writing and revising a portfolio.

If we take seriously the current call in higher education for more emphasis on accountability, assessment, and improvement, the model of reflective practice demonstrated by the teaching portfolio emerges as one compelling solution to the need for professors to improve the standards of teaching and learning in the academy. Of course, other methods of strengthening the connection between teaching and learning exist and should be implemented just as carefully and widely as portfolio strategies.

As I have posited earlier, periodic portfolio revisions challenge us consistently to reexamine *what* and *how* we teach, but more importantly, *why* we teach, with the aim of improving the impact of our practice on student learning. Is the labor of developing and updating portfolios worth the effort? In my view, the answer is a resounding yes.

15

Key Points on Teaching Portfolio Revisions and Updates

John Zubizarreta

All teaching portfolios are living process documents, revised and updated periodically to capture genuine improvement in teaching and its impact on student learning. Here, I offer a current draft of my portfolio, developed personally for improvement but used practically for comprehensive merit evaluation. The portfolio includes numbered items that correspond to the following list of changes made after considerable self-reflection and collaboration with a peer mentor.

The portfolio integrates my work in teaching, scholarship, and service for merit review. Readers should compare the current version with an earlier draft shared in Seldin (1997) to see the ways in which the teaching portfolio has been adapted to merit considerations and the imperative of connecting teaching, scholarship, and service.

Descriptions of important observations and revisions are keyed to numbers in the margins of the portfolio draft.

1) *Revision.* Title of portfolio changed to reflect a more comprehensive, integrative approach for annual merit review.

2) Name of faculty member, department, institution, and date for clear identification and baseline for improvement.

3) Detailed table of contents, emphasizing institutional priorities for merit evaluation.

4) *Revision.* Added prefatory rationale for the purpose, content, and format of the portfolio, an important step in clarifying for an evaluator how to read and understand a portfolio.

5) *Revision.* Concise identification of the most significant items in the portfolio and appendix materials ensures that, in the context of evalua-

tion, important information is not overlooked. Also, the strategy assists readers in focusing on major items and finding pertinent evidence in a timely, directed manner.

6) Notice how the portfolio complements already established institutional requirements for annual reports so that the portfolio becomes an integral part of comprehensive review, not simply additional work.

7) *Revision.* An appendix for products of student learning is added to strengthen the merit evaluation case for the connection between teaching and its influence on learning outcomes. Such a connection is crucial in reorienting faculty evaluation decisions in a way that honors and rewards teaching improvement and the positive results of enhanced student learning.

8) Including advising, committee work, and professional involvement helps to diversify the representation of multiple faculty responsibilities.

9) *Revision.* For merit review, the portfolio goes beyond teaching to include scholarship and service, using portfolio strategies to reflect on the integration of varied faculty roles and provide multiple sources of evidence. The approach also brings the portfolio into alignment with established requirements for merit evaluation, serving institutional needs.

10) *Revision.* The teaching component of the portfolio is compactly subdivided into key categories for sound evaluation of teaching performance: philosophy, methods, learning outcomes, and diverse sources of evidence.

11) A specific, detailed example of teaching methodologies provides a glimpse into practice, accompanied by documentation in the appendix.

12) Notice one example among several throughout the portfolio of multiple references to appendix materials documenting a single example or claim in the narrative, creating a complex and strong web of evidence for evaluation purposes.

13) *Revision.* A major adjustment in moving from the original teaching portfolio to a more comprehensive and integrated profile for merit review is the incorporation of the narrative portion of the teaching portfolio into the appendix of the merit document. The choice retains the information and value of the teaching portfolio without overburdening the current draft.

14) *Revision.* The bulky appendix materials of the original teaching portfolio are made available upon request in convenient formats in order to acknowledge the wealth of evidence but keep the current merit document concise and manageable.

15) *Revision.* The strong emphasis on immediate, ongoing performance reveals the focus in merit review on current sources of information. As opposed to a more general teaching portfolio, the draft for merit is built predominately, if not exclusively, on the most recent year's worth of information.

16) *Revision.* The section on scholarship is included for merit review. Notice the stress on different modes of scholarship, setting a framework for a more appreciative review of different kinds of scholarly engagement. The portfolio allows for setting the context for review.

17) Another example of how to cite multiple sources of evidence to document a single item, strengthening validity and reliability of portfolio used for evaluation purposes.

18) Notice the integration of *curriculum vitae* into the portfolio, making the connection between the portfolio and other required elements of faculty evaluation seamless and less duplicative.

19) *Revision.* The section on service is included for merit review.

20) *Revision.* Student ratings, a prominent factor in teaching evaluation, are compressed and analyzed for easier yet meaningful presentation for summative review. A combination of numerical data for a specific population in a particular course over time and a few selected written comments offers a compact snapshot of student ratings information.

21) The scale used in ratings is clearly identified.

22) Both quantitative and qualitative rating items are selectively chosen to represent articulated philosophy, methodologies, and course goals. The complete record of ratings is included in an appendix.

23) *Revision.* Reflection on areas for improvement and description of improvement efforts are added to comply with stated requirements in merit review. Such additions are useful in establishing an assessment record of growth and vitality in teaching.

24) Peer reviews and feedback help to diversify information from others for the purpose of summative review.

25) Goals are specific and detailed, and a clear timeline is established for assessment. In further updates, accomplished goals are deleted, and new goals are added.

26) Appendices identify the *amount, type,* and *sources* of evidence, an important dimension of portfolios used for summative evaluation. One option in updating the portfolio for future personnel decisions is that the detailed appendices may be shifted to the Table of Contents for more immediate representation of evidence supporting the document.

The entire portfolio is placed in a three-ring binder with tabs for appendices. Bulkier evidence such as videotapes or posters is listed and annotated in an appendix and made available upon request. Some information may be online, and web addresses are given, with further description and analysis of content and relevance. Additional information, whether it is more reflection or more concrete evidence, can be relegated to an appendix, keeping the narrative portion of the portfolio compact and coherent, an especially practical choice for summative review.

The dynamic quality of developing and updating the portfolio suggests that the author can maintain the portfolio without continually adding to its size. The focus of revisions should remain on cogent, qualitative analysis for ongoing improvement, but the beneficial secondary result is that the portfolio also becomes a powerful, valid process and document for evaluation.

2002–2003 Faculty Merit Portfolio   1
John Zubizarreta
Professor of English
Director of Honors and Faculty Development   2
Columbia College
Spring 2003

Table of Contents   3

Portfolio Preface and Rationale   4

Since the first draft of my teaching portfolio over ten years ago, I have invested a considerable amount of my personal and professional energy to the virtue of reflective practice. My effort has been an endeavor that challenges teachers and scholars to improve their influence on students and the academy by continually examining the core principles and practices that distinguish the nature and efficacy of their work. Conducted continuously within a context of collaboration and formative peer review, such regular self-analysis and attention to diverse sources of documentation offer opportunities for improvement, authentic assessment, and sound evaluation.

This portfolio has the twin purposes of both improvement and annual merit evaluation of my multiple responsibilities in teaching, scholarship, service, and academic leadership. It is an ongoing, updated tool for strengthening my roles as teacher, scholar, program director, and academic citizen, while also serving as a frame for reflective analysis of my work with students, colleagues, my discipline, and the college. My primary focus is on how reflection and systematic documentation of my efforts can help me continue to learn and improve as a teacher-scholar.

For the secondary but practical purpose of efficient yearly merit evaluation, I direct attention to the following five crucial components of my portfolio narrative and accompanying appendix materials:

1) Multiple and diverse responsibilities   p. 1 (Appendices A, D, G)
2) Continual efforts to improve teaching and learning   p. 3 (Appendices B, J)
3) Emphasis on learning   p. 3 (Appendix J)
4) Consistent awards and peer recognition   p. 4 (Appendices E, K)
5) Extensive and current scholarly engagement   p. 4 (Appendices G, H, I)

Responsibilities

The standard load at the college is four courses each semester, but because of double administrative duties as Director of Honors and Director of Faculty Development, my contracted teaching load is one course per semester, though technically each position offers two courses of reassigned time (See **Appendix A** for annual faculty report). There have been semesters recently when I have taught two or three courses in a term. Here is a sampling of my ongoing teaching this year: In fall 2002, I taught Eng. 350: The Modern Short Story, an honors course I designed and have taught often; it enrolled over twenty students. I also taught two combined honors sections of Liberal Arts 100, a newly developed freshman seminar course; it enrolled close to thirty. In spring 2003, I taught Eng. 102 (H): Literature and the Myth of the Hero (enrollment of twelve), using a web-based course shell to involve students in partial online course work. The main feature of our online engagement was an exciting and productive threaded discussion that received outstanding ratings by students when asked to reflect on their learning in the course. (See additional information about ratings and collected forms in **Appendix B**.) Also, **Appendix J** contains samples of student work online, a compelling record of substantial learning and enhanced critical thinking and writing skills.

During the 2002–2003 academic year, I also served as advisor to a number of honors projects, and I advised seven English majors. In the last four years, while also serving as a dean, I have advised as many as fourteen majors and served as appointed freshman advisor for twenty-eight honors students across disciplines. See **Appendix C** for selective acknowledgements of my consulting with both majors and honors freshmen on academic and personal issues, including email and other correspondence from students and alumnae whom I have mentored this past year and before.

In addition to directing both honors and faculty development programs, I currently serve on four college and faculty committees, acting as chair of two, and on occasional ad hoc task forces for grant selections, academic and administrative searches, travel/study, and a start-up peer mentoring program. See **Appendix D** for a list of faculty and administrative service activities and **Appendix E** for faculty and administrative service awards, such as nomination in spring 2003 for Faculty Excellence Award.

Externally, in professional venues, I am currently the Immediate Past-President of the American Culture/Popular Culture Association in the South, the Vice President and President-Elect of the Southern Regional Honors Council, the Conference Program Chair of SRHC 2003, Faculty Representative on the Executive Committee of the National Collegiate Honors Council, and member of various other professional organizations and committees (see **Appendix G**).

PHILOSOPHY OF FACULTY ENGAGEMENT: INTEGRATING TEACHING, SCHOLARSHIP, SERVICE

9

Teaching
Philosophy

10

In my relations with students, I have learned that conscientious mentoring is a necessary dimension of transformative teaching and learning. Delivering information is a function of teaching which the competent teacher can perform. But the outstanding professor knows the value of working patiently with students on personal levels to help them achieve more significant learning. In a sense, the professor teaches more than content; he or she teaches habits of thinking, habits of being. Students discover in the process of engaged and active learning the rewards of controlled inquiry, the value of reasoned discourse, the delight of intellectual curiosity, and an earned respect for the process of questioning knowledge and moving freely among the linked components of learning which involve analysis, comprehension, synthesis, application, and evaluation—all underpinned by the benefits of reflection.

Methodologies and Products of Student Learning

One example of my intentional focus in and out of the classroom on the value of such a process approach to teaching and learning is my use of self-styled RLMs (Reflective Learning Moments) in my classes. An RLM is an

11

opportunity to stop immediately whatever learning activity is in process—a classroom conversation, an online threaded discussion, an exam, a group project, a pre-writing exercise, library research, a field experience—and ask directed questions about what, how, when, where, and why one has learned or not learned. Such recorded reflection deepens learning and makes it more durable. The impact of RLMs, combined with the use of learning portfolio strategies, has been powerful, and Appendices B and J include both formative and summative student assessments of the method and samples of student work in learning portfolios which reveal the positive effect of such reflective practice on learning.

Additional details of the various methodologies I explore and use in my teaching to promote reflection, critical thinking, creativity, active learning, and strengthening of fundamental disciplinary skills are developed in my *Teaching Portfolio*. Such strategies include role plays, simulations, case studies, disciplinary exchange, online threaded discussions, email listservs, lecture, classroom discussion, group work, field experiences, journals, fishbowl observations, gallery walks, guest speakers, peer teaching, and more. The portfolio also documents the learning outcomes of my work by providing descriptions and reflective analyses of a variety of samples of student work in process stages, demonstrating the relationship between my teaching and student learning (see Appendix F).

Diverse Sources of Evidence

Such values have directed my commitment to teaching beyond my contractual obligations at the college, for teaching and learning are my core passion, my chief challenge, my greatest reward. My complete philosophy of teaching, along with detailed evidence of effective practices and reflective analysis of disappointing teaching moments and efforts to improve, are documented in my complete *Teaching Portfolio*. The narrative portion of the portfolio is included in **Appendix F,** and the complete portfolio with appendices is available for review upon request in either hard copy or digitized formats. The full version contains selective information and evidence from student ratings and qualitative assessments, peer reviews, teaching awards, materials (syllabi, assignments, handouts, exams, electronic media), improvement efforts, letters from and for colleagues and students, and teaching goals. For the sake of concise merit evaluation, I stress only highlights here.

Awards

One of the features of my many teaching portfolio revisions of which I am very proud is the consistency of recognition awards over time. Appendix E lists and describes many lucky awards and nominations from sources such as the Carnegie Foundation/CASE, American Association for Higher Education, South Atlantic Association of Departments of English, SC Commission on Higher Education, Conference on Christianity and Literature, and the college. I am a fortunate and perennial nominee on campus for our Faculty Excellence and Students' Choice Awards, and I am heartened that my performance continues to earn notice and reaffirmation from students and colleagues.   15

Scholarship

The professor must demonstrate competency and currency by actively   16
engaging in the public, professional venues of publications, presentations, or creative work. I also believe that the *scholarship of teaching and learning* is an exciting change in academia which complements the traditional arena of disciplinary scholarship, professional work that validates expertise among communities of scholars. I continually engage in SOTL to improve practice and contribute to a dynamic agenda in higher education (see **Appendix H** for sample faculty projects and **Appendix I** for examples of grant-funded collaborative undergraduate research projects that demonstrate forms of SOTL). Such charges fulfill the responsibility of faculty tenure, offer a positive model for faculty colleagues, and connect to current initiatives in the changing landscape of faculty roles and rewards in higher education.

Appendices G, H, and **I** provide evidence of current scholarship foster-   17
ing a climate of faculty, student, and administrative reflective practice and collaboration. For example, the work included in the appendices reveals collaborative publications, conference presentations, and professional workshops this year with students, peers, deans, and academic vice-presidents at my own and other institutions worldwide. Such work, combined with my commitment to working with students in mentored undergraduate research, suggests the ways in which I try to integrate teaching, scholarship, and service.

In traditional scholarship, this spring, I finished a book titled *The Learning Portfolio: Reflective Practice for Improving Student Learning,* a chapter for a book on teaching portfolios, an article on student-moderated midterm formative assessment, and a collaborative journal article with a student on using asynchronous technologies to enhance learning. Also, in 2002–2003, I have presented numerous papers, workshops, and sessions at professional conferences such as the National Collegiate Honors Council, Professional and Organizational Development Network in Higher Education, International Sigma Tau Delta, Southern Regional Honors Council,

Popular Culture Association in the South, National Conference on Undergraduate Research, International Improving University Teaching, and others. I have also consulted on teaching and learning, academic program review, and other areas at several institutions here and abroad, applying my developing scholarly expertise in various academic arenas. My vitae in

18 **Appendix G** contains a complete list.

Service

19 The professor/academic leader is also responsible for meeting the obligations of *academic citizenship,* for engaging meaningfully in institutional priorities and goals. **Appendix D** contains a list of college, professional, and community services, including my various contributions to institutional program reviews, site visitations, faculty development consultations, convocation and keynote addresses, committee work, and more. My *Teaching Portfolio* (**Appendix F**) also documents how I have lived up to my own values and performance standards in the full arena of the academy and its imperative of service. This more comprehensive yet more concise merit portfolio adds another level of reflection to my professional growth, examining the interactions among my multiple roles and achievements in teaching, scholarship, and service.

Evaluations of Teaching

Because of the importance of both formative and summative feedback from students and peers in yearly merit evaluation, I emphasize for merit review the following information taken from my *Teaching Portfolio.*

20 My student ratings continue to be excellent, though I recognize areas for improvement. Here is a summary of quantitative results on selected rating items relevant to my teaching philosophy and course goals. To attain sufficiently meaningful numbers from a contractually reassigned course load, I compile the information from the last two years of Eng. 102(H), a course I teach regularly. The items represent areas that research on student ratings suggests are most appropriate for evaluating teaching performance. I have organized related items on rating forms into five simplified categories for more effective summative review.

Scale (the *lower* the average, the *stronger* the rating)		21
1 Strongly agree 2 Agree 3 Disagree 4 Strongly disagree 5 N/A		
Item	*Avg. Rating*	
1) Detailed, organized, clear syllabus, materials, and goals	1.64	
2) Fair, timely, appropriate feedback and grading	1.68	
3) Enthusiasm, increased interest, motivated and encouraged learning	1.08	
4) Available, responsive, flexible	1.08	22
5) Challenging, rigorous	1.08	

Qualitative comments on the rating forms include the following statements connected to components of the teaching philosophy I articulate fully in my *Teaching Portfolio* (**Appendix F**):

- "Dr. Z presented the materials to us with a certain personal passion that made everything we were studying seem important and relevant to our daily lives."

- "The whole atmosphere of the class was very welcoming."

- "I enjoyed the hard work...interest...and flexibility of the course...gave us room to delve into our ideas and develop them further."

- "I am a more critical thinker...a more mature person."

- "Class and threaded discussions facilitated the process of applying concepts...to everyday life. The videos helped us explore common themes in different mediums. The midterm assessment was helpful, too."

- "I worked harder in this class than others because it was challenging and interesting."

Some student feedback has suggested areas for improvement. For example, in one class, after placing a great premium on the value of reflection, active learning, and how both classroom and online asynchronous discussions help develop critical thinking and problem solving skills, I discovered through feedback that my use of objective exams—especially since questions tended to be designed more for knowledge than any other cognitive functions or levels of learning—seemed to contradict my stated philosophy and goals. Luckily, the feedback was generated at midterm, and I was able to alter my strategies, and students' evaluations at the end of the term revealed their appreciation of my taking their learning seriously; they also earned a new respect for themselves as engaged learners who take an active role in

23

their success. (See **Appendix B** for a record of student comments on midterm and end-of-term assessments.)

A compilation of additional midterm formative assessments using the student-facilitated "critical response" method innovated in honors at the college is included in **Appendix B**, along with documentation of student ratings and comments cited in the previous table and lists.

24 *Peer Review and Feedback*

In **Appendix K**, I include various examples of peer review information from class observations, feedback on teaching materials and methods, and written records of colleagues' responses to workshops and presentations on teaching and learning. Here are a few statements written by a variety of colleagues in this last year.

- "Very helpful . . . I've gotten some great ideas for my own courses."
  —from colleague at a professional presentation on teaching improvement.

- "Thanks for your leadership in many areas, but especially in developing opportunities for student—and faculty—growth."
  —from colleague in my department.

- "Thanks for such a thoughtful reading of my 'philosophy.' Your enthusiasm is inspiring. . . . You've been a real help, and your expertise in these matters is quite palpable in the response you gave to my writing."
  —from colleague at another institution, about collaboration on improving teaching.

- "Ever since John arrived on campus, he has dazzled students and faculty alike with his engaging classes and individual attention to students and their needs."
  —from department chair in annual review.

- "You have given the college wonderful leadership. . . . Your ideas about faculty development are known to be some of the best in the nation."
  —from provost in annual review.

- "If I were wearing buttons, they would pop with pride! Thank you so much . . . for the wonderful work you do with these students."
  —from president, about teaching and mentoring of honors students.

25 *Development Goals*

1) Summer 2003: Study ways of including more cultural diversity in my courses, especially an evening class that I will teach in fall to a population of diverse adults, a new challenge.

2) Fall 2003: Develop a new English honors course that draws on more recent interests and professional directions and that connects thematically with the spring term honors senior seminar, culminating in a travel/study venture in May.

3) Fall 2003: Work with a co-director colleague in coordinating a new grant-funded Lilly Mentoring program to encourage and support faculty new to the college with reading groups, practical teaching workshops, class observations, discussion forums, portfolio development, and other activities useful to beginning a career at the college.

4) Fall 2003: Collaborate with Student Affairs to implement a vital residence hall academic experience for honors students, involving strong faculty participation and cooperation with Resident Academic Advisors to bridge academics and residence life and to help build a stronger learning community among students in the program.

5) Spring 2004: Move forward with a plan to expand faculty development on campus, exploring the possibility of linking with major academic initiatives and programs to establish a cadre of Faculty Development Fellows who can provide leadership to ongoing faculty development work across campus.

6) Summer 2004: Begin plans for a new book on teaching and learning issues and strategies in honors education. A publisher has already expressed an interest in the idea, and I will submit a proposal during summer.

Appendices   26
A: Annual Faculty Report
B: Student Ratings, Midterm Assessment, and Feedback
C: Advising Information and Acknowledgements
D: Faculty and Administrative Service
E: Honors, Awards, Recognition
F: *Teaching Portfolio*
G: *Curriculum Vitae*
H: SOTL: Faculty Projects
I: SOTL: Undergraduate Research
J: Products of Student Learning
K: Peer Reviews and Feedback

Part V

SAMPLE PORTFOLIOS
FROM ACROSS DISCIPLINES

Part V is composed of 22 sample teaching portfolios from across disciplines. Though the appendix material referred to is part of the actual portfolios, it is excluded here because of its cumbersome nature. The portfolios are arranged in alphabetical order by discipline. Because each portfolio is an individual document, varying importance has been assigned by different professors to different items. Some professors discuss an item at length, while others dismiss it with just a sentence or two, or even omit it. *Important: You are urged to bear in mind that sample portfolios from other disciplines often provide helpful information and insights applicable to your own discipline.*

16

Teaching Portfolio
Joseph G. Donelan
Department of Accounting and Finance
University of West Florida
Spring 2003

Table of Contents

Executive Summary

The following points highlight the most important elements of my portfolio:

- A clear statement of my teaching philosophy (pages 3–4) supported by strategies for implementation (pages 4–7) and evidentiary documentation (Appendices A–M).

- A summary of my student course evaluations shows that 75% of respondents rated my overall teaching either 4 or 5 on a five-point scale where 5 = excellent.

- Ft. Walton Beach College of Business Instructor of the Year Award, 2000 (Appendix B).

- Published educational and pedagogical teaching materials that support my teaching philosophy and integrate my own research into the classroom experience (Appendices C and D).

- Integration of real-world experiences and examples is supported and enhanced by 1,400 hours of significant, recent, relevant work experience (see *Faculty Internships* section, page 7, and Appendix E).

- Over 450 hours of continuing professional education courses (see Appendix F).

- My teaching philosophy is supported by a wide range of pedagogical approaches (Appendix G), syllabi and chapter outline (Appendix H), and sample examinations (Appendix I).

- Integration of technology in all my classes, including use of a web-based courseware in all of my courses.

- Knowledgeable in my field, as demonstrated by student evaluations, peer evaluations, and record of refereed publications.

- A practicing CPA's evaluation of course materials (Appendix M).

- Academic peer's evaluation of course materials (Appendix M).

- An active learning environment that includes student participation and many hands-on learning experiences held in computer labs (Appendix G).

- Student feedback process (critical success factor analysis, Appendix L) provides a vehicle for continuous change and improvement in my teaching.

- Published research in the practice of public accounting and in effective academic preparation for the Certified Public Accounting exam. These research projects directly support my academic and career advising skills.

Teaching Responsibilities

My primary teaching responsibility is undergraduate and graduate accounting courses. Since arriving at the University of West Florida in 1999, I have taught six different undergraduate courses. In addition, I have taught three different graduate accounting courses. My teaching load is three sections per semester, and I have usually had three different preparations per term.

I view accounting as a communication art, and all the courses I teach emphasize the communication aspects of accounting information. My primary area of instruction is the managerial uses of information for planning, control, and decision-making.

Teaching Philosophy

Teaching and learning go hand in hand. I expect to learn as much from my fellow classmates as they learn from me. I also expect to work harder than my students every semester, every class.

I believe that I have three primary responsibilities:

1) My first responsibility is to develop the following lifelong learning skills:

   • *Technical skills* are knowing how to do something.

   • *Knowledge* is knowing what things to do.

   • *Attitude* is wanting to do things.

   • *Communication* is being able to explain the things you did.

   As an educator, I have a responsibility to nurture all four. As a servant to firms who hire our graduates, I have a responsibility to evaluate student performance in all four. As a student, I have the responsibility to continually improve in all four. (See Appendix K for a full description of the four lifelong learning skills.)

2) My second responsibility if to provide a learning environment where students develop and practice lifelong learning skills while mastering the subject matter of my class.

3) My third responsibility is to act as a role model and mentor. I believe this is important, because if my students respect me—view me as a role model and mentor—then I can create a learning environment that promotes the *attitude* learning skill. Moreover, I am able to provide more effective career and academic advising.

Strategies for Implementing Teaching Philosophy
Developing Technical Skills

Technical skills involve knowing how to do things. This requires reading, writing, speaking, and listening. To help students develop these skills, I use a wide range of classroom pedagogy. For example, ACG 3311 is a course that covers the managerial application of accounting knowledge. Therefore, it is important to be able to read, compute, analyze, and explain the results to management. Appendix G shows how I accomplish this by including an average of five cases, reports, and spreadsheet projects in each section taught. Moreover, all my courses include exams (see Appendix I for an example) that test a wide range of skills including computation, analysis, and written explanations of the results.

So that students are aware of the technical demands expected of them, and so that they prepare adequately for the rigor of my examination, I publish all my prior semester exams as part of my course materials. In this way, students begin to develop the necessary skills from the beginning of the semester. Moreover, I publish an essay on how to prepare for Dr. Donelan's exams (see Appendix K). The following excerpt demonstrates the importance I place on communication skills.

> *I believe that business students should have a thorough understanding of fundamentals. I often omit coverage of details; however, I expect a powerful understanding of the fundamentals. The student must be able to explain a fundamental concept to a lay person in a clear, insightful way. I believe that you do not fully understand a concept unless you can clearly explain it verbally and in writing.*

Developing Knowledge

As described above, technical skill is knowing how to do something. Knowledge is knowing what to do. All my classroom experiences and exams take students beyond the computational level to the application of those computations to real-world applications. For example, in one of my applied managerial accounting (ACG 3311) exams (Appendix I), most of the grading points attach to knowing what ratios to compute in a particular situation. In my graduate level class, more than half the points assigned to an exam are for the composition of the explanations of the results (Appendix I).

Developing Attitude

Developing a desire to learn is the most difficult lifelong learning skill to instill in others. However, there are things instructors can do to encourage a good attitude.

- Provide a participative environment that involves students in the learning process.

- Stay focused and on task.

- Provide a challenging academic environment.

- Enjoy your material and enjoy teaching it to others.

- Be fair.

One way to provide a participative environment that involves the students in the learning process is through collective determination of the course objectives. I accomplish this though use of critical success factor analysis (described earlier).

Creating a Learning Environment

My objective is to design and manage processes that help students develop their lifelong learning skills while learning the subject matter of the course.

The learning environment should include effective, up-to-date, real-world materials. For that reason, my class material includes case work with many possible solutions, case work/assignments with messy data, missing data, and/or unclear facts, and instructor's evaluation of case solutions based on the students' ability to clearly state assumptions, document solution process, and compose a clear, concise solution that addresses the issues at hand. The published teaching materials that follow provide further insights into my use of the case method.

Published Teaching Materials

I develop and use real-world case materials in my courses. My skill in this area is demonstrated by my publication in 2001 of three cases in peer-reviewed journals. (See Appendix C for more details of the case teaching materials.)

My most recent case publication was recognized by one of the top academicians in my field. Dr. Robert Kaplan, Harvard Business School, wrote,

> *I just came across your excellent "case" and teaching note based on the CD-ROM simulation Balancing the Corporate Score-card. This looks excellent. You clearly have invested much time developing this thoughtful teaching approach to the simulation.*
>
> *[Dr. Robert Kaplan, Harvard Business School, 2001 letter included as Appendix D].*

Faculty Internships

In order to develop case materials for my class, improve the real-world examples that I could bring to class, and energize my teaching with fun war stories, I accepted three unpaid faculty internships over the past six years. These internships involved approximately 1,400 hours at one Fortune 100 company and another in one of the largest regional CPA firms in the Southeast (see Appendix E for examples). Three published teaching cases have resulted from these internships.

Faculty internships improve my instruction and advising in yet another way—by gaining the respect of professional accountants. With such respect, students will allow me to become a role model and mentor. As such, I can create an environment where students seek my knowledge for its usefulness in life, and not just for getting a grade on an exam.

Evaluation of Teaching

Students' Overall Assessment of Instruction

Evaluations of my instruction are available from a wide variety of classes, both undergraduate and graduate. These evaluations include numeric and written responses included on my student evaluation of classes. In addition, I have included comments from my chair and the MBA director.

My student evaluations are overwhelmingly positive. The table below reports the "overall assessment of instruction" question from all 1,054 student respondents from 1999 through 2002, showing that 85% of all student responses were 4 or above. (Complete student evaluation data is found in Appendix A.) Moreover, the chart provides evidence that my courses are challenging, which suggests that I am not "buying" the evaluations with light material and easy grades.

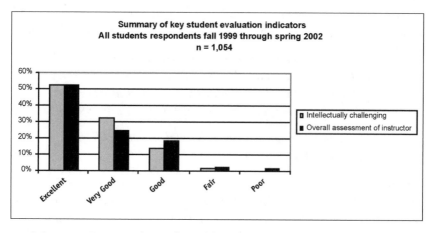

Moreover, I garner theses favorable evaluations in spite of

- Uninflated grades (see the GPAs reported in Appendix G).

- The rigors of my courses ("fast-paced and challenging," said one of my students in their written response).

- The fact that 70% of my responding students are nonmajors enrolled in a required accounting course that most students resist or fear prior to enrolling.

In addition to the numeric results, my students' written comments are very favorable. For example, several students commented on the quality of the real-world experiences that I bring to the classroom:

- *"I work in consumer and commercial lending. This class has been very useful and many of the [class] techniques are used in lending."*

- *"Assignments helpful. I could see a parallelism to professional work."*

- *"Dr. Donelan used 'real life' to explain situations."*

- *"Quite a professional man in his field."*

Students' Assessment of Technology Integration

I integrate the use of technology in all my classes. This includes:

- Use of hardware for in-class labs and demonstrations.

- Submitting, grading, and returning assignments via email.

- Integration of word processing, spreadsheets, and presentation software.

- Web-based material distribution, threaded discussions, and grade posting in all classes.

Selected student comments below report the favorable response to this integration.

- *"Communication using e-mail was very effective and useful."*
  (ACG 3401, fall 2001)

- *"The use of QuickBooks, Excel, Access, and Email was very productive."*
  (ACG 3401, fall 2001)

- *"Technology in this class helped make the class more interesting by letting me think outside of the box."*
  (ACG 3311, fall 2001)

Students' Assessment of Instructor's Enthusiasm

Student comments attest to my enthusiasm:

- *"Dr. Donelan is excited about this course. He is very thorough & organized."*
  (ACG 3401, fall 2001)

- *"Mr. Donelan was very energetic and enjoyed teaching the class."*
  (ACG 3401, fall 2001)

- *"Love the teacher. He's the best one in the MBA program."*
  (FIN 6406, spring 2002)

- *"Awesome Prof. Loved the class."*
  (ACG 3401, spring 2002)

Students' Participation in Setting Course Objectives
To accomplish mid-course corrections, I use a critical success factor process (see Appendix L for the instrument and measures used). At the beginning of the semester, students determine the ten most critical factors for the success of the class. Then, at midterm, the students assess our performance in those factors. We use quadrant analysis techniques to graphically display the results. I then draft an action plan for the remainder of the term that addresses corrections for improvement.

Peer Evaluation of Course Materials
The quality of my teaching materials are supported by peer evaluations:

- Mr. Edward Kaplan, Group Controller, Hilite Industries, Cleveland, Ohio (Appendix M)

- Dr. Timothy O'Keefe, Professor and Director of the University of West Florida MBA Program (Appendix M)

Goals

I have several goals to improve my instruction. A brief description and my timeline for accomplishing the goals are summarized below.

Goal	Completion Deadline
Have an academician review my course materials and examinations, assess my strengths and weaknesses, and make recommendations for improvement.	March 1, 2003
Have one of my colleagues (T. O'Keefe or S. Frank) observe my instruction.	March 1, 2003
Have a practicing professional review my course materials and examinations, assess my strengths and weaknesses, and make recommendations for improvement (E. Kaplan).	June 1, 2003
Retain records of my student learning cases with my comments: • Exam performances with my comments. • Unsolicited responses from former students. • Examples of my positive impact on graduates' careers. • Testimonials from students who changed their major to accounting because of a good experience in my class.	December 1, 2003

Appendices

17

TEACHING PORTFOLIO
Shivanthi Anandan
Department of Bioscience and Biotechnology
Drexel University

Table of Contents

1) Teaching Responsibilities

As a faculty member in the Department of Bioscience I teach several courses at the undergraduate and graduate level. At the undergraduate level I teach a required freshman level Genetics course (Bio 117), and several other elective courses: Microbiology (Bio 221), Biotechnology (Bio 480), Mechanisms of Microbial Pathogenesis (320), and Genetically Modified Foods (Bio 480). I also teach a required course at the graduate level, Microbial Genetics (Bio 530), and an elective course, Medical Microbiology (Bio 670). Appendix A contains the syllabi for these courses.

2) Teaching Philosophy

My role, as I see it, is to bring the field of biology to the students and to help them learn and understand its basic tenets. I aim to illustrate the uses and applications of basic concepts in biology in the real world. I work hard to foster my students' ability to learn and think critically while building their problem-solving skills.

To achieve this goal, there should be good rapport between the teacher and her students. This includes being accessible to the students, both within and outside of the lecture hall. To build rapport, it is also necessary to be accessible in attitude: to be open to hearing their questions, comments, and opinions. I foster an environment conducive to discussion and encourage my students to ask questions both in lecture and in lab.

3) Teaching Methods/Strategies

Using the Application of Biological Concepts to Motivate Student Learning

In keeping with the Drexel University mission statement to "educate men and women to live and work successfully in a technological world," I try to relate the concepts of biology to applications in the real world. This teaching method emphasizes to the students that the concepts they learn in their classes have applications in the every day world.

The Molecular and Cellular freshman genetics course (Bio 117) is lab-based and the students carry out a small independent research project using DNA fingerprinting, a technique commonly used in forensic science. A copy of the guidelines for this project, a sample poster evaluation sheet, and the course syllabus can be found in Appendix A.

The students in this course are an interesting mix coming from diverse backgrounds: Bioscience majors, students from the Nutrition and Food Science program, and students in the Environmental Science, Engineering, and Policy program. I designed this laboratory project to pique the students' interest in biology while teaching them practical skills. The students are initially trained to carry out the technique, and then use it to solve a small research problem. They then have to write a fictitious case study or scenario where the perpetrator is identified using DNA fingerprinting. While participating in this project, not only do the students have to learn the technical aspects, but they also have to understand the genetic concepts that allow this application to occur. By utilizing the techniques and gathering their own data, students are asked to come to a logical conclusion. To properly analyze their data, students need to integrate the basic concepts of genetics, such as the inheritance of traits from generation to generation, with the performance and limitations of this technique. Moreover, in a practical sense the students are gaining experience in performing a technique that they will use in their co-op labs.

I find that students really like this project and can readily relate it to the outside world, for example, the OJ Simpson murder trial or the identification of the space shuttle astronauts. This teaching innovation encourages students' interest in applications of scientific techniques, while at the same time stimulating their analytical and problem-solving skills. The results of this independent project are presented by each group in a poster format. This is an example of a teaching innovation that optimizes the delivery of course material by enforcing written communication.

Increasing Critical Thinking Skills and Building Teamwork

It is common practice to teach a graduate level microbial genetics course as a strictly lecture-based course. My microbial genetics course has, in addition to the lecture, a recitation section where the students learn to read, analyze, and present scientific papers. Most of the graduate students enrolled in the microbial genetics class work in pharmaceutical or biotechnological companies. Thus, to demonstrate to them how important the early, classical experiments in microbial genetics are, I show them how these experiments led to the development of strategies and methods for gene cloning. Since most students have some experience with gene cloning in their workplace, they relate to and retain the information better when they see how it impacts their world.

This is an example of my application-oriented style of teaching. This method personalizes learning and makes the students part of a cooperative learning experience. By analyzing scientific papers, students develop and refine a crucial skill requisite in their own research, that of critical thinking. The analytical exercise is carried out in pairs and focuses on team work. By consulting with two other people in the class (myself and another graduate student), each student becomes a member of a small research team. This reinforces the concept that research is not carried out in isolation. It also fosters teamwork among the students.

The Use of Portfolios to Innovate the Delivery of Learning Material

The course that I teach in microbiology is designed to be an introduction to the diverse world of microbes. One of the key wonders in biology is the incredible abundance and diversity of living organisms. This basic fact can be illustrated clearly in the microbial world. To arouse the students' interest and excitement in microorganisms and to give them the opportunity to do some independent research, I require that they each put together a portfolio on microbes in the real world with a unifying theme of their choice. I am a great believer in using portfolios to tie together course material with the outside world.

The student portfolio must contain entries from newspapers, magazines, and scientific journals, with accompanying annotations as to why the entry was chosen for inclusion and the student's personal feeling on the topic covered. The portfolio is a tool that makes the students realize that what we cover in lecture does not remain only in the pages of their textbook or in the classroom, but is of significance in the world outside their classroom. The students learn that newspapers, magazines, and the Internet all cover topics that relate to microbiology. They also learn that these topics impact their lives outside the classroom. In the classes that I teach I try to encourage this connection by bringing in articles from newspapers and magazines that relate to the subject matter covered.

I have used this approach in my genetically modified foods class to emphasize to the students the public debate on the social and ethical issues involved in this field. Using strategies that improve the delivery of course material results in students who are curious and eager to learn, and who are well equipped to be part of a technological world.

Making Oneself Accessible to Students

I believe that this an important strategy to motivate student learning. I have discovered from teaching freshman that they appreciate an instructor who is accessible and who they perceive as a willing participant in their learning. I achieve this by visiting each and every lab section and by discussing their lab assignments with them. I have also found that students respond positively when I send out emails to the class at-large with their homework assignments or with reminders of upcoming deadlines. This is documented in my student evaluation section with supporting student comments.

4) Additional Teaching Activities

Undergraduate Research Projects

Undergraduate students carry out independent research projects in my lab. I believe that this is a great way to integrate subject matter in science with the real world of how discoveries are made. Last year, one of my exemplary undergraduate students generated sufficient data that enabled her to present her results in the form of a poster at a national meeting. She had worked in my research laboratory for four years under my guidance. I mentored her through this time, teaching her laboratory skills and honing her analytical abilities by giving and discussing with her appropriate scientific articles. This is another avenue by which I motivate students. This particular undergraduate student is now in her first year of graduate school at Johns Hopkins University. Appendix B contains a copy of the abstract for this poster presentation.

Participation in a University Course

I participated in the university course (Univ 241) Great Works Symposium on Frankenstein by giving a lecture on the "Ethical and Moral Issues of Biotechnology" in winter 2003. The lecture was very well received by the students and gave rise to lively discussion on the topic. Appendix C contains the syllabus for this course.

Coordinator of the Department of Bioscience Teaching Circle

This year I have taken the role of instituting a teaching circle in the department. The idea of the teaching circle is to mentor junior faculty in all aspects of teaching, big and small. We have weekly meetings where we discuss issues in teaching. I also scheduled outside speakers from the university to talk to us on matters relating to teaching students. We have had speakers from the Learning Center, Student Life, Drexel Study Abroad, the Office of Disabilities, and the International Students office. In addition, we discuss topics dealing with the everyday teaching of students, including the use of homework, grading policies, and mentoring graduate teaching assistants.

5) Teaching Improvement

Staying Current in My Discipline

I stay current in my field by reading the primary scientific literature and by attending scientific meetings, both local and national. This influences how I teach genetics, microbiology, and microbial genetics, since I incorporate new and exciting discoveries into my lectures. I attend a scientific meeting every year to present my research as well as to learn firsthand about research in my field. A complete list of all the meetings attended can be found in Appendix K. In general, this allows me to present new discoveries to my students, or to update any long-held theories in these disciplines. For example, I recently discussed new irradiation methods for the preservation of foods in my microbiology class. The source of this information was a colloquium I attended at the American Society for Microbiology conference.

Participation in Teaching Portfolio Workshops

I first participated in a Teaching Portfolio Workshop at this university in the summer of 1999, just after I had completed my second year as a faculty member here. That workshop opened my eyes to how teaching excellence should be documented—with evidence and not mere statements. This was professionally an important milestone since it made me begin to analyze my teaching methods and strategies. I found it inspirational and have worked in the years since to evaluate my teaching methods objectively and to document the results with evidence. This current portfolio documents my growth as a teacher during my time at Drexel University. Appendix E contains a copy of my teaching portfolio from 1999 for purposes of comparison with my current portfolio, together with copies of my "graduation" certificates from these workshops in 1999 and 2003.

6) Information From Others

I have been evaluated by my students both with numerical scores and written comments. A student in my microbial genetics course describes the impact of the application oriented nature of this course.

> *"Microbial genetics was by far the best course I had this term. The material was interesting and relevant to anybody who does any genetics lab work. Dr. Anandan made the class work interesting and lively with her energetic teaching method. The student interaction through in class questions/experiment "design," weekly presentations and occasional group huddles really helps to keep me thinking and focused, which is saying something in a 5 hr class!"*

The following comments from students in my biotechnology course also address this aspect of my teaching philosophy:

> *"I enjoyed this class very much, I especially like the book Mutation and the discussions on genetically modified foods."*

> *"Made me think about all the issues on both sides of the arguments of Biotechnology."*

Comments from a student in my freshman genetics course also refers to the application-based nature of my teaching style: "Dr. Anandan is one of the best teachers I ever had. She always brings current applications in to the material being taught, making it more interesting."

A student in my genetically modified foods course wrote the following about creating a booklet on genetically modified foods.

> *"Overall, it was an excellent course. The quizzes were a good way to test us on the information presented in class. I also enjoyed and learned a lot by putting the booklet together and by reading articles that were handed out in class."*

Copies of student comments from all of my courses taught this past year can be found in Appendix F, and my complete set of student evaluations since I arrived in 1997 are available upon request.

Standardized Student Evaluation Scores for the Molecular and Cellular Genetics (Freshman) Course

The scores are for the "overall rating of the instructor." This is question 12 on the student evaluation form, which can be found in Appendix G.

Rating scale: 5 = excellent, 1 = poor	
Summary of Student Evaluation Scores	
Year	**Overall Rating***
Winter 98/99	4.118
Winter 99/00	4.08
Winter 00/01	4.87

*This value is based on the scores for question 12 on the student evaluation form.

As these scores demonstrate, my average scores for the freshman genetics course have always been higher than 4 on a 5-point scale. This indicates that my overall rating as an instructor has consistently been very good.

A copy of the letter from the Director of the university 241 Great Works Symposium: Frankenstein course lauding my participation in it can be found in Appendix C.

Copies of letters from participants in the Department of Bioscience Teaching Circle are in Appendix D. These letters indicate the value and utility of this Teaching Circle in their preparation for teaching as first-time instructors of a class.

7) Products of Student Learning
This section contains some examples of products of student learning from my courses. I have included them here to show some tangible outcomes arising from my teaching strategy.

Pre- and Post-Tests From the Microbial Genetics Course
I was interested to see whether the students' presentation experience in this course would actually match their expected outcome from the exercise. I hoped that this exercise would improve their problem-solving and analytical skills as applied to research methodology and also help to improve their formal presentation and communication skills. Appendix H contains an attitudinal test given to students in my microbial genetics course on the expected and actual impact of the paper presentation on their problem-solving skills.

Drafts for Portfolios From Students in the Genetically Modified Foods Course
At the start of the construction of the portfolio for my genetically modified foods class, I ask my students to give me an outline of the topics that they

plan to include in their final portfolio. I do this to make certain that the topics they wish to discuss are actually suitable for inclusion into the portfolio and also to see what creative ideas they have come up with. Appendix I contains sample outline drafts of the intended portfolios from students in my genetically modified foods course.

Student Letters

I have had several undergraduate students conduct research in my laboratory. Appendix J contains letters from those students describing my teaching and mentoring skills in the research setting.

Abstract of Student Poster Presentation at American Society of Microbiology Meeting

One of my best undergraduate students generated sufficient data from a research project that she was single-handedly carrying out in my laboratory to allow us to present this data at the national meeting of the American Society for Microbiology. Appendix B contains the abstract for the poster that was peer-reviewed prior to its acceptance. The poster itself was presented in an open poster session at the American Society for Microbiology meeting in Salt Lake City, Utah, in May 2002.

8) Closing Thoughts

My teaching goal is to be the best teacher and mentor that I can be to my students.

To accomplish this I intend to do several things:

- Improve and refine the project components of the freshman genetics lab.

- Participate in teaching workshops to improve my teaching strategies.

- Create and promote research opportunities for undergraduate students.

- Achieve peer assessment of my teaching.

- Mentor junior faculty in teaching.

- Achieve tenure.

9) List of Appendices

Appendix A: Course syllabi
Appendix B: Abstract of poster presentation
Appendix C: Syllabus of Univ 241 Great Works Symposium: Frankenstein course and letter from director of the course

Appendix D: Letters from Department of Bioscience Teaching Circle par-
             ticipants
Appendix E: Copy of 1999 teaching portfolio together with copies of cer-
             tificates from Teaching Portfolio Workshop 1999, 2003
Appendix F: Copies of student comments on my teaching methods
Appendix G: Question 12 from standard student evaluation form with tab-
             ulated student evaluation scores
Appendix H: Pre- and post-tests from the microbial genetics course
Appendix I: Copies of drafts of portfolio outlines from genetically modi-
             fied foods course
Appendix J: Letters from students that I mentored in my research
             laboratory
Appendix K: List of the scientific meetings attended

18

TEACHING PORTFOLIO
Abbey L. Berg
Dyson College of Arts and Sciences
Department of Communication Studies/
Communication Sciences and Disorders
Pace University

Table of Contents

Teaching Responsibilities

Each semester I teach 12 credits (unless awarded released time for research) in communication sciences and disorders. I currently advise 20 majors. I have responsibility for the teaching and the curricular development of the following courses:

1) Anatomy and Physiology of the Speech & Hearing Mechanism (SPP 253)
2) Introduction to Audiology (SPP 270)
3) Introduction to Hearing and Speech Science (SPP 350)
4) Introduction to Audiologic Rehabilitation (SPP 371)
5) Research Methods for Communication Sciences and Disorders Majors (COM 480)

Classes range in size between 19 and 25 students for all courses. These are required courses for all undergraduate communication sciences and disorders majors. Except for Anatomy and Physiology of the Speech & Hearing Mechanism (SPP 253), which is taken during the sophomore year, the remaining courses are taken during the junior and senior years.

Another responsibility is directing undergraduate student research. Though not all communication sciences and disorders majors present a directed research project, such supervision is expected in addition to a full teaching load. I am also very active in the Writing Enhanced Curriculum Program at Pace University and therefore spend much of my time working on a one-to-one basis with students on their writing.

Teaching Philosophy

All of the courses I teach are required. A minimum grade point average (2.7 GPA) must be maintained in order to continue in the program; hence, Pace students majoring in communication sciences and disorders are usually highly motivated. In addition, a graduate degree is required for certification. Most of our students go directly to graduate programs.

Of the five communication sciences and disorders courses I teach, four are heavily content based. Content-based information can often be dry and overwhelming, and I discourage my students from memorizing the material. I emphasize concepts that help students learn what "makes sense" and is logical. I use many visual aids (i.e., overheads, anatomical models, films, animation via software and links to web sites, computer technology), particularly in the Anatomy and Physiology of the Speech and Hearing Mechanism and Hearing and Speech Science I courses. Structures and functions are easier to remember and understand when visualized. In addition, two of the courses I teach, Introduction to Audiology and Hearing and Speech Science I, use instrumentation; because it is interactive, students can progress at their own rate and it is more interesting. As students learn in many different ways, I believe this engaged approach aids in the learning of important structures and functions and their connections.

Another technique I use throughout all my classes is a combination of traditional lecture and problem-based learning (PBL) formats. Students are given real clinical/patient/professional problems to solve. Specific etiologies are presented to students. By working through the problems, self-directed learning occurs. In addition, PBL helps students to connect and integrate structures and functions with evaluative materials, disorders, and pathology. This is not only more interesting for the student, but more relevant as well. The approach emphasizes the logical, and allows students to see the gestalt of communication sciences and disorders, as opposed to a series of isolated events. The combination of traditional lecture and PBL stresses analytical and critical thinking, and avoids just memorizing facts.

All of my classes are on Blackboard and/or FrontPage. This technology allows my students to download lectures and materials, as well as have direct access to materials on the Pace University Electronic Library Reserve and hyperlinked web sites.

Undergraduate research is another tool I use. Guided research requires students to apply knowledge learned in a structured classroom to a particular scientific question. By designing, implementing, and completing a research project, students must persevere, thus gaining self-confidence and responsibility for their own learning. Respect and enthusiasm for research develops. This format allows me to integrate teaching and research. I believe that scholarly research enhances effective teaching. By conducting and implementing guided research, I provide a good role model for my students. It is important for students to see that curiosity about topics or problems can be lifelong and exciting. Learning is seen as a continuum, not ending with the semester or graduation.

All of my courses require writing assignments, some accompanied by conferencing. Students are given the opportunity to revise their work without penalty. This allows students to see that writing is an ongoing process that requires editing and revision, as well as a means of providing feedback. Rubrics are given so that students know what is required to earn an "A," "B," etc. Examples of well-written, average, and poor papers are provided to guide students in the quality of their work. In addition, I developed a Writing Key to help students avoid common semantic and syntactical errors. In addition, this key also provides students with transitional phrases, appropriate word choice, vocabulary, and correct referencing for research papers. Oral communication skills are developed through individual and group presentations.

Service learning is another component that I use. Students apply the information gleaned not only from their communication sciences and disorders coursework, but from other disciplines (i.e., psychology, education, communication studies) as well.

Finally, excellent teaching requires feedback. Peer and student evaluations are invaluable in improving teaching, learning, and rewarding relationships. I encourage students and colleagues to confer with me, both informally and formally.

General Classroom Strategies

In addition to course syllabi, outlines of lectures, diagrams, tables, and figures are provided to students via Blackboard and/or FrontPage on the web. By providing detailed outlines of the course material, students are able to listen and digest the material rather than frantically writing down each word. This also allows me to cover more material in greater detail, and eliminates time wasted on note taking and the drawing of structures. Reference to previously presented material is used consistently. This allows students to see the interrelatedness of structures, functions, and pathology, as well as reinforcing concepts. Examples of outlines of lectures are provided in Appendix A.

Supplemental and suggested references are also provided and available to students. Such references reinforce the connection between scholarship and teaching and demonstrate that learning continues throughout life. The motivated and interested students will utilize these materials. On the course syllabi, direct links to web sites of interest and relevant references are provided by topic to aid students in further pursuing scholarship.

I rarely lecture from the assigned textbook. My lectures reflect a multitude of sources to which students may not have access. I believe that student learning is enhanced when sources used for the topic presented are varied. The readings may not be as clear as the lecture and vice versa.

Student proficiency is assessed in various ways. When exams are the method chosen, a study guide is given to students to reduce exam anxiety. It is explained that not all questions, but only questions, that appear on the guide will be covered on the exam. As the students do not know which questions will appear on the exam, they are responsible for learning all the material. Examples of review guides and exams are provided in Appendix B. Graded assignments are another format that I use. This may include the posting of pertinent and relevant comments on the discussion board of Blackboard, assignments requiring the use of instrumentation, research and written assignments that involve revision, compare/contrast, semester long and group projects. I encourage students to work together and believe this technique fosters collegiality and team dynamics. This is an important skill for my students to develop, as they will be in collaborative work environments. Further, it has been my experience that one of the best ways to learn information is when one has to teach the material. By working in groups, teaching is almost guaranteed.

Course Syllabi, Projects, and Assignments

Course syllabi (see Appendix C) reflect my teaching philosophy and strategies, and evolve through self-evaluation and the input I receive from peer and student evaluations. In addition, the syllabi provide documentation of my teaching development. They have become more precise in detailing course objectives and expectations. Readings, goals, methods, and assignments reflect variety and flexibility—characteristics essential to dynamic teaching. Further, these syllabi provide a thoughtful record of my teaching as I try to keep both the courses, and myself, fresh and alive.

Research Methods for Communication Sciences and Disorders Majors (COM 480)

In this course, students are required to design a study as the final project. This semester long research project reflects the culmination of all material presented (i.e., how to conduct a literature search, formulate questions, scientific justification, hypotheses testing, methodology, data analysis, appropriate use of graphs, figures and tables, discussion, and conclusions). Examples of assignments designed to facilitate this process are provided in Appendix D.

Anatomy and Physiology of the Speech and Hearing Mechanism (SPP 253)

The textbook used for this course has an excellent review and assignment section. Students are required to complete the assignments. These assignments are useful as supplemental study guides to the material presented in class. Anatomical models, demonstrating the respiratory, phonatory, and auditory systems, are used. Films, interactive and animated computer programs, and web sites are assigned.

Introduction to Audiology (SPP 270)

Students are required to analyze various audiograms (graphs of hearing sensitivity) and conduct five audiologic evaluations on individuals not enrolled in the class. Initial audiograms focus on proper notation and use of symbols while later audiograms require more complex analysis (i.e., analyzing and synthesizing test results for appropriate treatment, referral, and rehabilitation). Examples are provided in Appendix D.

Hearing and Speech Science I (SPP 350)

This course introduces the student to the study of the physics of sound, psychoacoustics, the decibel, and acoustics as they relate to the auditory and speech systems. A lab utilizing instrumentation for both clinical and research use is included. Students receive a multitude of hands-on experience with technology through lab assignments. Class time is also spent analyzing a rigorous research article.

Introduction to Audiologic Rehabilitation

This course explores the use of different types of assessments, technologies, and strategies for improving communication potential in the hearing impaired throughout the lifespan. A speech-language pathologist may be employed in a school, hospital, nursing home setting, or private practice. Controversial topics that include the ethics of cochlear implants in children, deaf culture, the World Health Organization (WHO) classification system for impairment, disability, functioning, and handicap are discussed. Further, this course includes a service-learning component. Students are required to conduct hearing screenings at a residential foster care facility for adolescent girls. This project not only services my students but the foster care facility as well. My students are role models for these adolescent girls as they are close in age. Equally important, the residents feel important—they are in the position of helping my students learn, rather than in the position of being helped.

Collaborative Research With Students

Student research at the undergraduate level is very important. Guided research allows students to begin to ask scientific questions that are of interest to them, rather than implementing research with known answers. Each year since I began teaching at Pace University, students have presented their research (refereed) at the annual New York State Speech-Language-Hearing Association Convention. This experience is immensely rewarding for both me as the faculty member and the student. Not only am I able to work closely and intensely with students, but also get to know more about them.

For the past two years, three students from Pace University have worked with me at the Children's Hospital of NewYork-Presbyterian screening well-born and neonatal intensive care infants for hearing loss. Students are exposed to working in a teaching facility with faculty and staff of various disciplines (i.e., neonatologists, developmental pediatricians, neurologists, surgeons, nurses, occupational and physical therapists, social workers, feeding specialists, speech-language pathologists, and audiologists).

Teaching Assessments and Evaluations

I believe that my teaching values have an effect on student behavior and achievement. When students feel my standards are high and fair, their achievement becomes that much more meaningful to them. A supportive, respectful, and professional manner encourages students to view themselves that way and, I hope, to emulate that behavior as well. I enjoy and take my teaching and mentoring responsibilities very seriously. Being respected by my students and colleagues is an indication that I have done my job well. On a scale of 1 to 5 (1 = poor teaching and 5 = excellent teaching) for student evaluations, my ratings for the 2002 academic year averaged 4.65 (range: 4.45 – 4.92).

Improving my teaching centers on reviewing peer and student comments and evaluations, staying current in my discipline, and participating in professional development. I try to provide a friendly, supportive, and open style to encourage students and colleagues to feel comfortable asking questions. In addition to the student evaluations required by Pace University, I have developed evaluations that give me a better indication of the value and usefulness of assignments. This has been especially effective for improving my writing and lab assignments. Student and peer evaluations and letters are provided in Appendices G, H, and I.

Professional development, which includes attending courses and conferences, is crucial to excellent teaching. I have participated, and will continue to do so, in a number of workshops designed to improve my teaching. These workshops have included Computer Technology in Teaching Introductory Speech and Hearing Science, Teaching Portfolio Workshop, Introduction to Smart E-Classrooms, BlackBoard, FrontPage, and PowerPoint. Further, my profession requires a minimum of 30 hours of continuing education units (CEU) every three years.

Future Teaching Goals

I would like to integrate and feel more comfortable with computer technology in the courses I teach. Recently, I took a course in how to utilize computer technology for teaching anatomy and physiology and speech and hearing science. Better incorporation into the curriculum and increasing my comfort level with computer instrumentation will help students develop the intellectual and technical skills required of the profession.

Proficiency in computer technology is an essential skill in order to compete in the workforce. One assignment I am considering is requiring students to locate references and information utilizing only high quality web sites, resulting in the writing of a research paper. This would expose and increase the comfort level using advanced information technologies, aid the student in discriminating among web sites, and integrate writing skills. I would like to make better use of Blackboard for discussion. I have canvassed several of my colleagues for advise and am exploring their suggestions.

Clearly written goals and objectives are important, as well as challenging. The writings of Howard Gardner and materials from Harvard's *Project Zero* have been thought provoking and have helped me to clarify and communicate better what it is I want to teach. Finally, I am interested in including and developing assessment measures, particularly in reflective practices, that compliment and supplement the service-learning component in the Introduction to Audiologic Rehabilitation course.

Appendices

Appendix A: Student Handouts
Appendix B: Review Guides and Exams
Appendix C: Course Syllabi
Appendix D: Student Assignments
Appendix E: Examples of Students' Work
Appendix F: Research Papers From Students
Appendix G: Student Evaluations
Appendix H: Peer Evaluations
Appendix I: Letters From Students and Colleagues

19

TEACHING PORTFOLIO
Kathleen A. McDonough
Department of Communication
State University of New York College at Fredonia
Spring 2003

Table of Contents

Statement of Teaching Responsibilities

I teach courses in three different areas in the communication department: video production, multimedia, and media criticism. In the video area I teach CM 354 *Video Field Production,* an intermediate course for sophomores and juniors with an enrollment of 18–20 students. This course is required for TV/digital film majors. I also teach CM 452/462, the two semester senior capstone course in *Documentary Production.* Students in the video/digital film major choose either *Documentary Production* or *Video Drama* for their capstone experience. This course usually has 12–15 students.

I teach two computer media courses: CM 312 *Multimedia Integration* and CM 314 *Multimedia Supervision.* The integration course is an upper level elective for audio/radio, media management, and TV/digital film majors. The enrollment is limited to 18 students so that each student has his or her own computer in the multimedia lab. The purpose of the one unit supervision course is to train lab proctors. It usually has between five to ten students.

In the media studies area I teach CM 155 *The Rhetoric of Vision and Sound.* It is a core course for all communication majors and it fulfills the arts requirement for the College Core Curriculum. Designed for freshmen and sophomores, this course is usually offered in two sections with 35 students per section.

I also designed and supervised two independent study production courses: *Experimental Video Production* and *Interactive Game Design*. At State University of New York College at Fredonia, independent study courses are considered volunteer work in addition to a full teaching load.

I generally have between 40–45 advisees. I have a 30-minute formal meeting with each of them during advising week to help with their course selection for the next semester. In addition I have at least three formal meetings per semester with my advisees who are on academic probation.

Curricular Development

An aspect of teaching that I particularly enjoy is developing new classes. During my first semester at SUNY Fredonia, I designed and taught CM 312 *Multimedia Integration*. The course allows students to integrate other electronic media into interactive projects using the application Macromedia Director. That same semester I created CM 314 *Multimedia Supervision*. It introduces the computer lab proctors to the Macintosh operating system, troubleshooting techniques, and the applications used in the lab. These courses were accepted as a permanent part of the curriculum *(see Appendix A)*.

Teaching Philosophy, Methods, and Strategies

Many of my teaching strategies and methods vary depending on whether I am teaching production or media studies classes. Other themes and methods are common to all of my classes.

Video and Multimedia Production

As a production teacher, my goal is to help students find their voices as media producers. In order to be well-rounded media producers, students should have a mastery of the basic technical skills, exposure to a wide variety of films, an opportunity to experiment with different stylistic elements, and a familiarity with film theory, history, and criticism. In my field production class, I incorporate and build on the theories taught in *The Rhetoric of Vision and Sound*. In the first semester of the documentary class I closely integrate production and studies. I assign readings about the various theories and elements of style in documentary and screen film clips for close analysis. Students then respond to the reading and screening by producing short documentaries. They also write a statement of intent explaining how their pieces relate to the screened documentaries. Students critique each other's work following the model of the readings.

Of primary importance is mastery of basic technical skills and respect for the equipment. To ensure mastery, I provide demonstrations, supervised practice sessions, written examinations, and practical tests with opportunities for remediation if necessary. I encourage a relaxed and cooperative atmosphere in the classroom so that students with less technical or computer experience are allowed to thrive. I am vigilant about not allowing a gender gap to develop in the technical areas. With group projects, I assign the roles if less dominant students are being relegated to subordinate positions. In the documentary class, two of the three projects are individual ones that guarantee each student is familiar with every aspect of production.

All of the creative projects in *Multimedia Integration* are individual ones. One major purpose of this class is to teach students how to create good interface design and to become proficient at writing Lingo, the scripting language for the authoring software. Functionality rather than appearance is what is assessed. This emphasis takes the burden off students who do not have strong artistic/graphic design skills. I do not want students who are not artists to feel threatened by this class. This division of labor is reflected in the multimedia industry where the design team is different from the authoring team.

For all of my production classes, critical feedback, both in the form of individual consultations with the instructor and discussions with the whole class, is essential for the development of a media producer. Students need to be guided on how to look at a work-in-progress and how to give constructive criticism. Presentation and critiques of completed projects force students to be analytical in their reactions. They also give the producer an opportunity to defend his or her vision and to discuss his or her work in terms of the intentionality and the critical framework that informs it.

By the time they graduate, students should have the skills necessary to make the transition into the professional world. I stress professional behavior and industry standards. I also teach the survival skills necessary for an independent producer: grant and proposal writing, pitching a project, budgeting, scheduling, distribution deals/self-distribution, and promotion. Assignments in advanced production classes provide students with material for their reels and portfolios. Ideally, capstone projects have a life beyond school: in festivals, broadcast, and distribution.

Media Studies
My goal in the studies classes is to introduce students to the ways the elements of production are used to shape the meaning of the content and to manipulate the perception of the audience. Major themes I explore are intentionality of the media producer, the influence of culture on perception,

and media ethics. I particularly emphasize perception in different cultures and draw on my experience in teaching in Europe and Southeast Asia. Americans in general and students in western New York in particular are very insular in their outlook.

I believe that the best way to understand media is to try production. Therefore, students are required to produce creative work and write a short analysis of that work explaining why they made the choices they did. Writing is also an effective tool to promote integration of lectures, readings and screening, and to encourage critical thinking. Throughout the semester I require short written analysis of various types of media that specifically focus on the concept under discussion *(see Appendix A)*.

I enjoy the give and take of classroom discussion and my goal is to be the conversational traffic director rather than the fount of all knowledge. I enjoy using teachable moments, as this adds spontaneity to class. Some of the most stimulating discussions have occurred during one of these digressions. In all my classes, I encourage students to draw on their outside experience during discussions. I frequently use stories from my life experience to illustrate concepts. One purpose of this is to model how to make the connections between life and the academic subject.

Common Themes and Strategies
Social Responsibility
It is essential that all students, both in production and studies, are aware of the power of the medium and become socially responsible. They should become aware of how their work reflects the dominant cultural ideology or breaks away from it. I cover issues of representation, perception, stereotyping, cultural dominance and multiculturalism, racism, and sexism in the *Rhetoric of Vision and Sound* class. Since it is a required course for the entire department and a prerequisite for the production classes, I can build on the concepts in my other classes. In the multimedia production class, each student gives a presentation about some aspect of the effect of new technology on society. Topics include privacy, censorship, identity on the Internet, commerce, copyright, the global digital divide, and governance. *(Samples of student presentations are available on request.)*

Motivating Students
I allow students to resubmit assignments and projects for a better grade. I give specific critiques of the work and make clear what steps they would need to take to improve that assignment or future assignments. This policy

is similar to the rewrite and resubmit practice of academic journals and client requests for revisions in media production industries.

In order to encourage students to do their best in group projects, I ask each member of the group to write a report on what he or she did to contribute to the project and write an assessment of how the group functioned.

Learning Outside the Classroom

I frequently have informal meetings with my students to help them with resumes, cover letters, and to chat about how their semester is going and their plans for the future. Learning that takes place outside the classroom is as important as learning in a more structured environment. I enjoy being a mentor to my students, meeting with them informally, and encouraging them to grow as humans as well as media professionals. Many students commented in course evaluations about my accessibility on weekends and outside of office hours *(see Appendix B)*. I enjoy hanging out in the Sheldon Lab, the communication department Mac lab for electronic media production and video editing, and seeing what the students are doing both in my classes and in other production classes.

Improving My Teaching
Rhetoric of Vision and Sound

I am continuing to revise this course. In the fall semester of 2000, I completely restructured the course to meet the guidelines for course adoption as a College Core Curriculum course under the category of arts *(see Appendix D)*.

Last semester I made the course content more inclusive of the different types of media. I used more examples drawn from fine art, advertising, web sites, and television commercials in addition to film. In the past, students had complained that the course seemed geared to production students and wasn't relevant to studies students. I now emphasize the connections between the concepts presented and their application to all areas of communication in lectures and encourage students to make their own connections in discussions and in the creative projects they choose. I am constantly reviewing textbooks to find one that is stimulating and reasonably priced. I now use a different textbook that is more inclusive of print and electronic media. In the previous text, all examples were drawn from film and television.

For the major research paper I tried ideas about writing partners learned from a writing across the curriculum workshop. Students exchanged first drafts with their writing partners and wrote critiques of each other's work. Students were graded on the quality of their critique but not on the draft. I was disappointed in the results of this procedure. The majority of the critiques were very poor in spite of a class discussion on how to critique a paper. I ended up critiquing the drafts myself to aid the students in polishing their papers. With 70 students in the class, it was quite a burden to read these research papers twice. I think the problem was with the initial writing assignment, as I let the students choose the topic for their papers. I need to impose a narrower focus and methodology so that the student reviewers will be able to critique from a shared knowledge base.

Multimedia Integration

As requested by students in the course evaluation, I increased the in-class hours to four hours per week in keeping with studio courses in other disciplines. I am very pleased with the results. Students have more time in class for supervised work on their projects and the quality of the projects is uniformly high. Because good oral communication skills are essential for pitching projects and working with clients, I revised the course so that it would meet the requirements of a speaking intensive course for the College Core Curriculum. It was accepted as such by the College Core Curriculum Committee *(see Appendix D)*.

I am continually creating different materials for demonstrating how to write the computer scripting language. I put all my demonstrations on the lab server so students can access it at any time to review the code. *(Examples of demonstrations are available on request.)*

Improved Assessment

One of the areas I am working on for all of my classes is assessment of student performance. I now use check sheets in addition to written comments so students can see immediately what the strengths or weakness of the assignment are. As a result I am receiving favorable student comments about my fairness in grading. *(See Appendix B for student evaluations and Appendix E for assessment check sheets.)*

I also serve on two curriculum assessment committees: the campus wide College Core Curriculum Assessment Committee for Arts and Humanities and the departmental Core Courses Assessment Committee. In both of these committees I have developed assessment instruments and conducted pilot assessments of student learning *(see Appendix F)*.

Evaluating My Teaching
Peer Review

Peer evaluators have reviewed classes in the three areas that I teach. In her report about *The Rhetoric of Vision and Sound*, Dr. Linda Brigance wrote, "I was impressed with Kay's sound presentation of the material as well as her interaction with the students and her enthusiasm for the course material" *(see Appendix G).* Dr. Ted Schwalbe observed *Multimedia Integration* and noted

> *... how thoroughly organized she was. This is especially important (and difficult) given the nature of the material (coding various sound techniques). Her material was well organized. She had samples prepared to demonstrate each new piece of code. She used both the projection system and the chalkboard to show how coding worked. She had examples for the students to use when they were working in the lab in out of class time. (See Appendix G)*

After observing a lighting demonstration for documentary production, the assistant chair, Jane Jackson, wrote,

> *The material she presented was clear and reinforced with a hand-out... She easily explained then demonstrated the difficult concept of exposure latitude and lighting ratios. This hands-on activity reinforced the earlier material and gave the students an opportunity to develop these skills. Her students will easily manage different lighting situations after this lecture and activity. Her knowledge and practice model clearly works. (See Appendix G)*

Course Approval and Adoption

Two of my courses have been favorably reviewed by various college committees. CM 155 was adopted as a College Core Curriculum course under the category of arts. In the approval notice Dr. Len Faulk, associate vice president for academic affairs, called it an "excellent submission." CM 312 was approved as a speaking intensive course for the College Core Curriculum. Dr. Ray Belliotti, Distinguished Teaching Professor and chair of the College Core Curriculum Committee, wrote that it was "enthusiastically approved" *(see Appendix D).*

Student Evaluations

The communication department uses a standardized evaluation form developed by the campus assessment committee. It uses a scale of 1 to 5, with 5 being the highest rating. The chart below shows the ratings for the most recent semester I taught the class.

Course Title	Overall Rating of Course	Overall Rating of Instructor
Rhetoric of Vision and Sound F 02	4.33	4.55
Multimedia Integration F 02	4.55	4.45
Documentary Production F 02	4.36	4.45
Video Field Production S 02	4.38	4.59

One student wrote,

> *I loved this course! I found it very interesting and it made it clear to me that film production is what I want to do. I would absolutely take another course from Ms. McDonough. She was so enthusiastic about the subject matter and I could tell she really loves teaching. Her grading was fair and she was always willing to help outside of class. (See Appendix B)*

Student Achievement

In the production classes, a major source of satisfaction is comparing student projects from the beginning of the semester with final projects. In the multimedia class, the first project is a linear animation with minimal interactivity. All of the final projects have complex interface designs that are transparent for the user. I encourage students to create final projects that will be useful to them outside of class. Several students have created interactive resumes; others have made enhanced CDs for their bands *(see Appendix C)*. One student created an interactive educational game. In an independent study class he fined-tuned the game, researched potential distributors, and created a marketing package *(available on request)*.

Another source of pleasure is receiving unsolicited praise from students and former students. A student from *The Rhetoric of Vision and Sound* as well as one of my advisees wrote,

> *You are the true definition of what a teacher is: always willing to help your students and even those of us who weren't. . . . Thank you for helping me find what I really want to do with my life. My grades have been through the roof ever since, 3.95 this semester! (See Appendix H)*

Teaching Goals

While teaching at Ngee Ann Polytechnic in Singapore, I had the opportunity to work closely with the lecturer who taught *The Individual in Society*, a required first-year course that covered issues of representation, perception, stereotyping, cultural dominance and multiculturalism, racism, and sexism. Each week I was able to reinforce the concepts presented in her course in my first year *Film History* course. It was extremely satisfying to watch the students making the connections and start thinking laterally. I am eager to team-teach in this manner at SUNY Fredonia. I hope that, as the department continues the self-assessment process, we will find ways to facilitate this type of team teaching.

Next year, I would like to start an informal gathering or listserv for the instructors who teach film studies classes. We are scattered in several different departments: communication, history, political science, English, and modern languages. Meetings or a forum for communication would enable us to share methodologies and resources.

Appendices

Appendix A: Course Syllabi
Appendix B: Student Evaluations
Appendix C: Student Projects
Appendix D: Letters Regarding Course Adoptions and Proposal Packets
Appendix E: Student Assessment Check Sheets
Appendix F: Assessment Committee Work
Appendix G: Peer Review Letters
Appendix H: Unsolicited Student Letters

20

TEACHING PORTFOLIO
Bridget Thomas
Division of Language and Literature
Truman State University
Spring 2003

Table of Contents

Teaching Responsibilities

I have taught 14 different undergraduate courses at Truman State University: all levels in both Latin and Greek, as well as three classics courses. Each of these courses counts in some way toward the Liberal Studies Program and/or the classics major or classical studies, Greek, or Latin minor. Two of these courses (CLAS 361 and 461) are required of all classics majors.

Because so many of these courses fit into the Liberal Studies Program, during a typical semester I interact with students of all levels and majors. I enjoy the opportunity to reach students who have such different interests: some of the best rewards in teaching come from unexpected places, like watching a math student find elegance in the order of a Latin sentence, or hearing an African-American student delight in the sound of his voice reading Greek poetry aloud. I look forward each semester to the opportunity to encourage another group of young people to fully engage in their studies so that they might truly find lifelong value and enjoyment.

The following is a complete list of the courses I have taught, along with an indication of their role in the curriculum:

COURSE #	COURSE NAME	ROLE IN CURRICULUM
CLAS 361	Greek and Roman Mythology	required for majors; optional for minors
CLAS 363	Women and Gender in Antiquity	writing-enhanced; intercultural; optional for majors/minors
CLAS 461	Classics Capstone Experience	writing-enhanced; required for majors
GREK 100 and 101	Elementary Greek I and II	language requirement for BA, BS
GREK 200	Intermediate Greek I	language requirement for BA
GREK 300	Greek Epic Poetry	optional for majors/minors
GREK 301	Greek Drama and Lyric Poetry	optional for majors/minors
LATN 150 and 151	Elementary Latin I and II	language requirement for BA, BS
LATN 250 and 251	Intermediate Latin I and II	language requirement for BA
LATN 351	Latin Historians	optional for majors/minors
LATN 353	Vergil's *Aeneid*	optional for majors/minors

Teaching Philosophy

I was a good teacher when I was appointed to the faculty in 1998, and I think I have become an even better teacher during my time here. As I have come to know this institution and these students, my approach to teaching has become more defined. I now realize that the following three points are essential to my successful teaching of the classics.

A Commitment to Encouraging Careful, Critical Attention to Primary Materials

The discipline of classics is at its least vital and interesting when it is considered the possession of an elite minority. I consider myself (a woman from a lower middle class background) a fairly unlikely classics scholar, and I derive considerable energy from this. I urge students to join me as I question the assumptions lurking behind popular misconceptions about classical antiquity. I begin most courses by assuming that my students have no background in the subject matter and insisting that—even if they do have some background—they will learn the most from putting aside any preconceptions and focusing on the ancient sources themselves. This emphasis on attention to the primary materials helps us dodge some of the common traps of interpretation, and at the same time as it enables all students to feel equally prepared for the challenge.

The Ability to Create a Comfortable and Respectful Classroom Environment

Latin and Greek can be difficult subjects, and students often find the classics intimidating. As an antidote I strive to create a positive, friendly atmosphere in my classrooms. I frequently emphasize our common enterprise and hope that my emphasis on collaboration encourages students to work together, share their knowledge, and learn from each other. In written comments I try always to strike a balance between positive feedback and constructive criticism. As part of this effort to be respectful and appreciative of student effort, I make myself readily available to students: In addition to my regular office hours, I also occasionally hold review sessions or schedule additional office hours in the days leading up to major exams. I encourage students to send questions via email (even if it is only a small grammatical question) and I respond promptly. I invite students to talk with me if they are unsatisfied with their progress or level of understanding. As I respond to students in and out of the classroom, I make an effort always to be respectful: I try to listen carefully to students' opinions and make constructive, affirming responses whenever possible. I encourage students to listen and respond to each other in a similar manner.

The Acknowledgment and Accommodation of Diversity—Whether That Be in Goals, Interests, Backgrounds, or Learning Styles

Since I frequently teach students who are taking a class because it fulfills a requirement, it is important for me to be mindful of their different needs. I aim to be aware of my students: I inquire about their interests on the first day of classes and plan some aspect of the course to respond directly to those interests; in this way I remind them of the larger significance of our topic of study. By referring to materials that interest individual students, I find that I ultimately increase the level of interest of the whole group. Whenever possible I try to introduce variety into the subject matter, my presentation style, our classroom activities, as well as quiz and exam formats to accommodate students' different talents. I plan a variety of assignments in every class that I teach so that there are many ways to earn points for the desired grade.

Student Evaluations

Student evaluations indicate a fairly high level of satisfaction with my abilities, efforts, and practice in the classroom. My overall average scores for my first nine semesters at Truman have consistently been above the division average. I routinely earn high scores for those questions that rate prepared-ness, a syllabus with objectives in plain language, fairness, and a reasonable return time on exams and papers. These things are relatively easy to achieve, and so I take no special pride in them. What I am proud of—and what takes some effort on my part—are my scores for five particular questions that cor-respond to my understanding of effective teaching (as described above):

- The instructor appeared to be thoroughly competent in his/her area.
- The instructor was enthusiastic about the subject being taught.
- The instructor seemed genuinely concerned with the students' progress and was actively helpful.
- The instructor was readily available for consultation with students.
- In general, the instructor was an effective teacher.

I should acknowledge in advance that these are not exact matches with my stated teaching philosophy; I am working with student responses to the standard form used in my division. In the future I plan to add several of my own questions to this form to get more accurate results. For now, the best measure of my "commitment to encouraging careful, critical attention to primary materials" might be a combination of "enthusiasm" and "compe-tency"; the best measure of my "ability to create a comfortable and respectful classroom environment" might be a combination of "concerned with the students' progress and was actively helpful" and "readily available"; and finally, since there is no measure for "the acknowledgment and accommoda-tion of diversity," I have included "effective teacher." (See Appendix A for the summary and interpretation of data for individual courses.)

The scale is 0–4, with 4 being the top score.

	Elem. Greek	Elem. Latin	Int. Latin	Advanced Latin	Mythology	Women in Antiquity
Number of Students	50	160	56	22	66	37
Thoroughly competent	3.86	3.84	3.86	3.64	3.74	3.89
Enthusiastic	3.90	3.83	3.93	3.91	3.83	3.89
Actively helpful	3.74	3.66	3.71	3.73	3.39	3.76
Readily available	3.78	3.63	3.71	3.86	3.55	3.81
Effective teacher	3.64	3.49	3.71	3.59	3.32	3.62

I am pleased that my numbers for competence and enthusiasm are fairly consistent across the board. This is important to me since I aim to inspire my students by example: By communicating to them that I think this material is worth reading and rereading, I hope to inspire in them a similar passion for learning as an ongoing endeavor.

These numbers suggest that I am most effective with small groups of students. Students in their first year of Greek (average class size of 18) and the intermediate Latin courses (average class size of 11) report more overall satisfaction than students in the mythology course (average class size of 35 students). This isn't surprising, as it is easier for me to build a comfortable and respectful classroom environment with a smaller number of students than with a larger one. Also, students in these smaller classes tend to take more responsibility for their own learning: they are more inclined to ask questions and initiate contact with an instructor. Still, I recognize the opportunity to improve instruction in the larger class.

The following comments from anonymous student evaluation forms speak directly to my practices in the classroom. (See Appendix B for the complete texts.)

> *For the first time in 2 or 3 years I felt like my Latin and understanding of grammar actually improved considerably. I liked how willing Dr. Thomas was to provide extra help sessions for us and it is obvious that she cares quite a bit about us succeeding in the class. (LATN 353 Latin Historians)*

> *The material was very interesting—I read a lot of stuff I would've never read, I also really, really liked the featured articles of the week because they raised some interesting & provocative issues. . . . I liked the VARIETY of assigned readings. (CLAS 363 Women and Gender in Antiquity)*

> *I cannot stress enough how thoroughly competent Dr. Thomas is. Not only is she a genuine wiz at Greek, she has a real knack for discerning when students do not understand. She is really good, when this happens, at re-conveying the material in a way I understand. (GREK 101 Elementary Greek II)*

> *Latin became interesting. I was not interested in the material before taking this class, though I've had a year of it already. Dr. Thomas is so passionate about her work and so in tune*

with the students that she makes learning about dead philoso-
phers interesting. (LATN 250 Intermediate Latin I)

Course Syllabi and Exams

A good syllabus sets up objectives and expectations in clear language so that students and instructors know what to expect from each other. I include in Appendix C a syllabus for each of the 14 courses that I have taught at Truman. Each syllabus includes a list of course objectives, course requirements, attendance policy, as well as dates for the semester's exams. The sample exams in Appendix D illustrate my efforts to use a number of different types of exercises to accommodate a diversity of learning styles. I have included a LATN 250 exam, a GREK 100 exam, as well as a CLAS 361 (mythology) exam.

Efforts to Improve Teaching

Although I have many good days in the classroom, I tend to reflect more on the bad days; since I would rather do things well, I look at those disappointments as opportunities for improvement. I also look at my lowest numbers on student evaluation forms: They indicate that I could be better at communicating expectations, knowing when they don't understand something, and presenting lectures. I am constantly working to improve in these areas.

I attend different professional conferences every year—sometimes the regional (Classical Association of the Middle West and South) or national meeting (American Philological Association), but other times conferences with more specific topics (for example, Gender in Antiquity, Women's Dress in Ancient Greece). Regardless of whether or not I make a presentation at the conference, I find that I always come back to campus with new insights and ideas. I make a point of sharing with my classes something of relevance immediately upon my return. I find that students benefit from hearing anecdotes from these meetings—it reminds them both that the field of classics is still active and evolving, and that I am still involved in teaching and learning from my peers.

While attending these professional conferences, I regularly attend panels devoted to issues of pedagogy. Most recently I attended a panel titled *Helping Marcus Read: Some Approaches Toward Bridging the Transition from Elementary Latin to Reading Roman Authors* (see Appendix E for more complete information). Members of the panel stressed that the transition to reading real Latin can be eased by using earlier levels as an opportunity to prepare for LATN 251. I am now convinced that our best strategy is the gradual introduction of our targeted author via the early introduction of appropriate vocabulary, grammatical concepts, and other background material. This panel inspired me to urge my colleagues at Truman that we reconsider the texts we read in LATN 251 in order to ease our students' transition.

Other curricular changes were inspired by a panel on *Teaching Courses on Women in Antiquity.* Members of the panel specifically addressed two topics: 1) the challenge of making this subject relevant to students who might have no background in classics, and 2) the problem of avoiding/combating group depression—which often seems inevitable in a course that focuses on the ways that ancient societies restricted women's lives. Since attending this panel I have significantly reorganized my version of this course (CLAS 363 Women and Gender in Antiquity). I have eliminated some of the most difficult secondary reading from the course in order to leave the students room to consider the primary texts for the first time. I also make it a priority to emphasize parallels between the past and the present so that students realize that part of the purpose of this course is to scrutinize their own society's organization of gender.

I have also attended several teaching workshops on campus. Dr. Tom Angelo, in a workshop on student assessment, stressed that useful conversations about improving student writing begin with a comparison of student and instructor assessments of an early draft: Any area where the ratings differ is a great place to begin talking about expectations and strategies for improvement. Angelo distributed a sample assessment form that I have since modified and used with considerable success in my CLAS 363 Women and Gender in Antiquity course. I have also used assessment forms for peer review in CLAS 461 Classics Capstone Experience (see Appendices E and G). Such forms not only facilitate conversations about writing, but—when I hand them out to students well in advance of any deadline—they also clarify my expectations for the assignment.

Finally, since attending a workshop on the use of Course Info for producing course-based web sites, I have regularly maintained web sites for most of the courses I teach. I have used these sites to share such things as interactive practice quizzes, updated syllabi, additional review material, online course packets, and current lists of assignments.

Descriptions of Curricular Additions and Revisions

I have developed two new courses at Truman: Women and Gender in Antiquity (CLAS 363) fulfills the intercultural and writing-enhanced areas of the Liberal Studies Program, and also serves as an elective for the classics major program, classical studies minor, Greek minor, Latin minor, as well as the women studies minor. The CLAS 363 syllabus documents my use of peer-reading and peer-response in the context of a writing-enhanced course:

Within the semester students exchange six short papers summarizing, analyzing, and responding to a scholarly discussion on some aspect of gender in the antiquity. The second new course, LATN 450 Latin Prose Composition serves as an elective within the major and minor programs. (See Appendix E for these materials.)

After teaching my first advanced Latin course here at Truman, I was discouraged by students' tendency to give up on the toughest passages instead of using their skills and background to work through any difficulties. For this reason, as I prepared to teach my second advanced Latin course (LATN 353 Latin Historians), I devised a new sort of assignment: the Puzzle. When I assigned the next week's work, I would also hand out the next week's Puzzle—an especially problematic sentence with additional grammatical help and some questions designed to help students think the problem through to its solution. A written solution was due at the next class meeting before we would discuss the passage in class. In the case of most students, I saw a gradual rise in Puzzle scores; it turned out to be a useful tool for review. (See Appendix E for sample Puzzles.)

Intermediate Latin II (LATN 251) is the last semester for many of our Latin students. In order to enable them to have a significant final Latin experience, a colleague (Alex Tetlak) and I designed a set of projects that encourage students to make connections between what we are reading and their outside interests. (Appendix F contains the full text of the prompt.) We have had terrific results. This past semester one student composed a piece of music for strings and marimba based on Apuleius' "Cupid and Psyche," another created a "movie soundtrack" for Ovid's telling of the story of "Apollo and Daphne," and another picked out a moody piece of music on the banjo in imitation of a particularly stormy poem by Catullus. (Find several student responses in Appendix F.)

Student Achievement

In October of 2000 I traveled with a student who presented a paper in Athens, Georgia, as part of an undergraduate panel at the meeting of the Southern Section of the Classical Association of the Middle West and South. The paper was a product of my CLAS 363 course. In March of 2000 I served as mentor for three students from my LATN 351 course who presented papers at Truman's Undergraduate Research Symposium. All of these students have subsequently enrolled in graduate programs in classics or a related field.

Appendix G contains several examples of student work on exams and papers. I have included final exams from outstanding students in LATN 250 and GREK 101. I have also included—as an example of excellent work in CLAS 363—a pair of papers (a first and revised draft), complete with my comments. An assessment form is attached to both of these papers.

Statement of Teaching Goals

First, I am interested in gaining additional insight into my teaching. To that end I would like to have someone observe my teaching in a variety of formats so that I can get a better sense of my weaknesses and strengths. I plan to arrange this visit with the help of our faculty development director within the next 12 months.

Second, I aim to continue to generate materials which enable students to read authentic texts during their first semesters of studying the languages. I am planning to create notes and vocabulary for select Catullus poems as a replacement for the texts currently available, many of which omit the most interesting poems. This will be an ongoing project, but I will plan to complete a draft before I next teach LATN 251 (Spring 2005).

Third, I would like to integrate audio/visual aids into my mythology presentations. To this end, I have already had hundreds of photos from my recent trip to Greece saved in jpg format. Last semester my student worker assisted me in building this collection. I feel that the regular and formal incorporation of a visual element into the course will greatly enhance both instruction and student learning.

Appendices

Appendix A: Summary and Interpretation of Student Evaluations
Appendix B: Select Written Comments From Anonymous Student
            Evaluations
Appendix C: Course Syllabi
Appendix D: Sample Exams
Appendix E: Curricular Additions and Revisions
Appendix F: Student Achievement: LATN 251 Projects
Appendix G: Student Achievement: Outstanding Exams and Papers

21

Sally L. Fortenberry
Associate Professor and Department Chair
Design, Merchandising, and Textiles
Texas Christian University
Spring 2003

Table of Contents

Teaching Responsibilities
As the department chair I am given a one-course reduction per semester; consequently, I am only teaching five different classes during each academic year. In the department, my area of expertise is in the merchandising and textiles program. All the courses I teach are required for fashion merchandising undergraduate students majoring in the program. Students who are minoring in our program or those who want elective credit may select these courses. I have had several MBA students take the entrepreneurship course for elective credit in their MBA program. Because I teach these classes only one time per semester per school year, the average class size has fluctuated between 30 and 60 students. In the fall semester I teach the following courses.

DEMT 40243 International Trade of Textiles and Apparel

This course is taught on an accelerated basis typically for five hours each week during the first eight weeks of the fall semester for our senior students planning to complete their internship during the fall. The general enrollment for this class is between 40 and 60 students.

DEMT 40286 Fashion Internship

This course is taught on an accelerated basis during the first eight weeks of the fall semester or during the first week of the summer term to our senior students prior to starting the work component of their internship. After the on-campus course is over, I visit each of the interns at their internship site, maintain communication with each student and their supervisors through weekly progress reports and evaluations, and then facilitate a final wrap-up session at the end of the semester. In the summer the enrollment is typically between 15 and 20 students and in the fall, enrollment is between 30 and 40 students.

During the spring semester I teach the following courses.

DEMT 30091 Career Development

This junior level course is the prerequisite course to the internship. This is a one-day-a-week course that prepares students for their job search and gives them the necessary resources to obtain a position in the industry. The enrollment in this class is typically between 40 and 60 students.

DEMT 40013 Entrepreneurship

This course primarily explores the challenges and satisfactions of starting a business related to the design, merchandising, and textiles industry. This is a university curriculum requirement critical inquiry class that requires students to prepare a complete business plan for their final project. The enrollment in this class is generally between 45 and 60 students.

DEMT 40263 Merchandise Buying

This course is primarily applied accounting and focuses on the mathematical formulas used in the merchandise buying process. The enrollment in this class is between 45 and 60 students.

Advising

I am also responsible for advising majors, minors, new freshmen, and transfers regarding their academic program. For the past three years, I have advised at least 70 majors each semester, and that number continues to go up. I have attended numerous advising workshops sponsored by the TCU

Center for Academic Services which has given me the strategies required to properly advise these students. My advising was last evaluated in 1995 during the formal review of tenured faculty. I have included comments received from current students at that time in **Appendix K**. These students were requested by the department chair to respond to a series of questions about my advising skills as part of the review process.

My Personal Teaching Philosophy

I endeavor to help students learn, internalize the information presented, and be able to apply this information in realistic situations. I maintain high expectations for myself and for all students. I try to be as fair and as objective as possible. I strive to eliminate the power struggle between teacher and student. I believe that it is necessary to establish an environment that is conducive for productive learning within the classroom. I encourage and solicit questions and I applaud diverse opinions (see **Appendix F**). I believe that my primary mission as a college professor and advisor is to assist students to become self-starters, independent thinkers, and self-confident in their personal abilities and attributes.

I consistently maintain an open door policy at all times. Furthermore, I encourage students to contact me at home or work, if I can be of assistance to them in any way. I do not believe that my "job" ends when the class is over. I consider it imperative to be available to the student's learning process both inside and outside of the classroom. I also endeavor to continue my personal contact and counsel with these students as they complete their studies and begin the learning process in their chosen career field (see **Appendix G**).

Teaching Methodology, Strategies, and Objectives

Since the courses I teach tend to be so different, I incorporate a variety of methods into each one depending on the requirements of that particular class.

- In general, I provide students with different evaluative exercises so that everyone has an opportunity to show their level of learning in the class—since many students do not necessarily do well on tests.

- Every class has at least one project, except for buying, and requires students to apply the knowledge they gain in the classroom to that project.

- I always bring in guest speakers from the specific aspect of the industry that the course relates to. This is very effective since those who are practicing professionals can reinforce what really needs to be learned in that subject area (see **Appendix H**).

- I also use visuals—videos, overheads, slides, PowerPoint, and examples—to illustrate what I am talking about. I believe this is important since so much of our industry requires visual skills.

- I try to give personal examples since I have worked in both the textile and apparel industry in several capacities prior to teaching in higher education.

- I use lecture, student discussion, in-class teamwork, and student-led presentations. I use a variety of methods in each class period so that the student is able to grasp the material based on what may be their best learning style—and also to prevent boredom.

I would really like my students to know that I only have their best interest at heart. When I make them work hard and challenge them, it is because I know that they will be expected to do the same in their career position—as in life. I want to encourage them to learn everything and to actually enjoy learning, since that will be so valuable for them when they do enter their first career position. I want to instill a passion for lifelong learning and not just memorizing information to pass a test or doing a project just to get it done.

- I encourage them to internalize the information and not just memorize. I provide relevant examples of how the information can be applied.

- I give the students review sheets for major exams.

- I provide a variety of ways for students to demonstrate their level of learning: tests, quizzes, projects, demonstrations, and in-class participation.

- I work with students outside of class, especially in the merchandise buying class since many of these students have a math phobia.

- I give students my home phone number so they may call me if they need assistance, especially prior to an exam or before a major project is due.

- I try to use encouraging words during class and be patient with those who are struggling with new concepts.

- I review tests and discuss the correct answers or processes that should have been used so that students know where they need to continue to focus their learning.

- I provide a very detailed syllabus and class schedule so that students know what is expected and what will be taking place each day in class.

Description of Unique Course Materials Including Syllabi, Handouts, and Assignments

International Trade

In this class I ask the students to write their own personal position paper on whether or not they believe in free trade or protectionism. This is written at the end of the course after they have been exposed to the pros and cons of both positions. I believe that this truly helps the student internalize what they have learned into their personal value system. It is usually an eye-opener for them. (See **Appendix A** for a course syllabus and representative assignments.)

Entrepreneurship

This course requires the student to do several small projects, which lead up to the final completed business plan. I have them do a competitive analysis for the business they hope to open with actual businesses that could be their competition. The students must also go through the process of gathering the necessary paperwork to start their business, such as a tax permit, articles of incorporation, health department permit, Occupational Safety and Health Act requirements, FICA information, etc. It is at this point that they realize that starting your own business is not all that simple. I also have them interview an entrepreneur about their business and their successes and failures. (See **Appendix B** for a course syllabus and representative assignments.)

Career Development

This course is made up of about eight projects culminating in the student obtaining an internship. They must prepare a resume; complete a cover letter, a thank-you letter, and an acceptance or rejection letter; write a paper on the company they hope to work for; interview with at least three different companies; and register with the career services office at TCU. Everything that they learn in this class is applied to their projects. The final result is if they get the internship they hope to obtain. (See **Appendix C** for a course syllabus and representative assignments.)

Merchandise Buying

The only projects that the students do in this class are take-home quizzes and end-of-chapter tests. I invite buyers to come into the class to speak, and sometimes the entire class will visit a small retailer to discuss their buying process. (See **Appendix D** for a course syllabus and handouts.)

Internship
The ten-week, full-time work component of the internship is one large project that requires total application of all that students have learned up to this point in their college career. However, students are also required to complete a final paper and portfolio of their internship experience so that they have tangible examples of all that they have accomplished. This is used to obtain a career position. (See **Appendix E** for a course syllabus and packet of assignments.)

Efforts to Improve Teaching

The textiles and apparel industry is dynamic and global in nature. Consequently, there is a need to continually update my terminology, materials, and information presented within each class. The classes I teach tend to be focused on professional application of knowledge gained in the classroom. Therefore, I believe it is imperative that I maintain consistent communication with industry professionals either formally via workshops or informally via luncheon meetings. By continuing to aggressively network with practicing professionals in the textile and apparel industry, I believe I am better able to instruct my students about career opportunities and the realities of the industry.

There are a variety of ways which I choose to stay current in my discipline. Since TCU is located in a major metropolitan area and a major market area for the textiles and apparel industry, I am able to participate in a large number of local seminars, workshops, and meetings geared directly to my area of teaching.

Student Ratings on the Student Perceptions of Teaching Evaluations

Evaluation by students is depicted in the following charts. Student Perceptions of Teaching Evaluations are administered every semester.

DEMT 40243 International Trade of Textiles and Apparel
*1 Compared with all instructors in same department
*2 Compared with all instructors in same college
Rating Scale is 1–5: 1 = Poor and 5 = Excellent

Term	Respondents	Overall Class Average *(1) (2)	Department Average *(1) (2)
Fall 97	23/28	4.70/4.70	4.23/4.17
Fall 98	22/23	4.68/4.50	3.95/3.93
Fall 99	Evaluations were not available to administer prior to final class day of Oct. 15 since class is accelerated and ends after the first 8 weeks		
Fall 00	40/40	4.55/4.45	3.86/3.77

Student Comments

> *Dr. Fortenberry made the class very interesting and clear. If we didn't understand she didn't mind re-teaching the material until we understood. She gave good ideas for reviews and allowed students many possibilities to raise their grade if needed. Her tests were fair and covered the material, which she extensively covered in class.*

> *Dr. Fortenberry is good at bringing in the opinions of students of other cultures. She relates the real world to what she is teaching to emphasize importance. Dr. Fortenberry is excellent at maintaining a professional standpoint, but is not too proud to get at the student level and give the respect that she intends to receive in return.*

DEMT 40263 Merchandise Buying

Term	Respondents	Overall Class Average *(1) (2)	Department Average *(1) (2)
Spring 97	25/25	3.54/3.50	4.25/4.22
Spring 98	18/21	4.56/4.50	4.02/4.00
Spring 99	34/38	3.76/3.74	4.17/4.10
Spring 00	29/36	3.32/3.24	3.73/3.68
Spring 01	41/59	3.93/4.02	3.83/3.77

Student Comments

> *She explained the material very well (especially since I am not a "math" person). She was always willing to stay after and help with problems that I did not understand.*

> *She presented the materials, which could sometimes be confusing in the book, on a level that we were able to understand and relate to. Always willing to help us and make sure we understood concepts. I learned so much that I feel I can actually use this in my career.*

DEMT 40013 Entrepreneurship in Merchandising and Textiles

Term	Respondents	Overall Class Average *(1) (2)	Department Average *(1) (2)
Spring 97	18/18	4.50/4.50	4.25/4.22
Spring 98	Class was taught by an adjunct for my one class reduction as I took on role of department chair		
Spring 99	28/32	3.56/3.59	4.17/4.10
Spring 00	23/35	3.57/3.55	3.73/3.68
Spring 01	45/59	4.20/4.09	3.83/3.77

Student Comments

> *I loved Dr. Fortenberry's endless amount of information! She knows her industry very well and is interested in everyone learning.*

> *She loved working with students and teaching. She brought lots of outside speakers which were very interesting and helpful and definitely added to the class.*

The students in the Career Development class and the Internship class fill out an evaluation developed by the instructor, which is specific to that course since the evaluations used for lecture classes do not necessarily apply to these two classes. Additionally, more recent ratings are not available because the university adopted a new format for the Student Perceptions of Teaching Evaluations, which is not consistent with the previous format used. All numerical student evaluations and student comments of courses may be found in **Appendix I**.

Evidence of Student Learning

I have maintained communication with a large majority of the students that I have taught and or advised over the past 14 years while at TCU. Many of these students are now in management positions within the textile and apparel industry in Fort Worth, Dallas, New York City, London, and California. Additionally, many of these same students are now acting as internship supervisors for my current students. The following is a sample list of successful former students:

- Ajiri Aki, Associate Fashion Editor, *DNR,* New York City
- Deana Giles, General Manager, The NBA Store, New York City
- Nicole Dabbert, Marketing Director and Assistant Manager for Lilly Dodson/Escada in Dallas
- Donna R. Hale, Director of Visual Merchandising, Pier 1 Imports, Fort Worth

Several of my former students aspired to go to graduate school in order to teach in higher education in the field of textiles and apparel. Karol Blaylock, Ph.D., Ellen McKinney, M.A., Stephanie Bailey, M.A., and Nicole Bettinger, M.S., have taught as adjuncts for our program at TCU. Dr. Blaylock is currently an assistant professor at Southwest Texas State University in San Marcos, Texas, and Ellen McKinney teaches at the Art Institute of Dallas. I have included letters from former students in **Appendix G** and articles and work that relates to the student's profession in **Appendix L**.

Teaching Recognition
By Professionals in the Discipline

I have been invited to make presentations, review or edit textbooks, or had peer-reviewed papers accepted that relate directly to my teaching expertise. The following is just a sample of the recognition I have received for my teaching capabilities:

- Invited to present Store Planning for Profit at the Dallas International Apparel Market Buyer Symposium
- Invited to present two teaching workshops on the U.S. Textiles and Apparel Industries in the Global Economy at the Texas State Education Association annual meeting for junior high and high school teachers in family and consumer sciences
- Invited to be primary editor of the Textiles and Apparel Production and Management Text and Reference book for the Texas Education

Association for use by all family and consumer science teachers in Texas public junior high and high schools

- Invited to be expert guest on educational broadcast video via the Texas Education Agency network to all schools in the state regarding the textiles and apparel industry and the need for a skilled and educated workforce

- Selected as the Social Science Division Nominee for the TCU Dean's Teaching Award

- Invited to write the Textiles and Apparel Summary document for the College Board 2003 Reference Manual

I made my second invited presentation to the Texas State Teachers Association annual meeting related to my teaching International Trade of Textiles and Apparel and Consumer acceptance of non-U.S.-made products. Supporting documentation can be found in Appendix J.

By Current and Former Students

I have received 30 TCU Senior Appreciation Program recognitions since it was established in 1990. Seniors make a monetary gift to the university paying tribute to those who have influenced their lives. I consider this a very special honor and one that confirms that I am doing something right as a teacher and mentor. I have included one of the letters indicating the recognition in **Appendix J**.

In the fall of 1999 and the spring of 2002 I was nominated by my former students for the TCU Wassenich Award for Mentoring in the TCU community. Students were asked to nominate individuals who had made a difference in their lives by providing personal support, assisting them with academic and career concerns, encouraging active involvement in learning, and serving as role models. I have included the letters of recognition in **Appendix J**.

Teaching Goals: Short- and Long-Term
Short-Term Goals

- To continue to evaluate the content and methods of teaching the various courses that I teach each semester with outcome assessment in mind, specifically, DEMT 30091 Career Development, DEMT 40243 International Trade, DEMT 40263 Merchandise Buying, DEMT 40013 Entrepreneurship, and DEMT 40286 Internship.

- To investigate more efficient ways of teaching larger classes if enrollment continues to stay at its current level.

Long-Term Goals (after my term as department chair)

- To be granted a sabbatical and use the time to complete instructional internships related to the content areas of the courses I teach.
- To participate in one of the Global Study Programs offered through TCU in order to enhance my teaching of the International Trade class.
- To investigate the use of web-based instruction within the context of my current classes and participate in the training offered through the TCU Center for Teaching Excellence.

Appendices

Appendix A: DEMT 40243 International Trade
Appendix B   DEMT 40013 Entrepreneurship
Appendix C: DEMT 30091 Career Development
Appendix D: DEMT 40263 Merchandise Buying
Appendix E: DEMT 40286 Internship
Appendix F: Current Student Comments and Letters
Appendix G: Former Student Letters
Appendix H: Announcements of Guest Speakers
Appendix I: Student Perceptions of Teaching Evaluations
Appendix J: Teaching Recognition
Appendix K: Advising
Appendix L: Evidence of Student Learning

22

TEACHING PORTFOLIO
Amy E. Seldin
Department of Education
Westfield State College
Spring 2003

Table of Contents

This is my first year of college teaching. My portfolio covers only the data for this year at Westfield State College.

Teaching Responsibilities

My teaching responsibilities in the Department of Education include teaching undergraduate and graduate courses in reading and literacy. I have taught EDUC 303: Early Literacy and Reading, which is a required reading methods course for all elementary and early childhood majors in their third year of the undergraduate program. The average class size for this course is 25–30 students.

Undergraduate courses EDUC 335: Individualized Instruction in Reading and EDUC 317: Analysis and Correction of Reading Disabilities, and the graduate course EDUC 662: Innovative Practices in Teaching Reading, are elective courses within the major of reading, but are also required of students majoring in reading. Average class size for these elective courses ranges from 11–20 students.

In addition to my classroom teaching, I also supervise graduate student teachers in their full-time student teaching reading placements in local school districts. As supervisor, my role is that of liaison among the college and the elementary school, mentor from the college, and collaborator with each college student and their classroom reading teacher. I go into different schools, meet with teachers and student teachers, observe and discuss student teacher-taught literacy lessons, and act as a support to both college student and cooperating elementary teacher. I enjoy going into the schools. Each time I do I am reminded of the colorful variety of schools, teachers, learners, principals, reading programs, and the multitude of ways of combining all to help children learn to read.

Philosophy of Teaching

It is my belief that all children can learn to read and that all individuals can learn. It has been my long-held belief that a teacher's job is to help *all* students learn. If there are students who do not learn in the ways that other students do (and this is almost always the case), it is my job to find other ways for the student to access and practice using the material. This applies to struggling readers, college students, adults much past college age, and individuals in-between these groups. It is my job as a teacher educator to raise my college students' awareness of teaching all of their students, and to have different teaching approaches in their repertoires to teach those students who do not learn as their peers do.

It is important for me as a teacher educator to be aware of my own experiences, interests, and biases about teaching and learning reading to all types of students. It is also important for my students to reflect on their experiences as students, to examine their own assumptions about teaching and learning, so that they may be aware of their own beliefs and biases about teaching children of different races, ethnic backgrounds, first languages, and physical and academic capabilities.

In teaching, knowing the content and instructional plan is certainly important. But it is also important to observe and listen. It is my job to inquire about what students bring to the classroom and incorporate students' lives into their learning. As teachers, we need to create engaging classrooms, lessons, discussions, and to build communities of interested, motivated students who participate, listen, and respond to each other.

I firmly believe that it is important for each teacher to reflect upon his or her own work—daily and over time. We can learn a great deal from thoughtful, personal reflection about why we think and teach in the ways that we do. Reflection and discussion with other educators about the work that we do is additionally beneficial to our individual growth as teachers. In the end, effective teachers are lifelong learners.

I believe that it is important for all students to realize that they can become great reading teachers even if they do not love reading. It is also my belief that they will improve their own reading as they learn to teach others. Students learn by getting feedback from peers or from me.

Teaching Methodology and Objectives

People learn by different modalities or a combination of several: listening, discussing, observing, practicing, reflecting orally or in writing. By using different means, students may more thoroughly understand ideas as well as teaching techniques and strategies. Students learn by talking and writing (thinking) about the material. It is important that my students have opportunities in and outside of class to discuss issues and questions about the material and teaching methods. I build in time each class for students to ask questions they have previously written about the reading, or to write on a question, discuss it with a colleague in class and then have a few pairs share their ideas or issues that were raised in the conversation. Having to form and articulate an idea provides students a chance to clarify it for themselves and others.

I use a variety of teaching methods. Lecture, discussion, and small group activities are a part of each class. I use lecture/discussion to check for understanding and opinions about the readings, and ask for student observations from their experiences in schools. Small and large group activities are used to provide opportunities for students to clarify their understandings of theories, ideas, and strategies.

In each class, students keep inquiry notebooks throughout the semester (see Appendix A). They write a reaction, a summary, or answer a question about the readings, and also write down several questions. I read the students' responses and questions in the notebooks and respond in writing several times during the semester in a "conversation" style. In addition, I use videos, such as *Guided Reading,* by Fountas and Pinnell, *The Reading/Writing Connection,* by the Center for the Study of Reading, and computer software, such as Kid Phonics, A to ZAP, and talking books, by Broderbund, for students to examine and critique. I give students clear assignment guidelines (see Appendix B) with criteria to address in order to receive the full number of points. I often give time in class for students to discuss assignments and to get feedback from each other.

I keep my classes moving and typically do several different things during a class: lecture, discussion, small group, individual, or whole class activities, such as participation in professor-modeled lessons, creating student lessons, presenting lessons or ideas to peers for feedback, and asking and answering questions.

In my classes, students learn many different literacy assessments to do with students in classrooms. Examples include running records and miscue analyses, reading conferences, reading interviews, retellings, and anecdotal notes (see Appendix C). They practice several assessments in class. Then they practice with a single elementary school student, analyze their findings, and reflect on what they learned or didn't learn. Practice in both the assessments and the analysis/reflection is essential to student development of solid and thorough understanding of the reading process and of teaching reading.

In teaching students about models and methods of reading instruction, I model them and put them into practice for the students to experience. For example, instead of simply talking about literature discussion groups, I ask my students to choose a novel to read independently and to come to the college class prepared to hold discussions on their text (as they would teach their students to do in their own elementary classes). After the experience, we discuss how actually holding and doing literature discussion groups looked and felt to them as college students as well as what it could be like for them to organize and facilitate them in their own classrooms.

Whenever possible, I present examples—concrete examples—such as actual books from a Basal reading series, model lessons to describe what different reading methods can look like, effective teaching materials and activities, scenarios from my classroom teaching experiences to illustrate an idea, and student stories about their experiences in classrooms as both teachers and learners.

Student Motivation

During classes, I try to find out what students know, what kinds of classroom teaching experiences they have had, and what they have observed in classrooms. I tell them that their experiences and ideas are important and that I'd like to hear them in class. Further, I tell them that we are all learning together. I connect what we are learning to things with which the students already are familiar.

I let students know that I am available in my office to talk about their projects, coursework, or interests and issues. In addition, I ask student presentation groups to meet with me to show them that I am a resource and available to help them with their research or to sort out presentation ideas. I give students the opportunity to improve their work on assignments after feedback is given. I provide the consistent support needed for students to feel successful (see Appendix E).

Community Outreach

In February 2003, I began a project with a first grade teacher at a local West-field elementary school. This project involves volunteer Westfield State College (WSC) education students going into a first grade classroom to assess elementary students in reading. It provides an elementary teacher help in assessing her students as well as an opportunity for WSC education students to practice current reading assessments. The Westfield students learn about the theory and practice of using running records and miscue analysis in my EDUC 303: Early Literacy and Reading course, and then go into a first grade classroom to take running records with first graders and to discuss and analyze the results with the teacher. The project began in one classroom and we plan to expand it soon into other first grade classrooms in the school.

Conference Work

Over the last seven years, I have participated in local and national reading, literacy, and educational research conferences. Each year, I have participated in researching, writing, and presenting at these conferences both individually and as part of a team. I have been an active participant in the New England Educational Research Organization (2000 to 2003), the American Educational Research Association (1999 to 2002), and the Massachusetts Reading Association (1997 and 2000). In addition, I have made a number of presentations to Boston Public School teacher groups from 1997 to 2002 on Reading Workshop, Writing Workshop, and Literacy Technology. (See Appendix F for a more complete listing of these presentations.)

Student Evaluations

I am in my first year of teaching at Westfield State College. The numerical student ratings are not yet available. I have selected three unsolicited quotes from student correspondence that describe their view of me as a professor. It pleases me to hear that they feel that I am a supportive teacher who is responsive to their individual needs. In addition, I am glad that students believe that they have learned a good deal while taking my classes.

> *Dr. Seldin—Thanks for your help with the running record. It made a lot more sense to me when I left your office. Most of all, thank you for being so understanding. I learned a lot from you this semester.*
> —Jillian T., December 2002

Thank you for caring about us as students. See you next year!
—Michelle, H., December 2002—note at the end of final exam

I learned so much from you. I'd love to take another class with you.
—Chassity W., December 2002—note at end of final exam

Efforts to Improve Teaching

Informal student feedback during the fall term in EDUC 303 suggested to me that it would be beneficial to consider making several changes for the spring semester. Based on informal student feedback, changes I made included changing the textbook to one that was more accessible to beginning teachers and reorganizing course material to increase the time spent on fewer topics. In addition, based on student feedback, I have made sure that clear expectations are articulated throughout the semester for assignments, and that I consistently check in with students to see their understandings about topics and methods throughout the semester through oral discussion, questions, and "one-minute" papers.

Student Learning

At the end of the semester, I asked students to write me a note saying what readings or activities for the class benefited them the most (see Appendix D). This is what a sampling of students have said:

I will walk away with a better understanding of students' involvement in their own learning and how important it is for students to have meaningful experiences rather than straightforward instruction without involvement. I enjoyed the phonics lesson plan and learned from it how to think about addressing phonics from many different angles.
—Cassandra S., December 2002

Our discussion on multicultural issues was especially helpful for me as an education student. I found it beneficial because it gave me a different perspective on cultures and how to respond to them in the class. Creating the Phonics lessons and learning about phonics elements were the most beneficial for me.
—Kate M., December 2002

I really liked working with the running records and miscue analysis. Actually sitting down with a child having him read to me and then assessing him I thought was a bit hard. I really thought hard on how I was assessing him. But after much revision I received a 100 on the written portfolio. That makes me much more confident.
—Angela K., December 2002

The observation of the Reading Recovery program and the group's presentation of the program in class was most beneficial. Even if my school doesn't have this program I can implement some of the strategies and skills with my students. I already have done some of them with my own son.
—Christine L., December 2002

There is so much I will take with me from your class, such as running records by Marie Clay, Fountas & Pinnell's writing workshops, Routman's chapter on guided reading. I got to see how to use texts to motivate students to think about vocabulary and history.
—Christine F., December 2002

Making the phonics lesson helped me because up until this point I didn't know how to read a book and isolate a specific skill that I could teach. Knowing the different phonics elements, I am now able to recognize them and can develop lessons more easily. Reading the Brisk and Harrington article on Bilingualism also helped. I never realized how much effect culture has on the way we write.
—Jaime G., December 2002

This class has taught me a multitude of ways to go about teaching phonics, spelling and reading... I also really enjoyed reading the "Knapsack" article. It brought a new perspective to me and made me think about white privilege.
—Rebecca W., December 2002

The running record information and project was most beneficial to me. I can take this skill and actually see myself using this as an assessment tool within my own classroom. All our conversations/readings of children's books allowed me to see

what great literature is. I can choose books of quality and will bring this knowledge to my own classroom.
—Lindsey K., December 2002

Having a book discussion group helped me see what kinds of things need to go on and what to focus on and talk about. The presentations on reading programs helped me see how I would gather information on a program and what the important elements are as well as what to look for.
—Jessica M., December 2002

Goals

I have several goals for the future.

- I will expand the use of web sites in my classes with students within the next six months.

- I will expand the use of technology—such as PowerPoint presentations—in my classes with students within the next six months.

- I will integrate more "one-minute" writing-for-understanding student evaluations.

- I will have a formal observation by my department head within the next four months.

Appendices

Appendix A: Course Syllabi
Appendix B: Sample Assignments
Appendix C: Sample Reading/Literacy Assessments
Appendix D: Student Evaluations
Appendix E: Successive Drafts and Graded Student Lessons
Appendix F: List of Presentations and Workshops Taught

23

TEACHING PORTFOLIO
Clement A. Seldin
Collaborative Teacher Education Program
University of Massachusetts, Amherst
Spring 2003

Table of Contents

1) Teaching Philosophy
2) Teaching Responsibilities and Strategies
3) Representative Course Syllabi Including Assignments, Examinations, and Supplementary Reading
4) Advising
5) Evaluation of Teaching
6) Honors Relating to Teaching
7) Teaching Improvement Activities
8) Reflective Statement
9) Appendices

Teaching Philosophy

The following eight statements provide fundamental structure for me as teacher and learner. They support a strategic filter through which I place my courses, advising and supervision, writing and research, and other faculty activities. They help maintain my sense of balance and professional direction.

- Growth is developmental and requires time and patience. We are the instruments of our own growth.

- Teachers must focus on strengths and use feedback and support to help learners grow academically, socially, and emotionally.

- Critical thinking helps students internalize learning.

- Structure and shared decision-making are significant to the learning process.

- Success stimulates further success.

- Teachers must strive to meet all learner needs and be keenly aware of social, emotional, and physical variables that affect the learning process.

- Teachers and learners must value diversity and seek unity in a multicultural nation.

- All teachers must seek continuous renewal and growth.

Teaching Responsibilities and Strategies

My teaching assignments are centered broadly on foundations of education and specifically within the Collaborative Teacher Education Program (CTEP), a five-year master's/licensure program in elementary and early childhood education. Courses are framed on a vigorous knowledge/research base and I utilize a lecture, discussion, and problem-solving approach. Students are systematically urged to actively contribute to class discussions and learning activities.

The Socratic dialogue is used in my classes—a method of argument and proof using a question and answer approach. I developed a series of case studies for the foundation courses and the controversial issues course to encourage debate and critical thinking. These multifaceted case studies focus on contemporary problems to which students can easily relate. Given their diverse backgrounds, students bring unique perspectives to class which create a fertile environment to explore various issues represented in the case studies. I want students to appreciate the complexity of every issue. My aim is to illuminate the conclusion that being an absolutist on controversial issues undermines children and education.

Various teaching technologies are used to enhance class presentations by improving the overall quality of the material through dynamic presentation. Systematic use of presentation graphics (PowerPoint), integrated video and audio clips, slides, and animation graphics serve to stimulate discussion and analysis each week. Regular use of the SMART Board has generated a powerful, interactive tool for my classes.

I teach the following courses:

- Educ. 351, Social Foundations of Education (two sections each semester)

- Educ. H01 Controversial Issues in Education

- Educ. 645, Inquiry Into Schooling

- Educ. 282E Pre-Practicum I Field Experience

In previous years, I have taught Foundations of Education: An Urban Perspective; Developmental Education; and Principles and Methods of Teaching Social Studies.

Educ. 351, Social Foundations of Education

This course focuses on the culture of the American public school. It enrolls 25–30 students in each of two sections. The course explores the teaching/learning process, the sociology and history of public schooling, teacher roles, and philosophical and psychological aims of education. Importantly, I have designed the course to help students identify the degree to which their interests and strengths are consistent with those demanded by the teaching profession. During this course, or shortly thereafter, students apply to CTEP. Much time is devoted to helping students prepare their applications and position themselves for successful interviews. In addition, substantial energy is committed to helping nonaccepted students regain emotional equilibrium and refocus their academic directions. (See Social Foundations syllabus in Appendix A and Supplemental Reader in Appendix B.)

Educ. H01, Controversial Issues in Education

Designed for university honors students, this course explores fundamental educational topics and investigates multiple solutions. With a maximum enrollment of 12, the course attracts honors students from many university disciplines and involves extensive readings, discussion, presentation, and debate. (See Honors Course syllabus in Appendix A.)

Educ. 645, Inquiry Into Schooling

This required graduate course examines contemporary educational practices for master's/certification students in their fifth year of the program. Among the issues examined are ability grouping, character education, teacher testing, bilingual education, standardized curriculum, schools and technology, inclusion, charter schools, and community service. (See Inquiry into Schools syllabus in Appendix A.)

Educ. 282E, Pre-Practicum I Field Experience

This course is designed for students enrolled in Social Foundations. Working with a team of graduate student supervisors, I have constructed a comprehensive system to place the students with local teachers in elementary schools one morning each week for ten weeks. In weekly meetings with supervisors, I coordinate their directed observations and three-way teacher/supervisor/cooperating teacher conferences. (See Pre-Practicum Booklet in Appendix C.)

Honors Research and Theses

Given my focus on undergraduate education and my role as advisor to Kappa Delta Pi, Education Honor Society, I have also chaired many undergraduate honors theses. This involves working closely with the honors student to design the thesis, direct its research and writing, and chair a thesis defense before an honor's committee.

Independent Studies

Every semester I work closely with many undergraduates and graduate students who wish to pursue independent study in areas in which I have knowledge and interest. My students explore an array of topics related to teaching and learning in the public schools.

Representative Course Syllabi Including Assignments, Examinations, and Supplementary Reading

My comprehensive syllabi include course descriptions, specific academic requirements and expectations regarding course organization, examinations, and papers, as well as a grading rubric. Required and recommended readings are identified. A detailed weekly breakdown of topics and readings is presented. (See Course Syllabi in Appendix A.)

It is my belief that a comprehensive syllabus is a fundamental teaching tool. For students, it provides essential information and expectations about the course on the first day. For the teacher, it is a formal vehicle that conveys a blueprint for the course and expectations for student learning and academic performance. For the academic department, comprehensive syllabi collectively describe the department's curriculum, its scope and focus, and its academic rigor and standards.

Advising

My students are told that my door is always open. I announce this in every class. In addition to maintaining regular office hours, I meet daily with students. My goal is to equip them with tools to find answers for themselves rather than to rely on my suggested solutions.

In addition to receiving many appreciative letters and e-mails from students for numerous years, I also have standardized evaluations regarding my advising role that are very positive. Specifically, in terms of **showing a personal interest in helping students,** student ratings are consistently very high. Mean student rating from 1 (*almost never*) to 5 (*almost always*) is 4.92 (N=518) during the previous five-year period in H01 and all sections of 351 (see Appendix D).

I currently serve as the primary academic advisor to 26 undergraduates and 21 graduate students. Although my responsibilities are at the undergraduate level, I have served on masters and doctoral committees in the

School of Education and doctoral committees in the psychology department (Clinical Psychology Program). I have also chaired many undergraduate honors thesis committees.

Evaluation of Teaching

Student evaluations are vital to my efforts to improve courses. I have used a two-prong approach to gaining student perceptions. I have regularly administered a student evaluation instrument since my initial part-time faculty appointment 25 years ago, and I routinely request anonymous written student assessments at the conclusion of courses. Therefore, I have longitudinal statistical and descriptive data focused on both presentation and content. Evaluations are consistently at the highest levels in all categories (see Appendix D). Illustrative of the very positive student evaluations are the following student ratings by 518 undergraduate students in courses (H01 and two sections of 351) during the past five-year period. Mean student ratings on a scale from 1 (*almost never*) to 5 (*almost always*) follow:

4.94	Instructor was well prepared for class.
4.91	Instructor used class time well.
4.92	Instructor explained course material clearly.
4.95	Instructor inspired interest in the subject matter.
4.89	Instructor provided useful feedback.
4.93	Instructor stimulated useful participation.
4.96	Overall rating of instructor's teaching.
4.94	Overall rating for course.

Anonymous student evaluation narratives reveal significant strengths of my courses and instruction (see Appendix E). Representative examples from different classes in the past five-year period are as follows:

> *Throughout our amazing semester, you have repeatedly pointed out my academic strengths, gave me superior critical feedback on my work, and helped me to become more knowledgeable and confident. Thank you for your commitment and dedication to Education and your students.*

> *I was so impressed by your grading system. You used varied approaches including different types of questioning— multiple choice, matching, true/false, short and long essay questions.*

You carefully evaluated our group work, both large and small. You graded on project work and the quality of participation in class. I know it was a great deal of work for you but you should know how much we all appreciated it. Thank you!

Simply the best course at UMass. I had no idea there was so much to learn but you made every class fascinating. The lectures, discussions, readings, and debates were outstanding. I never missed a class.

Honors Relating to Teaching

- **Faculty Grant for Teaching,** Council on Teaching, Learning, and Instructional Technology, Center for Teaching, University of Massachusetts, 1998–1999. Proposal to develop a new course on contemporary educational issues.

- **College Outstanding Teacher Award,** School of Education, University of Massachusetts, Amherst, 1997–1998.

- **TEACHnology Fellowship,** Center for Teaching, University of Massachusetts, 1997–1998. Ten senior faculty (one from each school and college) were awarded fellowships to study technology in classroom teaching.

- **Mortar Board Award for Outstanding Teaching,** University of Massachusetts, Amherst, spring 1993. For outstanding teaching at the University of Massachusetts.

- **Distinguished Teaching Award,** University of Massachusetts, Amherst, 1984–1985. Regarded as the university's most prestigious award for classroom instruction, this recognition may be received only once in a professor's career.

Teaching Improvement Activities

As documented in my teaching philosophy, all teachers must seek continuous renewal and growth. I work diligently to improve my knowledge base and instructional methodologies. The following briefly identifies my efforts:

Columbia University (Teachers College) National Study of Schools of Education at Colleges and Universities

This research focuses on teacher education, administration/leadership programs, and doctoral programs. As a member of Site Visit Teams, I have studied schools of education in North Carolina, Michigan, Virginia, Kansas, and

Missouri. I have been had the opportunity to conduct extensive interviewing of administrators (chancellors, provosts, deans, chairpersons), professors, graduate and undergraduate students, principals, and teachers. In addition, we study handbooks, reports, reform plans, pamphlets, and handouts to help provide context, policy, and procedures. After each Site Visit, a technical report is written.

Teaching Portfolio Development

As an invited member of training teams, I have helped faculty in many disciplines to develop teaching portfolios in four-day programs at universities in Georgia, Texas, Ohio, and Missouri.

Interactive Conferencing Model

Researched parent/teacher communication and developed a new model for parent/teacher conferences that has been presented for teachers and parents in communities in Massachusetts, New Hampshire, and Vermont. This model has also been presented at a research conference and has been published in *Capstone Journal of Education* (see Appendix F).

TEACHnology Fellowship

Center for Teaching, University of Massachusetts. Ten senior faculty were awarded fellowships to study technology in classroom teaching.

National Studies on Off-Campus Teaching

Directed two national studies and have presented findings at conferences which have been published in *Educational Research Quarterly* and *Educational Horizons* (see Appendix H).

Presented Workshops

University of Massachusetts Teaching Assistant Orientation titled "Course Design, the Syllabus, and the First Day of Class," every August since 1989 at the invitation of the university's Center for Teaching.

Reflective Statement

I often reflect on how fortunate I am to have found a profession that provides a multitude of personal and professional rewards. I feel elated when I receive letters from former students who express genuine appreciation for my teaching, advising, and general support as they take aim at distant goals. I derive great pleasure from the challenge of designing a new component to a course and witnessing the nods and expressions of understanding on the faces of my students. On the first day of every class, I tell my students, "You are my priority." They are. My responsibility as teacher is profound. I strive to improve content and delivery and to teach at my highest level every day. John F. Kennedy said, "The exemplary teacher instructs in realities and suggest dreams." That is my mission.

Appendices
Appendix A: Course Syllabi
Appendix B: Supplementary Course Materials
Appendix C: Pre-Practicum Booklet
Appendix D: Student Evaluations
Appendix E: Student Evaluation Narratives
Appendix F: Parent/Teacher Conference Model
Appendix H: National Studies
Appendix I: Unsolicited Letters of Support of Support

24

TEACHING PORTFOLIO
Mary Barrows
Department of English
Barton County Community College
Spring 2003

Table of Contents

Teaching Responsibilities

As an instructor for foundation courses in English, I encounter students with varying degrees of achievement, apathy, and apprehension. These students challenge me to present a course in which they can learn, improve, and ideally, understand and demonstrate proficiency in written communication. As a full-time tenured instructor, I prepare syllabi, write and deliver lectures, plan and prepare student assignments, design and grade tests, and evaluate student performance for classes in English Composition I (ENGL 1204), English Composition II (ENGL 1206), Introduction to Literature (LITR 1210), World Literature (LITR 1215), and College Reading Skills (READ 1111). I provide office hours to accommodate my students who need direction regarding their lessons.

Teaching Philosophy

My philosophy of teaching is multifaceted and multidimensional. It is such because teaching requires and transcends a multitude of endeavors, skills, and personalities. Because learning can be so overwhelming for many college students, it is important to carefully choose methodical steps to assure their continual commitment to their own education.

Similarly, writing is a complex process that matures over time with continued practice and informed guidance, as does any worthwhile endeavor. What students learn in the classroom with any discipline transcends into many other aspects of their personal and professional lives. The same is true with writing.

I believe the achievement of learning, the creation of knowledge, and the understanding of subject matter in a course is an interactive process. As such, the amount of understanding and knowledge a student gains from a course is directly proportional to the amount of solid effort given in preparing for the course by the student and the instructor. Classroom meetings with students must be orchestrated to allow for the exchange of ideas and interaction between students and instructor, yet stress to students the desired level of achievement. Only through interaction can each student's ability be identified and developed.

Consequently, I believe in the empowerment of students. By guiding students to adopt certain principles and tools, we as educators empower them to become effective partners in their own education, giving them the outer behaviors and inner qualities to create greater success in college and in life.

Following the English department goals and objectives, I emphasize a process writing approach focusing on planning, drafting, and revising. Delivering information in the classroom, assessing student academic achievement, and administering grades comprise the basics of teaching; however, it is my belief that the personal interaction between student and teacher forms the foundation for student success. By working individually with students, a teacher not only reinforces academic skills but also promotes development of the whole person. Because the act of writing is both personal and social, this one-on-one communication allows the student to express his ideas, frustrations, and struggles with writing in a constructive way, thereby bolstering his confidence and willingness to persist. Similarly, students learn by interacting with each other. My role, then, becomes one of facilitator. As each class takes on a culture of its own, I attempt to adapt classroom discussions to meet each class's needs. In an environment where student communication is valued, the students are more likely to contribute to discussions and to share personal opinions and experiences related to the course. Quality instruction teaches more than content: Quality instruction encourages curiosity and the importance of lifelong learning and investigation.

Foremost, I believe that students should take personal responsibility for their work, their actions, and their behavior not only in the classroom but also in their personal lives. In so doing, they learn the benefits and the power to be gained when they seek opportunity to learn all through their lives, both formally and informally. Only then will the role of American education come full circle in providing functioning, contributing members of society.

Teaching Strategies, Objectives, and Motivational Techniques
Strategies and Objectives

For many entering freshmen, writing is a mystery that they believe they can never fully master. As an instructor, I attempt to separate the writing process into manageable steps with each step building the foundation for effective writing. These steps—planning, drafting, and revising—are essential to any writing task, and by mastering this process, students will have the competence to tackle any other writing situation they may encounter. With the accomplishment of every writing task, the students gain more experience, more confidence, and more competence.

Throughout all my classes I demand that students reach for more than they would otherwise. Specifically, I work first to lay the foundation of the material to be covered and then move into application, technique, modeling, and demonstration of the concept of the skill being taught. From there I challenge my students to perform using the tools taught. At times, I expect students to over-emphasize or exaggerate a particular concept, assuring me that they have a full grasp of the concept. On one English Composition I assignment, for example, I ask students to overemphasize transitional words and phrases and other coherence devices by inserting a transitional expression into each and every sentence. Most find this task challenging since they previously have not focused on or have not learned to appreciate the power of effectively placed transitions. To aid them in this task, I provide them with an extensive list of transitional and other coherence devices. This requirement forces students to reexamine and analyze the progression of their ideas and arguments and to prove how their ideas tie together. As a result, students learn the importance of clarifying the relationships between their ideas.

To teach students to write involves having the student write and then responding to what they have written. Initially, in-class time is devoted to generating ideas by using brainstorming, mapping, and listing techniques. These sessions allow students to interact with one another as well as with the instructor while discovering that differing viewpoints about the same topic are not incorrect. At the beginning of the writing course, the student's individual needs and strengths demand that they follow a closely regimented writing process, sharing and evaluating each other's ideas. Often this collaborative learning environment helps the student to experience less anxiety as he or she begins writing cohesive paragraphs.

Likewise, through guided class instruction, I maintain control on the academic writing skills necessary to eventually move the student to a level where he or she composes clear, coherent expository, persuasive, and argumentative essays. As the class moves from the planning to the drafting stage of the writing process, I attempt to work with students individually as much as possible. Working with students through one or two drafts before they turn in the final product allows me to reinforce concepts we have been studying and practicing, and allows the students to ask questions, clarify any misunderstandings, and ultimately, obtain feedback before I determine a grade. Students have often commented that writing multiple drafts with teacher guidance eases their anxiety. I have found that this extra in-class effort results in a more solid final effort.

As the semester progresses, my role changes. At the beginning of the semester, I am an instructor, both showing and telling. I point out errors, explaining the problems and showing the students how to correct them. As the semester progresses and as their confidence in their abilities increases, I attempt to become more of a facilitator, still finding problems and errors but encouraging the students to offer their solutions and corrections. It is at this point that I rely on peer editing and revising suggestions as a means of increasing their writing skills.

In a broader sense throughout my Introduction to Literature class, I focus much attention on the vocabulary of the discipline. Since the course is an introductory survey in nature and design, students need a solid foundation to draw concepts that all can understand, and they must continue to draw upon this vocabulary through the course and apply it from one genre to another. For example, I require that students apply the segments of the plot covered with a Faulkner short story to the design of the Elliot narrative poem to that of a Shakespearean tragedy to a short novel by Chopin. In so doing, not only are students forced to remember the concepts and to apply them, but they also learn the interconnectedness of literature ideas and principles.

A major portion of all my classes, especially literature, is discussion based. In so doing, I direct students' reading through informal writing assignments or through student-generated questions over particular issues that we then discuss and debate in class. My role as a teacher is to pose the questions, clarify student comments, encourage debate, explain misunderstandings or challenge risky interpretations, and keep the discussion on task.

Motivational Techniques

Simply stated, learning requires effort. It is not always easy, nor is it always fun. For that reason, students must be motivated to develop and use strategies that are effective and that they perceive will lead to success. A relatively small number of students come to the English classroom with strategies that will effectively enable them to complete the course. For whatever reason, these students are already intrinsically motivated to learn the subject matter. Perhaps they enjoyed a positive experience in a high school English class; perhaps they believe they are "good at English," and that this class will allow them to practice an activity they enjoy; perhaps they enjoy an intellectual challenge. These students are a special joy, but they are rare.

The majority of students who enroll in English bring with them negative perceptions of themselves, the subject matter, and the "English teacher." Through their past disappointments to master the subject matter, they have learned that English is not relevant to their lives, that it is too complicated to ever understand, and that "English teachers" are unreasonably picky people who expect students to meet unstated expectations. Thus, a critical part of motivating these students is to help them overcome their preconceptions about themselves and English. Some of the keys I have found to motivating students include:

1) Encourage students to do well. Praise them for their efforts, however minimal. Give them as much positive feedback as possible.
2) Make expectations clear.
   - Write assignment directions in nonambiguous, coherent language.
   - Provide feedback relative to those expectations on an individual basis.
   - Let students know I expect them to do well by allowing them to revise and rewrite unsatisfactory papers.
   - Outline general class expectations on the syllabus.
3) Use concrete learning examples to help students grasp concepts.
4) Make the material relevant by creating writing assignments that allow students to draw upon personal or real-world experiences.
5) Teach with enthusiasm.
6) Demonstrate concern for what students are learning and involve them in the learning process.
7) Be accessible. Arrive early. Repeatedly encourage students to come to my office for one-on-one help.

8) Provide prompt feedback to questions in class and to tests and papers. Use tests and written assignments as learning tools. Evaluate written assignments using the stated expectations.

9) Solicit feedback about what students understood and did not understand.

Supervisory Evaluations

Each spring at Barton County Community College both the instructor and the division supervisor, Dr. Gillian Gabelmann, complete a Full-Time Faculty Annual Performance Appraisal-Evaluator form. After the instructor submits the evaluation instrument, both the instructor and the supervisor meet and discuss the contents of the evaluation instrument. In the three areas of the teaching appraisal instrument—Teaching, Professional Growth and Performance, and College and Community Service—I have consistently scored a score of 7 on a scale of 1 to 7.

Student Evaluations

Student evaluations are gathered each semester at Barton County Community College by using the Individual Development Educational Assessment long or short form. The evaluation includes a separate data collection form for the instructor to complete for each class. Among other things the form asks the instructor to prioritize certain skills and intellectual activities. Feedback from the student evaluations then provides the instructor with information about the prioritized items from the students' perspective. In that way, the instructor can see if her perceptions of the class match those of the students, and if not, she can make the necessary changes. Included below is a chart of my most recent Individual Development Educational Assessment evaluations for English Composition II (ENGL 1206). The following three categories were selected:

1) Oral and Written Communication Skills
   Question: Developing skill in expressing myself orally or in writing.
   Response Choices: In this course, my progress was: 1 = Low, 2 = Low Average, 3 = Average, 4 = High Average, 5 = High

2) Improve Thinking Skills
   Question: Learn to apply course material (to improve thinking, problem solving, and decisions).
   Response Choices: In this course, my progress was: 1 = Low, 2 = Low Average, 3 = Average, 4 = High Average, 5 = High

3) Excellent Teacher

  Question: Describe the frequency of your instructor's teaching procedures.
  Response Choices: 1 = Hardly Ever, 2 = Occasionally, 3 = Sometimes, 4 = Frequently, 5 = Almost Always

Results	FA00 Norm & No. of Students Responding		SP01 Norm & No. of Students Responding		FA01 Norm & No. of Students Responding		SP02 Norm & No. of Students Responding	
Oral and Written Communication Skills	4.9	22	4.8	12	4.4	17	4.6	16
Improve Thinking Skills	4.6	22	4.6	12	4.5	17	4.4	16
Excellent Teacher	4.7	22	4.6	12	4.2	17	4.2	16

The feedback form also includes suggestions for teacher improvement. I have chosen to concentrate on those areas for future improvement. In addition to these quantitative measures, I also have solicited comments that speak directly to my teaching goals. These narrative comments I often find the most enlightening as well as encouraging.

Honors and Awards

I have been fortunate to be nominated and to receive several teaching awards. Twice I was named the University of Kansas Outstanding Community College Instructor. This award recognizes a community college instructor who made an impact on a current University of Kansas student. Additionally, I have received the Master Teacher Award from the National Institute for Staff and Organizational Development given by the University of Texas at Austin. Recipients are nominated by their peers and receive a special medallion. Next, I have been honored with the Who's Who Among American College Teachers Award. Again, this award is from a former student who recognizes a teacher's influence on his life.

The greatest compliment that a teacher can receive is to be recognized by her peers. In 1998, a Barton County Community College faculty member nominated me for the Distinguished Instructor Award. This award recognizes teaching excellence and commitment to the institution. The application process is rigorous, involving not only the nominee, but also her peers, community members, and students. A panel of five reviews the nominees' applications, ultimately deciding on a recipient to be announced at the spring commencement ceremony. I was both humbled and honored to be chosen Distinguished Instructor among many worthy candidates.

Syllabi and Curricular Revision

English Composition I (ENGL 1204), English Composition II (ENGL 1206), and Introduction to Literature (LITR 1210) courses have evolved over the past three years. This evolution has been a result of a sharpening of my own perception of what areas in these subjects require elaboration or additions as well as the concentrated effort of educational institutions to be more accountable for student learning. For example, each course syllabus identifies specific information concerning classroom policy, how the course is viewed in the total curriculum, and broad course objectives as well as the specific course competencies that students must be able to complete and to demonstrate before successful completion of these courses. Also included are instructor's expectations of his or her students, methods of instruction and evaluation, attendance requirements, and general course outline.

A comparison of the earlier syllabi with the current version reveals how the objectives and competencies are now more specific and complete. Though students may not initially understand what all of these mean, by the end of the course they should be able to view the objectives and competencies as a checklist of their accomplishments, thus validating all of their effort and perseverance.

For the English faculty the syllabus revisions provide guidance and continuity. As each of us designs his or her individual courses, the syllabus serves as a blueprint for creating lessons, assignments, and tests. Even though the faculty methodologies may differ, by semester's end all students will have been exposed to the same concepts and mastered the same objectives. The syllabus also allows for individual faculty members to write additional competencies, thus providing flexibility for the faculty member.

Examples of Student Work

Included in this teaching portfolio are two examples of student work. For English Composition II, I have included the final draft of a précis and essay based upon Plato's "Allegory of the Cave." This paper exemplifies the standard of excellence which I hope my students will attain. The second example, an English Composition II final research paper, represents the achievement of mastery of English Composition II competencies. Though not perfect, both papers show student improvement and coherence.

In the future, I intend to collect multiple drafts for the purposes of tracking student improvement more closely. This will not only aid me as an instructor but will also contribute to the English department's assessment efforts. My plan is to pilot spring English Composition I classes and eventually include all writing classes.

Future Goals and Timeline

As I continue to be an English instructor at Barton County Community College, I have several goals for the future, some immediate and some long-term.

1) At the beginning and end of the spring 2003 semester, I intend to administer and to collect both pre- and post-tests in English Composition I (ENGL 1204) and English Composition II (ENGL 1206). I will use these assessments as a tool to evaluate a student's growth in English. These test scores will then be accumulated by the English department to compile data for future assessment.

2) Beginning in the spring 2003 semester, I intend to develop a portfolio of products that document the results of my teaching in English Composition I (ENGL 1204) and English Composition II (ENGL 1206). I will systematically track the progress of three students functioning at various achievement levels to determine whether or not I am meeting their diversity of needs.

3) In general, and as an ongoing goal, I want to work toward a greater variety of experiences in the classroom. First, I intend to focus specifically on peer editing. By working with fellow classmates, students begin to recognize and to understand the complexities in written communication, and to become more cognizant of their own errors.

4) In the spring 2003 semester, I intend to incorporate Grade Quick to track students' scores and absences. Using this computer program, I can readily help a student know his standing in English Composition I and English Composition II, including any missing assignments.

Appendices

Appendix A: Transitional Devices
Appendix B: Paragraph Format
Appendix C: PowerPoint Presentation
Appendix D: Supervisory Evaluation
Appendix E: Performance Appraisal
Appendix F: Individual Development Educational Assessment Evaluation
Appendix G: Honors and Awards
Appendix H: Spring 2003 Course Syllabi
Appendix I: Previous Year Course Syllabi
Appendix J: Student Papers

25

TEACHING PORTFOLIO
Jane Collins
Department of English
Pace University
1998–2003

Table of Contents

I. Teaching Responsibilities

I teach a broad range of classes in literature and writing. My doctoral dissertation was on 16th and 17th century English literature, which I use specifically when I teach LIT 211 Early British Literature and Shakespeare. However, my graduate and doctoral education prepared me to be a generalist, able to teach in many genres and periods. I regularly teach the required core courses, LIT 211 and 212, which usually fill at 30 students. I have also taught many upper-level electives such as Modern American Drama, The American Short Story, The American Short Novel, Chaucer, Shakespeare, and the Senior Seminar. The upper-level courses generally have run at 15–25 students. Although my department does not have a graduate degree, I usually have education graduate students in my upper-level literature courses.

My primary responsibility for writing courses is teaching ENG 100A and ENG 116. ENG 100A is a course designed to prepare students for whom English is a second language to write successfully in mainstream writing classes. ENG 116 is a required writing course for students transferring to Pace from two-year colleges. Both courses involve all of the challenges of teaching students effective writing skills, but both also have a social component of easing the student's entry into the Pace environment and preparing them to live up to Pace's academic standards.

II. Teaching Philosophy and Methods

My primary goal in organizing the classroom experience is student participation and engagement. My student evaluations, summarized in section V of this portfolio, attest to this focus. In three classes I outline, 100% of the students agreed that student participation was encouraged. I firmly believe in the idea of a student-centered classroom and a student-centered course. My objective is to bring complex and rigorous material to the students, and through a variety of pedagogical strategies, help them to rise to the challenge of learning. For me, good teaching is a mix of challenging and difficult material and teaching methods and strategies designed to make students feel comfortable with their own ability to master this material. While my course material is rigorous and often needs lectures to help students understand what they are studying, students need to feel that they have personal access to the material.

I believe that students learn best when they can form clear connections between what they already know and the new material they are approaching. To help students make these connections between their own body of knowledge and the material I am teaching, I use a combination of classroom and curricular strategies, designed to help students engage complex material:

- Collaborative and active learning

- Internet technology which allows students to become part of an intellectual community that extends beyond the classroom

- Bringing the "real world" into the classroom through service-learning courses and campus visits by Shakespearean actors and creative writers

I use collaborative and active learning strategies as an integral part of most of my courses. In literature classes in particular, I find that students have a greater sense of ownership of literary texts when they can work on directed group projects to exercise their own critical faculties. A typical literature class I teach might include a brief lecture that included discussion questions on the text, followed by a group collaborative exercise in which students apply the ideas and skills described in the lecture to the text for that day. In Appendix A.1, I've included several collaborative exercises that I have developed that have successfully engaged students studying difficult literary texts.

In most of my literature courses, from 1998 to the present, I have used the software Blackboard, an interactive Internet software that allows students to post their ideas to a class bulletin board. This software allows students to be instantly published on the World Wide Web, changing their role as passive consumers of knowledge. Through this computer publication, students become producers of knowledge, part of a larger discourse community of intellectuals who make meaning. I described this pedagogy in my essay, "Practicing Public Discourse: Network Theory and the Social Production of Knowledge," which I delivered at the Mid-Atlantic Popular Culture Association Conference in October 1999. I have also used the electronic classroom to teach writing courses. In Appendix A.2, I include a list of innovative technological strategies I've used to teach literature and writing.

I also believe strongly that students need to be able to see the uses of literature and writing in the "real world" outside of the college. In the two service-learning courses I've developed, students come to see the power of language by working with underprivileged children in an after-school program and interviewing elderly residents of low income housing. These two courses are described in Appendix B. In addition to sending my students out into the world to learn the value of their own skills, I have brought performers and writers to Pace to allow my students to see themselves as consumers of culture. I have brought groups of Shakespearean actors to perform plays and workshops for students as well as 16 contemporary poets in the Poets at Pace reading series I direct. These interactions have helped my students to see how literature, even literature from 400 years ago, has meaning for the world at the end of the 20th century. I include a complete list of performers and writers I've brought to campus in Appendix A.3.

III. Curricular and Course Development

I have developed several courses in four important areas: the senior seminar, service learning, distance learning, and multiculturalism. In 1998, I created a course for the Dyson College Senior Capstone Experience titled The Writer and Society (see Appendix C for the course syllabus). This course was featured by Dr. Robert DiYanni in the NEH seminars on teaching at Pace (his letter regarding the course is in Appendix E).

I have also developed two service-;earning courses. In 1999, I created the service learning course called Writing and Social Identity, which has run two times and garnered much praise from both students and the university community. Pace University students enrolled in this advanced writing course served as creative writing mentors to children in the Southwest Yonkers YMCA's after-school program (see Appendix C for the course syllabus). In

1999, I developed a course titled Oral Literature and History, which ran as a tutorial in the spring of 2000. This service-learning course focuses on the traditions of oral literature and history, including storytelling, folktales, and song. In addition to classroom discussion and analysis of selected texts, students engage in the act of gathering oral literature and history by visiting senior citizens in Westchester County to record their memories.

In 1998, I created a distance learning course as part of a pilot program initiated by the dean of Dyson College. I developed an asynchronous, web-based course that has run successfully for three semesters with capacity enrollment. I have given workshops at Pace and other colleges describing my work on this course. In Appendix B, I include sample web pages from this course, including the syllabus and a section of the course on the Harlem Renaissance. Since then, I have created four online courses and taught one per semester.

Also in 2000, I developed a course in African-American literature to help fill the multicultural needs of the literature and communications department.

I developed two graduate courses, Writing for Business and Images of Work in American Culture, for the master's degree in professional communications being created by the Department of Literature, Communications, and Journalism.

IV. Representative Course Syllabi
I believe students need a clear and accurate vision of the course from the very first day they arrive in the classroom. To this end, I work to create syllabi that are detailed and complete. My syllabi include course descriptions and learning objectives, grading guidelines, attendance policies, lists of required texts, as well as specific due dates for all readings, assignments, and exams. Whenever I can, I also include detailed descriptions of the major assignments with the syllabus, so students can organize their time for the semester. I have chosen to include here four syllabi which are representative of the kinds of courses I teach:

1) A syllabus for ENG 100A, a writing course for students who have English as a Second Language

2) A required literature course LIT 211: World Literature I

3) A senior seminar syllabus for a course I created: The Writer and Society

4) A service-learning course I created: Writing and Social Identity

These syllabi are collected in Appendix C.

V. Evaluation of Teaching
Student Evaluations

Student evaluations are the primary resource I use for revising and improving my courses. I try to determine whether students feel they have learned the material of the course and whether they were satisfied with the methods I used to present that material. Because the general Pace student evaluation form does not always give me specific information about which texts, teaching methods, and assignments they felt worked best for them, I have also developed an informal survey for many classes that aims to get more specific feedback from the students.

Overall, my student evaluations have been positive. I particularly value the anonymous nature of the student evaluations because the narrative comments seem to be a reliable measure of the student's feelings. In the chart below, I have collated the number of students who answered "strongly agree" and "agree" in five categories. I chose representative categories, which cover student participation, my own knowledge of the subject, the quality of the syllabus, the perceived fairness of the evaluation, and the student's overall feelings about my teaching.

Course	Student participation encouraged	Professor knew material well	Objectives were clear	Exams were fair	Student recommends professor
Shakespeare	12 of 15 (80%)	14 of 15 (93%)	14 of 15 (93%)	13 of 15 (87%)	11 of 15 (73%)
Chaucer	17 of 17 (100%)	17 of 17 (100%)	17 of 17 (100%)	14 of 17 (82%)	17 of 17 (100%)
Short Novel	21 of 21 (100%)	21 of 21 (100%)	21 of 21 (100%)	Not applicable*	21 of 21 (100%)
Service Learning	7 of 7 (100%)	7 of 7 (100%)	7 of 7 (100%)	6 of 7 (86%)	7 of 7 (100%)
ENG 100A	11 of 12 (92%)	12 of 12 (100%)	10 of 12 (83%)	Not applicable*	7 of 12 (59%)
British Literature I	24 of 28 (86%)	22 of 28 (79%)	18 of 28 (64%)	17 of 28 (61%)	17 of 28 (61%)

*Essay portfolios replaced exams in these courses.
Copies of the evaluations for these six courses are in Appendix D.

I have also been very pleased over the years by the number of students who have kept in touch with me via email and private notes and letters. Even after they graduate, students often contact me to make connections between their work or graduate experiences and the courses they took with me. Susan Luft, who took three literature classes with me, emailed me to say, "I miss your classes. No one uses the class time the way you do." Since Susan will be a teacher herself, I appreciate her comments. Another former student who went on to become a teacher, Robin Maslanek, wrote to tell me how her work in my service learning course Writing and Social Identity became the basis of her graduate thesis: "The final paper we had to write planted the seed in my brain for this independent research project I have to complete before I get my masters. I have developed a rabid interest in literacy, and its various implications, especially for poor people and people of color. I just wanted to thank you for creating a course that enabled me to think about something so differently and passionately!" In 1999, Faye Roberts-Paul wrote about the seminar class, "Great class. I was much inspired by the way the group worked together. At one point I thought, 'this IS how people learn.'"

Full texts of these letters and others are available in Appendix D.

Peer Evaluations

Colleagues in my department have observed my teaching on five different occasions. I have included all five evaluations in Appendix E, but would like to present some pertinent quotes here. I think a common thread in the evaluations is their acknowledgment of my deeply held passion for teaching and for engaging students in their own learning process.

Dr. Robert DiYanni, a full professor at Pace University, wrote about my 1998 Senior Seminar, "I was impressed by the quality and the overall level of discussion conducted throughout the evening by the entire class. This was a model of what engaged and engaging teaching and learning can be." Dr. DiYanni noted that he had also used my syllabus for this course in a Pace faculty development workshop as "an example of what a Senior-year Capstone experience could be."

Dr. DiYanni also observed a 2000 class I taught in freshman writing. He noted,

> *Professor Collins clearly enjoys her work and, as a result, demonstrates a decided enthusiasm for what she is teaching. Her conversations with students were interesting and engaging for them, and were genuinely helpful in moving students through the revision process. It is quite clear that Jane Collins is a dedicated and committed teacher.*

Dr. Linda Anstendig, the director of Writing at Pace Pleasantville, visited my upper-level service-learning course in January 2000. Dr. Anstendig wrote,

> *Dr. Collins conducted an excellent, beautifully orchestrated class. Students were thoroughly and actively engaged in practicing real-world writing situations. . . . We are lucky to have such a progressive, creative instructor as a faculty member of the Lit/Com department.*

Dr. Rebecca Martin, associate professor at Pace University, observed an upper-level literature elective. She noted,

> *The class had a positive atmosphere. Students felt comfortable expressing their ideas and Dr. Collins and the students seemed to feel a shared sense of intellectual purpose. . . . Dr. Collins's engagement with the material was unmistakable; her excitement about literature and teaching is palpable. Her enthusiasm was mirrored in students who vigorously pressed points and joined the discussion eagerly.*

Dr. Susan Gannon, full professor at Pace University, observed the online American literature class I created and teach. Dr. Gannon noted that

> *Dr. Collins has put a great deal of effort into pioneering the on-line teaching of LIT 212 and her department has benefited from her initiative. . . . the archive of the class postings and responses evidences her success in the formation of a real, though on-line, writing community.*

Full text of these evaluations are available in Appendix E.

VI. Participation in Teaching Development Seminars

I firmly believe in the usefulness of workshops and seminars to improve teaching. Over the past few years, I have more often than not been the leader of such workshops, but I have found that in such settings, I have learned a great deal from other participants. Each year, I have done a number of workshops for faculty members here at Pace, and recently, I have been getting invitations from colleagues at other universities to share my experiences using technology to enhance student learning at their faculty development workshops.

At Pace, I have led workshops on helping second language students, on diversity and international educational issues, and on using technology in the classroom. In 1998 and 1999, I led workshops to help literature and communications faculty evaluate and grade writing by students who have English as a second language. In September of 2000, I led a workshop on diversity at the freshman orientation. In the spring of 2001, I was asked to lead a workshop on multiculturalism in the classroom for the Pforzheimer Center for Faculty Development.

In the summer of 1999, I led a two-day workshop, with Dr. Linda Anstendig, for Dyson faculty who wanted to create their own teaching web pages and include technology in their courses. In March 2000, I led a workshop for Dyson faculty on creating and running a distance learning class. In May 2002, I ran a workshop called "Technology in the Classroom" for the Pforzheimer Center.

I have been invited twice to Nassau Community College. In April 2002, I gave a talk at a workshop titled "Improving Student Learning: Computers in the Classroom" and in May 2002, I led a workshop on using a networked writing lab to teach composition. In January 2002, I visited Centenary College to introduce faculty to writing software to improve student communication. In April 2002, I was a featured workshop leader at Bergen Community College at the New Jersey Faculty Development Tenth Annual Conference. Records of these workshops are in Appendix F.

VII. Presentations and Publications on Teaching

I have published four articles and delivered two conference papers on teaching over the past five years. I feel that publishing on teaching is an important avenue for improving one's own teaching. The rigor of publication challenges me to keep current with the debates in teaching and to maintain a high level of professionalism.

In 1998, my essay, "Creating Communities: Strategies for Supporting Working Minority Women in the Classroom," was published in the *Proceedings of the Eighth Annual International Conference on Women in Higher Education.* This essay details a graduate course I taught at Queens College before coming to Pace.

My 1999 essay, "Writing for a Community: Using Internet Newsgroups for a Student-Centered Classroom," was published in the online *Guide to Writing in the Twenty-first Century* created by the Epiphany project. This essay grew out of strategies I used to help Pace students see themselves as an intellectual community by publishing their own writing in listservs. With the development of Internet software, I revised this student writing project and did a series of student surveys to determine the impact of this published writing on the students' sense of their own writing ability. I delivered a paper on this research, "Practicing Public Discourse: Network Theory and the Social Production of Knowledge," at the 8th Annual Mid-Atlantic Popular Culture Association Conference in November of 1998.

In 2000, my article, "The World is Smaller Than You Think: International Students Bring Their Cultures to Pace," described the importance of diversity on Pace campuses for a textbook created especially for Pace freshman enrolled in the mentoring course UNIV 101. This textbook, *Connections: A Text Compiled for Pace University Freshman Seminars*, was published by Simon and Schuster.

In 1999, *Shakespeare Magazine* published my article "Boy Actresses in the Classroom." This article details an innovative performance exercise I developed for Pace students, which allows them to imagine the stage conventions of Shakespeare's time. I also delivered a workshop on this performance technique at the 2nd International Teaching Shakespeare Conference sponsored by the National Council of Teachers of English in Chicago in February of 1998.

A chronological list of these publications and conferences papers is in Appendix F.

VIII. Student Accomplishments

In addition to introducing students to challenging material and helping them to learn, I extend my role as a teacher beyond the classroom and try to act as a mentor for students. This role often takes my relationship with students beyond the one-semester course. I have worked with many students over the years, both those in trouble academically and those who have achieved great success. I have chosen several students to represent the kinds of enhanced student learning that can arise from this mentoring relationship.

Primarily, I try to introduce students to new ways of seeing themselves as "professionals" or "intellectuals." I look for experiences that can move the student from a traditionally passive role into a more active and mature role. I have chosen to describe student accomplishments from several kinds of courses (writing, literature, and service learning), which are representative of the range of courses I teach. Further evidence of these student accomplishments is included in Appendix G.

Dyson Academy of Fellows

My student Angela Nally was inducted into the Dyson Fellows based on the quality of an essay she wrote for my course The American Short Novel. I recommended Angela to the Society of Fellows as an excellent writer and thinker. Once her essay was accepted, I worked with Angela on revising her ideas and research on American writer Kate Chopin. Her essay was chosen to be read at the opening Plenary Session as an example of the best work being done by Dyson students. At the November 8, 1998, meeting, I was proud to introduce Angela to a large audience of Pace students and faculty. In the spring of 2000, I supervised Angela's independent study project on oral history and literature (in conjunction with Via Pace), which completed her Dyson Fellows requirement for a major independent research project. Her work from this project was published on the literature and communications web site and also in a local newspaper for senior citizens.

Service Learning Recognition Dinners

Three of my students from the service-learning course Writing and Social Identity were asked to address the annual Via Pace Service Learning Recognition Dinner. Sara Whitman, Jean Salvia, and Christine Molougney each gave brief speeches about their experiences teaching creative writing to underprivileged students in an after-school program.

NEH Conference Student Panel

In fall 1998, I taught a Dyson capstone seminar in literature titled The Writer and Society. Four of my students presented work from this class at a panel at the Dyson College Conference on Environment Day as part of the Dyson NEH grant. Our panel, "The Writer and the Environment," included a diverse group of Pace students, including a Morroccan student, a graduate student, and two Pace undergraduates, who shared their original research on the Nigeria writer Ken Saro-Wiwa and his campaign against environmental racism.

Prize in Ethics

In the spring of 1999, I encouraged all of the students in my ENG 116 writing course to enter an essay in the Annual Essay Competition in Ethics run by the Pace Center for Applied Ethics. My student, Don Ventrice, was awarded an Honorable Mention for his essay, "Primal Sensitivity," which he read at a panel with other finalists on May 22, 1999.

IX. Goals

1) To create and evaluate the successfulness of multimedia classroom presentations with PowerPoint. I took a course in PowerPoint at the Computer Learning Center in Spring 2002. In the coming year, I hope to begin creating multimedia classroom presentations to make lectures more accessible and digestible for students. The presentations would help students absorb complex information and show them graphics and

images that would allow them to visualize the historical period of a literary work.

2) To continue my work directing the Teaching, Learning, and Technology Roundtable here at Pace.

3) To continue to improve my teaching by developing a new survey for evaluating the ways students learn with technology.

Appendices:
Appendix A: Teaching Methods
Appendix B: Courses Developed
Appendix C: Representative Syllabi
Appendix D: Student Evaluations
Appendix E Peer Evaluations
Appendix F: List of Presentations, Publications, and Seminars
Appendix G: Student Work and Presentations

26

Teaching Portfolio
Saundra K. Liggins
Department of English
State University of New York College at Fredonia
Spring 2003

Table of Contents

Teaching Responsibilities

I taught three undergraduate courses in the fall semester of 2001: ENGL 209: Novels and Tales, a required course for English and English education majors, as well as a general education requirement; ENGL 240: Introduction to African-American Literature and Culture, that serves as a requirement for the African-American studies minor, as well as also an elective for English and English education majors, and may count as a general education requirement; and ENGL 341: The Harlem Renaissance, a course that qualifies as a "period" course for English and English education majors, and may count as a general education requirement. The enrollment for these courses was 25 students, ten students, and 25 students, respectively. In the spring semester of 2002, I taught four undergraduate courses: two sections of ENGL 209; ENGL 338: Contemporary American Literature, a course that qualifies as a "period" course for English and English Education majors; and a new course, ENGL 399: African-American Autobiography, a course that serves as an elective for the English and English education majors, as well as for the African-American studies minor. The enrollment was 17 and 22 students for ENGL 209, 25 students for ENGL 338, and 23 for ENGL 399.

Teaching Philosophy

I believe that as a teacher it is my job to help students to expand their knowledge base of a particular subject matter. I find that the student body at SUNY Fredonia knows very little about African-American literature, which is the basis of most of the courses that I teach. This can serve as both an advantage and a disadvantage. More often that not I have found that the students are very enthusiastic about learning new material and it is exciting to know that upon leaving my classroom the students have at least a rudimentary knowledge of African-American culture.

Since a large portion of my students are English education majors, it is also rewarding to know that the students often take what they learn in my classroom and incorporate the material into their own lesson plans. There is a risk, however, in presenting the material. It would perhaps be very easy for students to perceive me as the authority on all things related to black American culture. I try to stress to my students that I am serving more as a guide, rather than as a sole and definitive expert. Learning about the literature and culture of a group of people requires more than a semester-long course. My job is not to show the students every single aspect of black culture, but to illustrate signposts, if you will, of the culture.

It is not only crucial that students are able to understand the material, but that they also can assess it and question its significance. What may be more important than the actual subject that I teach are the analytical skills that the students develop in the classroom. These are abilities that span many, if not all, disciplines, and transcend any specific subject matter. It is imperative that students be able to think on their own about the information that they receive, to formulate arguments, and make and apply judgments to present and future knowledge.

Teaching Strategies

Finding a balance between lecturing and leading the class in discussion is one of the most difficult tasks of teaching. To understand the literature and culture, it is also important to provide the historical, cultural, and social background in which this literature was produced. Especially since students know very little about African-American culture, much less African-American history, it is crucial that I give them important factual information. Therefore, I primarily use lectures to provide a historical context. Lecture is also useful when we are reading a difficult article or text. My job, however, is also to facilitate discussion. In class discussion I guide the students' reading (through writing assignments and study questions) to particular themes or issues.

Because literature is often a subjective discipline, open to many interpretations, I highlight what I think are the important issues regarding the material that we're reading, without dictating any single reading of a text. I also use class discussion and writing assignments, to be done both at home and in class, to allow the students the opportunity to engage in a more direct manner with the text.

Analyzing a piece of literature is an investigation or a process of discovery, and students frequently learn more when they explore on their own. In some courses I also require a group or individual presentation, or that a student lead a brief class discussion. These methods are useful because they give the students an opportunity to do research and examine an aspect of the material on their own. In addition, student-led presentations can also facilitate other students' learning, since many times students learn better from their peers than from the professor.

Efforts to Improve Teaching

In January 2002, I attended a workshop at SUNY Fredonia facilitated by John Olsafsky, "Introduction to Blackboard," which assisted me in using the Blackboard technology in my classroom. I believe that as technology advances, more and better use of the Internet will be a crucial aspect of most college courses. And while I do not subscribe to a "technology for technology's sake" attitude, instruments such as Blackboard, if used properly, can only enhance one's teaching.

In March 2002, I attended a workshop at SUNY Fredonia led by Peter Seldin where I learned how to create a teaching portfolio. This workshop served many practical purposes. Professionally it assisted me in preparing materials for renewal, but it also gave me an opportunity to really reflect upon the ways that I teach. The clearer focus gained from this workshop is reflected in my instruction.

Student Learning

In the fall semester 2001, I worked with undergraduate Melanie Yaskulski on a paper to fulfill a requirement for her African-American studies minor.

The focus of her paper was on the depiction of female friendship in Toni Morrison's *Sula.*

During the spring semester 2002, I worked with Marcel Freeman, an undergraduate, on a paper to fulfill a requirement for the African-American Studies minor. The focus of the paper was African-American film.

A student, Anne Fearman, submitted a paper that she had written for my Harlem Renaissance course to the SUNY Fredonia Rosa Parks Scholarship Competition. She was one of a select group of winners and presented her paper at the campus celebration and reception.

Syllabi and Assignments

Appendix A includes copies of my syllabi for the 2001–2002 academic year. My syllabi reflect not only the diversity of the courses that I teach, but also the diversity that I include within the courses themselves. Fall semester of 2001 gave me an opportunity to repeat two of the courses—ENGL 240: Introduction to African-American Literature and Culture and ENGL 341: The Harlem Renaissance—that I had taught the previous fall semester, and I welcomed this opportunity to improve upon the design of these courses.

In my second year of The Harlem Renaissance, I had a better understanding of what texts and activities work in the classroom, and both classes were better organized than in my first year. A more careful selection of texts also improved the dynamics of the course; we covered other aspects of the time period, including history and music and the arts, giving the students a much broader perspective of the era.

My Introduction to African-American Literature and Culture course was much improved as well. This course, too, had much better organization. Rather than designing the course purely on a chronological basis, I structured the readings more thematically. This, I believe, added a broader scope. For this course I would still like to incorporate more "culture"—discussing music, film, or television, for example—rather than solely discussing African-American literary texts.

The major adjustment that I made to the Harlem Renaissance class was the requirement that each student lead the class in a discussion of the material. This assignment gives the student an opportunity to closely analyze the text and then engage his or her fellow students in a discussion about the material. I believe that student-led discussions are often a better teaching method than lectures, and with some modifications I believe that more students will find this exercise useful.

Spring semester 2002 was very challenging and exciting since I was teaching two new courses: ENGL 338: Contemporary American Literature, and a new course that I had proposed, ENGL 399: African-American Auto-biography. For ENGL 338 I incorporated Blackboard on a limited basis. The discussion board section of Blackboard, a space that operates similar to a listserv, has been most useful in that it allows for more opportunities for students to discuss issues related to the texts we are reading (for example, while reading an excerpt from Art Spiegelman's *Maus,* the students discussed on Blackboard a controversial art exhibit that had shown at the Jewish Museum in New York).

I enjoyed teaching ENGL 209: Novels and Tales because I was still able to experiment with texts and other teaching strategies. Of all of the courses that I teach, this is perhaps the one that I find most unpredictable. Because this class is a requirement for English and English education majors, and it also is a general education requirement, there is often a mix of English and non-English majors in the classroom. The students come into the course knowing very little, if anything, about gothic literature, or about how to analyze literature in general, but by the end of the semester they have at least a rudimentary understanding of the conventions and themes of the genre. To demonstrate their understanding of the literary genre, I give the students an opportunity to write their own gothic short story, if they choose, for their first or final essay. The students who choose this assignment appreciate that it allows them to be creative, an opportunity that they don't often have in college.

Appendix B includes copies of representative assignments for three of my courses. A short story written by one of my students in ENGL 209: Novels and Tales, has been included to indicate the originality that many students bring to this assignment. The example from ENGL 338: Contemporary American Literature stemmed from a class discussion assignment. The students were to either give a presentation or lead the class in a discussion of the day's reading. I like to encourage free-thinking in the classroom, so I was happy when one of the students went beyond the standard class discussion exercises (providing discussion questions) for our readings about New Journalism and had the students take a newspaper article and write their own New Journalism–style account. The final selection is a paper written for ENGL 341: The Harlem Renaissance.

Student Evaluations

Appendix C includes summaries of my student evaluations for the course that I taught in the fall and spring semesters, compiled by other faculty members in the department. English department faculty have the option of choosing which particular format they would like to use for their student evaluations. Rather than using the more traditional format, where different qualities of the course and teacher proficiency are rated using a numerical scale, I choose to utilize the format that allows the student to write more of a narrative of their experience in the classroom. I find that the way in which the students respond to particular questions gives me a better idea of the students' feelings about the course.

The summaries provide a good overview of the areas of instruction that are most successful, and of those places where improvement is needed. As indicated, most of my students appreciate my helpfulness and friendliness and believe that I provide a challenging classroom atmosphere. Some students felt that I should more fully develop my skills in facilitating classroom discussion and clarify the requirements for written assignments. As a whole, my classes have been very successful and enjoyable.

Teaching Related Activities, Advising, and Committee Work

- Advised 12 English and English education majors.

- Moderated, as co-advisor to the Black Student Union, several film screenings in the Williams Center Multipurpose Room: *Black Is, Black Ain't; Bamboozled;* and *Sankofa.*

- Recruited two new students into the African-American studies program while I was interim coordinator for the minor.

- Assisted in spring semester 2002 academic advising for the English department on January 23, 2002.

- Attended Professor Bruce Simon's Honors Seminar class as a guest participant in a discussion about the Great Migration, the Harlem Renaissance, and Toni Morrison's *Jazz.*

- Facilitated a workshop for the Black Student Union and other students regarding professional letter writing and telephone etiquette for student organizations in April 2002.

Scholarship of Teaching

In December 2001, I presided over a special session at the Modern Language Association (MLA) Convention in New Orleans, Louisiana. Sponsored by the MLA's Committee on the Status of Graduate Students in the Profession, the session, "Narratives of the Graduate School Experience," gave graduate students the opportunity to discuss different challenges faced.

In June 2002, I presented a paper, based on a novel that I had taught in the Contemporary American Literature course, "Colson Whitehead's *The*

Intuitionist (1999): An Urban Gothic Vision," at the annual American Literature Association conference in Long Beach, California (Appendix D).

Future Teaching Goals

In the coming year I anticipate proposing three new courses: 19th Century African-American Literature; 20th Century, or Contemporary, African-American Literature; and a course on gothic literature. I feel that new African-American literature courses in particular are essential additions to the department and would be good companions to the courses already in existence: Black Women Writers, The Harlem Renaissance, and African-American Literature and Culture.

In my two years at Fredonia I have noted (and been told of) the lack of awareness of African-American literary texts, and minority texts in general, on the part of Fredonia students. These courses will not only add to our students' knowledge base, but they could fulfill a number of categories, from serving as an elective for major and minor programs, to being possible "period" course options.

I also plan on implementing new techniques in the classroom that will better facilitate discussion among students. All too frequently the class lapses into silence as students are unwilling or unable to actively participate in discussing the material. Determining more and better ways of consistently engaging the students in a conversation among themselves is a constant challenge.

Appendices

Appendix A: Course Syllabi
Appendix B: Sample Assignments from ENGL 209, ENGL 338, and ENGL 341
Appendix C: Summary of Teaching Evaluations
Appendix D: Abstract for American Literature Association Conference

27

TEACHING PORTFOLIO
Alan Shepard
School of English and Theatre Studies
University of Guelph
Guelph, Ontario, Canada
March 2003

My portfolio falls into two parts—a brief collection of materials I have assembled while teaching at the University of Guelph, whose faculty I joined in 2002, and a larger collection of materials created in the previous 12 years I taught at Texas Christian University (TCU).

Table of Contents
1) Teaching Responsibilities
   - Formal Courses
   - Directing Graduate Theses and Dissertations
   - Mentoring Graduate Instructors and Junior Faculty Members
2) Teaching Philosophy
3) Teaching Goals and Strategies
4) Syllabi, Assignments, and Responses to Student Work
5) Evidence of Teaching Effectiveness
   - Statements from Peer Colleagues, Students, and Alumni
   - Student Perceptions of Teaching Data
   - Student Outcomes and Achievements
   - Awards and Other Recognition
6) Goals for Improving My Teaching in the Future
7) Appendices
   - A: Courses Taught at Guelph and TCU, with UCR designations and enrollments
   - B: Courses I Have Developed for Guelph and TCU's Curricula
   - C: Graduate Theses and Dissertations; Undergraduate Senior Honors Theses
   - D: Programs Designed to Mentor Graduate Instructors and Junior Faculty Members
   - E: Sample Syllabi and Assignments
   - F: Sample Responses to Student Work

- G: Statements About My Teaching From Peer Colleagues
- H: Statements About My Teaching From Undergraduates, Graduate Students, and Alumni
- I: Representative Data From Student Perceptions of Teaching, 1996–2003
- J: Sample Achievements of Former Students
- K: Copies of Teaching Awards and Professional Recognition, Including Web Sites

1) Teaching Responsibilities
Formal Courses
Like most faculty members I teach at all levels of instruction—from first-year courses through midlevel ones aimed at English majors to graduate seminars in my research areas, early modern English literature and culture and contemporary Anglo-American drama. It gives me great intellectual and professional pleasure to teach beginning students and nonmajors, and I regularly do so.

Having joined the University of Guelph in 2002, I am teaching for the first time a new seminar in Early Modern Autopsy narratives, my current research project, to 16 students in the Bachelor of Arts and Sciences program (B.A.S.) here. The small seminar format has allowed me to retain teaching techniques I developed at TCU, where I never taught more than 35 students in any course.

Beginning next semester, however, my Guelph assignments will include a large lecture course on Shakespeare and his contemporaries that is likely to have from 80 to 100 students enrolled, as is common at public universities. My Guelph colleagues have already shared with me and other new faculty members in our school some strategies for teaching a relatively high number of students effectively—the school has held its own internal seminars on strategies and techniques, thus taking responsibility for inventing new teaching methods while the teacher-student ratios are higher than anyone would freely choose them to be.

In 12 years at TCU, I taught 24 different courses, several of them writing intensive. The average enrollment in my undergraduate courses during this period was 22 students, consonant with the goals of a private university. My assignments included occasional team teaching: in semesters one and three of the Honors Intellectual Traditions (HIT) sequence, for example, and in the English department's first-year graduate course The Profession of English, where I taught the section on professional ethics, and in the TCU-in-Edinburgh program. I have directed four undergraduates in their senior honors theses. A fifth, with whom I did a directed study in my final semester at TCU, has subsequently presented her paper at an academic conference, a sure sign of her interest and effort in planning to do a Ph.D. herself.

For the Edinburgh program I created a site-specific course in Renaissance literature and 16th century witchcraft trials that took advantage of Scottish artifacts and locale. I invented several other courses for TCU's curriculum in the English and honors programs, including courses in the effects of the AIDS epidemic on American life, on early modern drama and war, and on Shakespeare and Marlowe. The most significant course, in terms of my own development as a researcher and teacher, was Renaissance Literature and the "New" Science, which I taught as both undergraduate and graduate courses.

Directing Graduate Theses and Dissertations

As a member of the graduate faculties at TCU and now Guelph, I spend a modest amount of time working individually with students who are completing doctorates, either in my areas of expertise or, because both are small programs, outside those areas. To date, I have directed four Ph.D. completed dissertations, with a fifth in progress, and acted as second or third reader on several more. As a prelude to directing students' dissertations, I occasionally do a directed study in an area not covered by regularly offered coursework; a recent example is one in Renaissance Humanism (spring 2001). My most recent Ph.D. student to finish is now a tenure-track assistant professor at Penn State University.

Mentoring Graduate Instructors and Junior Faculty Members

I am continuing to work as an academic administrator at Guelph, and both here and at TCU I have held several roles that have made it possible to mentor graduate students and junior faculty (both full- and part-time members). From 1996 to 1998 I served as director of undergraduate studies in the TCU English department and as chair from 1998–2002. At Guelph I am director of the School of English and Theatre Studies.

All of these appointments have significantly shifted my teaching responsibilities. Typically, I teach no more than one formal course each semester. While serving as director of TCU's Self-Study in 2000–2002, for 18 months my teaching was confined to directed readings and informal mentoring. But as a department chair/school director in a department with some 50 to 60 people teaching in English and theatre in any semester, I do a substantial amount of informal teaching, advising, and mentoring in my office, especially in helping the graduate instructors and junior faculty teach effectively in the first years of their careers.

At TCU, two programs aimed at the improvement of teaching emerged from the department during my service as chair: the Teaching Practicum, a one year program for all new graduate instructors in the department, and the Faculty Development Series. The practicum is typically staffed by three full-time faculty members, each of whom mentors three to four first-year instructors who are teaching first-year composition. The Faculty Development Series brings together the entire faculty once a week for the first half of each semester to discuss teaching and research issues and ways to integrate them. Below I have included the syllabus for my section of the Teaching Practicum from fall 2000.

2) Teaching Philosophy
I bring these expectations of myself to most teaching situations:

- To create an atmosphere of mutual trust, respect for learning, and joy in ideas

- To know that day's text(s) well; to learn something new about it before class

- To prepare a fresh set of notes for each class session

- To figure out what I want students to learn during a session, and offer an itinerary

- To encourage active learning in a variety of ways, in class and outside class

- To keep track of what went well and what didn't, and learn from those notes

- To listen at least as much as I speak; to hear students' questions, doubts, growth

- To be fair, honest, and patient with students

- To read students' work carefully, and respond in ways that propel them forward; to allow students to revise their work and learn from their mistakes

- To gauge when to push a student intellectually, and when to praise him or her

- To establish high academic standards and help students understand criteria for achieving them; to model those standards in my own scholarship

- To keep in mind that my own best teachers were active, publishing scholars; and that they were the ones who pressed me to grow intellectually and as a writer

- To engage occasionally in "productive estrangement" with students by challenging specific ideas and inherited narratives of what is/must be true

- To help students understand the larger contexts and virtues of the humanities

I bring these expectations of my students:

- To prepare for class in ways that can help to create a community of readers

- To be prepared to grow and stretch intellectually

- To work hard at expressing themselves in class and in their essays, and to become better writers and thinkers; preferably they accelerate their growth as writers

- To attend class regularly and participate actively in group discussions

- To research a topic sufficiently, and to ask for help in doing so if needed

- To think for themselves, and to understand how the positions they may take on any given topic relate to other analytical or critical positions that might be taken

- To treat each other and me with respect

- To collaborate with each other and me in learning the assigned material and developing ideas, and to do that work—and all other work in the course—honestly

- To voice their needs as students in my course in productive ways to take intellectual risks and to understand in retrospect, whenever that is possible, which risks succeeded and which did not, and why

3) Teaching Goals and Strategies

My goals include creating courses whose atmosphere encourages active learning, sophisticated intellectual engagement with complex texts and ideas, and growth as writers. Especially in lower-division courses for beginning majors and nonmajors, I try to emphasize that the study of literature and theatre is not simply about "preference" for one writer over another, or one genre over another, and especially not about finding the "right" answers in a text.

I acknowledge that human memory is often like a sieve, and that what students are likely to remember a year or two years or five years later are not the particular ideas that they learned in the course, but the "meta-lessons" they take away with them: how to read carefully for nuance and context; how to synthesize conflicting perspectives; how to pose subtle questions and research answers to them and how to make new knowledge; how to write lucid, persuasive prose, and why that matters. These acknowledgments lead me to certain kinds of assignments in my courses, as discussed below.

In the classroom, I employ what I would call a "mixed method," or what I sometimes refer to as my Oprah Winfrey mode: in any given class session, I do some lecturing; the students and I do call-and-response to specific questions regarding particular moments in the text we were studying, questions I have often given them in advance; and we attempt to integrate historical information, literary methods, and close reading of certain key passages. In approximately a third of the class sessions, I devote some space to small-group discussions that get groups of three to four students to work together to solve particular "problems" in the texts that I have posed for them in writing in advance. Typically these small groups will last approximately 20–30 minutes, after which time the large class reconvenes to share results to the problems.

A good part of the teaching and learning in humanities courses goes on outside the classroom. For me, this kind of teaching includes web discussion boards, web sites, and email exchanges with an individual student or the entire class, and especially my written responses to essays they have prepared for me and often for their classmates, too. Because so much of what I have to teach them is about learning to become more careful readers and more precise and persuasive writers, it's important that I offer them specific and extensive responses to their prose. In every course I teach, including the graduate seminars, I make provisions in the assignment structures and evaluation for students to do at least one revision of an essay, and frequently more than one. Samples of these syllabi and assignments are generally included in the appendices of my portfolio.

In most courses, I assign smaller chunks of writing, believing that students' writing improves from regular practice. Undergraduates' writing grows most effectively when students are *not* asked to write the traditional 10- to 15-page research paper. Over the course of my career at TCU, it was not unusual for me to return a student's first essay in a course with as much as a full-page of single-spaced commentary. Moreover, I kept most of those commentaries on my computer so I could refer back to them as the student progressed through the course. But I do not consult these previous comments before grading the student's next essay, as I also employ a mechanism to read and evaluate the essays without knowing who has written each one.

Students have praised this model for what they take to be its implicit objectivity, or at least as much objectivity as can be mustered. At Guelph, where the ratio of teacher to student is much higher than at TCU, I expect to modify these patterns of responding to students' work to accommodate the reality of larger courses. So far, however, I have taught only small-group seminars at Guelph, which have not necessitated a new model for my patterns of assignments and responses to students' writing.

In both undergraduate and graduate courses I require a conference with each student regarding his or her first piece of writing in the course; or in some cases, the second piece of writing. This allows me to break the ice with the student, demonstrate to him or her how I will be reading essays submitted to me, and hear from the student any concerns, reservations, or enthusiasm for the material we are studying together. During the sessions I also try to understand where the student "is" intellectually in his or her own education, and to make some plans for individualizing the instruction as much as it is possible to do. For example, when it is possible to do so I try to tailor a major research project to students' previous intellectual interests, showing them how those interests can be expanded.

4) Syllabi, Assignments, and Responses to Student Work

Over time my courses have become more effective at achieving the goals set out above, in large part because the goals themselves have become clearer as I have gained teaching experience. For example, in terms of encouraging active learning, I now put a premium on the small-group discussions that were suggested by my first department chair. To support that goal, I have striven to give more weight to out-of-class student writing than to in-class final exams, and to write exams that do not ask students to regurgitate only facts. I have adopted a strategy of handing out the final exam questions in advance, and inviting students to work together outside of class to create sophisticated and meaty answers that can be written in bluebook exams.

My students and I are also regular visitors to the rare book rooms of our libraries. At TCU we were able to take advantage of the university's extensive collection of early modern printed books, including a first edition of *Paradise Lost* by Milton. These field trips are crucial to developing students' knowledge of the early modern material world and its intellectual artifacts. One of my areas of expertise is theatre, from the 16th century to the 21st. When teaching these courses, I assign students to attend live productions of plays and ask them to write reviews of those productions. I also ask them to identify a popular journal, newspaper, or magazine they would like to imagine publishing their review in, and help them adjust the style and content of their review to that source.

In graduate seminars I ask students to develop a syllabus for a related but not exact replica of the course they are taking with me, so that these students can get practice in designing undergraduate courses. I then ask them to defend the structure and contents of the course they have imagined for their own students, and to make choices about which texts they would assign, and why, and how they would frame the course and assess their own students' learning.

Like most university faculty members, I am attempting to incorporate advances in technology into my courses. In the humanities generally, the area of humanities-computing is now an essential part of the field. I have experimented with assignments that ask students to explore and report on web sites that have helped them to learn the material we are studying. It frequently surprises them, for example, to learn that there are already hundreds of web sites devoted to early modern British and European culture, and that the web sites associated with research institutes at major universities can be of profound help in discerning the contexts for the materials being studied.

5) Evidence of Teaching Effectiveness
Statements From Peer Colleagues, Students, and Alumni
While I am only now teaching my first formal course at the University of Guelph, at TCU I was nominated three times for a college-level teaching award, and won it in 1999. As a part of my teaching portfolio I include several letters from former and current colleagues submitted in support of my nomination for the Teaching Award. I also include letters from a former associate dean of the college, a staff member working on her BA, graduate and undergraduate students, and alumni, some of whom are or were undertaking advanced degrees and are therefore in a position to comment on the ways I helped them prepare for future expectations.

Student Perceptions of Teaching Data
Although I do not yet have evaluations from my students at Guelph, I do have substantial data from my time at TCU. Here I present a small sample of data taken from Student Perceptions of Teaching reports at TCU. These show students' consistent responses to my teaching. The numbers below represent students' responses to this question, "Compared with all instructors I have had in this department, this instructor is...":

	Course Number	Course Title	UCR	Number	Class Avg.	English	Division
			Enrolled		Avg.	Avg.	
1996 Spring	20403	Major British Writers	L	33	4.28	3.72	3.93
1997 Fall	20403	Major British Writers	L	27	4.48	3.9	4.03
2000 Spring	20403	Major British Writers	L	20	4.88	3.94	4.07
1999 Fall	20433	Shakespeare	L	24	4.41	3.74	3.96
1997 Spring	30423	Early British Drama	W	25	4.46	4.47	4.39
1995 Spring	40483	Shakespeare & Marlowe	W	17	4.71	4.19	4.12
1998 Fall	40483	Shakespeare & Marlowe	W	25	4.29	4.38	4.43
1996 Spring	60433	Renaissance Drama		16	4.85	4.49	4.54
1999 Spring	60433	Renaissance Drama		9	5	4.27	4.3
2000 Fall	60433	Renaissance Drama		5	5	4.24	4.27

The scale is from 1 to 5, with 5 the highest mark.

Student Outcomes and Achievements

I continue to be in touch with a sizable cohort of former students. Some of this contact is informal, when they call or email me to discuss their careers, new opportunities, or their lives in general. Some of it is formal, as when I write a letter of recommendation for someone who is now applying for professional programs or graduate school. As examples, very recent contacts with students whose work I have closely supervised include one law student who has also clerked for a U.S. federal judge on the D.C. Circuit, one who completed an M.A. in linguistics at Helsinki University and is now pursuing a Ph.D. in English at the University of Hawaii, a Dallas lawyer, a Ph.D. candidate in Spanish at the University of Virginia, and students who have completed Ph.D.s with me, including one who is now herself a tenured faculty member in English and women's studies at Purdue University (Calumet) and two years ago a Fulbright Scholar in Minsk. These are representative of my contacts, and in Appendix J I name these former students and a host of others with whom I maintain some kind of long-distance contact. Such contact is for me a sign of effective teaching and mentoring in the recent past.

Awards and Professional Recognition for Scholarship on Pedagogy
At TCU I won the Deans' Awards for Teaching in 1999, and in recent years two students chose me as their Mortarboard Professor of the Year, and one alumna honored me with a Senior Appreciation Award. Beyond TCU's campus, I have received recognition regarding my ideas about the nature of teaching in relation to my own social class history. These ideas appear in my essay "Teaching 'the Renaissance': Queer Consciousness and Class Dysphoria," part of a collection I co-edited with Gary Tate and John McMillan, then a graduate student himself, and published with Heinemann Press in 1998. I consider the collection, *Coming to Class: Pedagogy and the Social Class of Teachers,* to be my most significant contribution to pedagogy in U.S. English departments. The collection is again being used in summer 2003 at the Bread Loaf Writers' Conference, and has been used in recent years, for example, to train new teaching assistants at Indiana University. It has also appeared on the syllabi of graduate courses at institutions such as Penn State, University of Iowa, George Mason University, and Wright State University. Before its recent demise, the journal *Lingua Franca* included *Coming to Class* on a list of books nominated by readers as one of "the most influential academic books of the 1990s."

6) Goals for Improving My Teaching in the Future
I have these goals for my teaching over the next three years:

- To make more effective use of humanities technology in my courses, especially drawing on EEBO (Early English Books Online)

- To make opportunities for more frequent "real-world" learning by creating alliances with rare book rooms and with theatres

- To follow up more consistently with graduate students seeking to publish papers that originated in graduate seminars they took with me

- To create new opportunities for undergraduates to engage in collaborative research projects with me, and to motivate them to seek these out, by creating a new undergraduate research course in the School of English and Theatre Studies at Guelph

28

Teaching Portfolio
Stephen W. Henderson
Department of Geology
Oxford College of Emory University
Spring 2003

Table of Contents

Teaching Responsibilities

I am responsible for all the offerings in the geology department at Oxford College. Thus, I have had the enjoyment and hard work of developing courses in a number of areas of expertise. I teach several courses on campus during the regular semesters and several courses with an off-campus field experience. At Oxford College we are responsible for teaching the entire course, both lecture and laboratory portions. Our students at Oxford College are freshmen and sophomores. The majority of my students are non-science majors taking my courses for science distribution requirements. In addition, my courses attract students to the environmental studies major. The syllabi for the following courses are found in *Appendix A.*

- *Meteorology and Climatology with laboratory (Geosciences 115):* This course commonly enrolls about 24 students. I have been teaching it every spring semester. Although it is designed primarily for the non-science major, it is also useful for the environmental studies major as one of their elective sciences.

- *Physical Geology with laboratory (Geology 141):* This course typically enrolls about 24 students per section, and I have been teaching two sections of it every fall semester. I consider this course to be the foundation course in geology. Although I realize that the majority of the students enrolled are non-science majors, I teach it on a level equivalent to the best of the physical geology courses for geology majors.

- *Evolution of the Earth with laboratory (Geology 142):* Offered during the spring semester in alternate years with Geology 250, it has Geology 141 as a prerequisite, and the enrollment is always low, generally about eight to ten students.

- *Mineral Resources, Energy, and Power with laboratory (Geology 250):* Offered during the spring semester in alternate years with Geology 142, it typically enrolls about 24 students.

- *Desert Geology with field laboratory (Geology 100N):* This course is offered as an interim course in alternate years with Geology 200N. Its enrollment varies from approximately nine to 20 students. The students that are attracted to this class are diverse; ranging from nonscience majors, to pre-med, to environmental studies majors. There are no pre-requisites, except for permission of instructor. The course meets weekly during the spring semester and is followed by a 12-day trip to the Chi-huahuan Desert of west Texas in Big Bend National Park.

- *Dinosaurs and Their World with field laboratory (Geology 200N):* Offered as an interim course in alternate years with Geology 100N, its enroll-ment varies also from about nine to 17 students, and like Geology 100N, the students are diverse. There are no prerequisites, except for permission of instructor. The course is taught with Dr. Anthony Martin of environmental studies through the video-conferencing facilities of Emory University. We have weekly seminars on the Oxford campus and the Emory campus.

Fieldtrips

A number of my courses involve fieldtrips. As such, I thought that it would prove insightful to have a partial list of the places that I have taken students, either as the primary focus of the course or as a component. The list can be found in *Appendix B.*

Community Outreach

In addition to my formal courses, I enjoy going to the local schools and being a guest speaker in various classes. Several letters written by students are contained in *Appendix C.* One of my most memorable occasions was a visit to my daughter's fourth grade class where I presented material on dinosaurs and fossils in general. I really ended up talking about the evidence that we as paleontologists have for interpreting what we know about ancient life forms.

I started off using a dinosaur hand puppet and then talked about how the puppet was colored tan and gray and other aspects of it that we don't have any evidence for. After that talk I decided that it was a good approach to my other courses. I have also given talks to local community groups, such as the Cub Scouts, Brownies, and Lions Club, on topics including Scotland, caving, and dinosaurs.

Teaching Philosophy

Like most newly minted Ph.D.s, when I came out of graduate school I was ready to do high-powered research in my limited area of geology. Fortunately, I had also been well prepared in all areas of geology. I found myself in a position as the entire geology department of a small liberal arts college, Oxford College. I have always had many interests. Among other things, I enjoy literature, history, photography, architecture, and art. I believe that it is artificial to try and separate one discipline from another. As such, I have tried to connect geology to these other disciplines in my teaching. Over the last ten years or so, I have become fascinated with the connections between geology and culture. Dr. Mark Auslander and I organized a one-day symposium on teaching about place. That is, how does a sense of place enter into teaching and what do students think of place? More and more, I see students who would like to spend their lives in a mall. They have no sense of the geology or landscape because it has never been pointed out to them. They don't know what to look for. I want students to see the connections between everything. Some of my ideas are contained within the Emory profile of myself that was published in the Emory Report on June 10, 2002 (*Appendix D*). If there is one thing that I try to do, it is to open their eyes and minds to what is all around them so that they can truly see, understand, and appreciate this world.

Teaching Strategies and Objectives

Students learn in many ways and I try to touch on the various senses as I am teaching. I have an introductory exercise on observation and interpretation that begins the learning process in science. What I have done recently in my classes is to spend the first several classes doing an exercise on observation and interpretation. This introduces students to the scientific method through doing science and not just memorizing the principles of the scientific method. I give specimens to small groups and ask them to carefully sketch them (and therefore observe them). We then go around the room and I solicit their observations. As soon as they start to give me interpretations, we talk about the differences between observations and interpretations. At that point we bring up the scientific method and discuss the nature of scientific theories. I would like to do this throughout the semester as I present new information, to always talk about observations versus interpretations. One thing that I'd like them to say is, "I finally understand what science is!" I have heard this, but I'd like to hear it from many more students.

So many people think that science is the body of facts that they don't completely understand. They get overwhelmed by it all and feel like they aren't any good in science because they've been told that all their lives. I would like them to understand that science is not the body of information, but a method of inquiry that can be exciting. It can change the way that they think and allow them to approach everything they hear and read in a more critical fashion.

One of the latest trends in learning is inquiry-based learning. I think that I do a lot of it in my field courses but not enough in my campus-based courses. In lab, I have them smell, touch, and taste minerals and rocks. Much of geology is visual. I believe in using many slides of geologic features that I have taken so that they have an image of the feature. If they are your own slides, the impact on the students can be greater because you really know the circumstances and geological significance of the place. The professor's personal experience is one of the reasons students come to class. Students have commented upon the benefit of slides (see student comments in the section on student evaluation and in *Appendix N*). I have included representative slides with captions in *Appendix E*.

Language is also important. There is a considerable vocabulary in geology for the students to learn. I even introduce word origins and how words reflect the history of geological exploration. Some can be found in *Appendix F*.

One of my strong attributes is curiosity and enthusiasm for learning. My students consistently rate me very high in this regard. Some of the relevant comments from students can be found in the section on student evaluation and in *Appendix N*. The students usually get enthusiastic about what I'm teaching if I'm enthusiastic. I began to develop my love of teaching and teaching style in graduate school as I taught various beginning and advanced laboratory portions of geology courses. What I found out in graduate school continues to be true today. Most students can't simply read a science book and get much out of it. They find science completely different from their other areas of study. Although much of what I say in lecture comes out of the book, they can understand it if I explain it to them. I also relate stories and other personal experiences that help them to remember the material. I try to provide everyday examples and simple analogies for complex ideas. In class, I frequently ask students to share experiences that they may have with such things as hurricanes, tornadoes, earthquakes, or volcanic eruptions. It's probably just as well that I don't have too many students with these experiences.

Another aspect of my teaching that I have found to be very effective is to have a sense of humor. It not only enlivens the class, but also is a great aid to remembering the material. One student wrote in Physical Geology from fall 2002: "I enjoyed the little jokes he made during the class. I realized later that this helped me remember what he taught in class easier." I go slowly enough for questions. If there isn't understanding, then I try and come up with another way of explaining the concept. It's extremely important to me that I am open in and out of the classroom to questions and that I am fair and consistent in grading. Relative comments from students can be found in the section on student evaluation and in *Appendix N.*

Laboratories are the main time for group work and individual understanding. The students can get frustrated if they don't get something right away. I try and gauge the timing of when I help them and how much I help them. I don't want them to get discouraged, and yet, I want them to develop the discipline to work through problems. In laboratory, I don't like to just give them the answer but, instead, I help them discover for themselves, through leading questions or pointing out features for them to observe.

In the field, I send them out to discover and then we have a group discussion about what was out there. One of my favorite things to do is to always reinforce basic principles of geology this way. They really get excited when they discover something on their own. I would like to do more of this, especially in the courses that are completely on campus.

Curricular Revisions and Additions

My main thrust in recent years has been to integrate other areas of study with geology and to develop more inquiry-based projects. In my meteorology course part of the first laboratory exercise is to go out and observe the weather and then discuss it as a group. The catch is that nobody knows much about the weather and we don't bring out any instruments to measure anything. The purpose of the exercise is to introduce the students to the concepts of scientific measurement and description. It's very similar to the observation and interpretation exercise involving specimens, but here we use the weather and the sky. At the end of the semester, we go outside again. Now, however, we are armed with knowledge and instruments and the students can see how far they have come. This Weather of Oxford lab exercise is in *Appendix G.*

The evolution of the earth course focuses on the methods of analysis and interpretation of the evidence for how we understand the history of the earth. I'm always asking students if the evidence supports the interpretation. We spend much of our time on modern environments and their ancient equivalents. One of our exercises is a fossil collecting trip to a limestone quarry south of Macon. I've had students tell me that it was one of their favorite memories of Oxford College. Students can still remember the scientific names of species of fossils that they collected and identified.

In my mineral resources course I have worked extensively on integrating geology with other fields of study. After I gave a series of lectures on the geology and history of the Industrial Revolution, Dr. Michael McQuaide in sociology gave a guest lecture on the sociology of the Industrial Revolution. I have related the history of the American Labor Movement to mining geology. I began my material on oil with whaling and a reading from Herman Melville's *Moby-Dick*. Our fieldtrip of the building stones on Oxford's campus includes history and architecture.

I have developed a number of inquiry-based laboratory exercises including a petroleum exploration project and a laboratory exercise distilling crude oil. Consulting Geologist Richard Gibson and I created a petroleum exploration exercise using real geologic data and situations. The details can be found in *Appendix H.* The whole project is a wonderful opportunity for learning how to work in a group. There is not enough group work in college. and yet so much of the business world requires being a successful member of a group. Mrs. Brenda Harmon in chemistry and I created the laboratory exercise on the distillation of crude oil. The exercise is in *Appendix I.*

In my desert geology course, we stopped on the way out to Big Bend at Vicksburg, Mississippi. I discussed how geology had influenced the Civil War Battle of Vicksburg as we drove through the National Military Park. Once we are out in Big Bend the students do a number of projects. One of our stops involves understanding relative ages of volcanic geologic events. I send them out to do observations and then we gather together to interpret them and discuss the nature of geologic theories. A reference to this exercise is the first quoted journal extract in the section on student learning.

I have had success in teaching the classroom components of both the dinosaur and Bahamas course using the video-conferencing facilities. The key is that in both courses I co-teach with Dr. Anthony Martin of Emory College. We run the courses in a seminar fashion and we have a professor in each classroom. In addition, because the courses are field based, we are able to have significant time with the students in person.

One of my students, Chris Sedgwick, did a project on the Island of Skye in Scotland that started out to be on the movement of sand on a beach. It ended up being a project that related the erosion of the beach sand to the building of a pier nearby that involved a political dispute. It was the perfect combination of geology and culture. There is more about it in the *Atlanta Journal-Constitution* article in *Appendix J.*

Ideas for Teaching Improvement

Before I teach a course, I look at the student evaluations from the last time that I taught it and see if there are some good ideas for changes. For instance, in my Evolution of the Earth class, the suggestion was made to break up the laboratory into individual sections about 30 minutes apart and go over it as a group before proceeding to the next section.

I used to give laboratory quizzes in my courses only at the beginning of the lab period over the introductory material in the lab for that day. The students suggested that they would know more after the lab is over. I'm sure they would, but I still wanted them to come prepared to lab. Now, I give a quiz at the beginning and the end of lab to see how much they have learned.

When I attended the Eighth American Association for Higher Education Conference on Faculty Roles and Rewards held in New Orleans in February of 2000, I participated in two workshops. One of these concerned "Linking Classroom Practice to Student Understanding: Documentation and Assessment in the Scholarship of Teaching and Learning." Among other things, the workshop gave me some good ideas for including more discussion of real-life geologic problems in the classroom and creating test questions that are more problem based.

I read Richard Light's book, *Making the Most of College: Students Speak Their Minds,* and I participated in his talk when he came to campus in November of 2001. One thing that was brought up in his book is that students strongly suggested that "substantive work in the sciences should be structured to involve more interaction with other students and with faculty members." I need to work on this. Of course, we have lab partners and group discussions, but I'd like to introduce more group projects into my curriculum. The best example that I have so far is the petroleum exploration exercise in the mineral resources course. I should work on creating a group project for each of my courses.

Student Learning
Testing

One of the aspects of my teaching that I am proud of is the quality of my test essay questions. As I tell my students, "You can go to a large school as an undergraduate but you run the risk of not getting to know your professors and taking tests where you don't really have to think." I try to create some of my essay questions as mysteries and problems to be solved and have included some of them in *Appendix K.*

Presentations and Publications

One of my students, Kathryn Orvold, took some of her geologic knowledge gained from my Evolution of the Earth course in spring of 1997 and applied it in a different fashion to another of her courses. After leaning about the famous 18th century Italian geologist, Giovanni Arduino, she did a presentation about him in Italian to her Italian class. I'm always excited when I see students integrating their knowledge.

After we learned about the geology of gold deposits in the mineral resources course, Dr. Christine Loflin of the English department and I worked with the students on writing short stories about the social affects of gold mining in South Africa. Several of my students' stories were published in the *Oxford Review* for 1999. Elizabeth Smith's *Ninjuni and Tuntuko,* Mandy Schmitt's *Constellations,* and Abbey Peterson's *Trapped* were featured. They are in *Appendix L.*

Post-Graduate Work

I have had a number of my students go on to graduate school and law school. Fred Nicol has started a master's program in science education. Nick Pyenson has begun Ph.D. work at UC Berkeley in vertebrate paleontology. Tera Compton is enrolled in law school at Georgia State University with an expected specialty in environmental law.

Journals

One of the advantages of some of the courses that I teach is that the students keep a journal during the field courses. Through reading their journals I get a chance to see what they have learned. Several portions of journals can be found in *Appendix M,* and one student comment follows.

> *I have to say I had low expectations for this trip. I thought it would be boring and the challenging parts, like hiking and the heat would break me. I still, 3 days later, cannot believe some of the stuff that I did. I am so proud of myself for this trip, for*

the things I have done, for the boundaries and limits that I've pushed.

Thank you for letting me be a part of this and thank you for making me feel welcome. Your job was to teach us, and you did, but you went above and beyond that call of duty to become friends and mentors.

Student Evaluation of Teaching

Although the summaries of student evaluations of my courses and my teaching of those courses are contained in *Appendix N*, some data from recent courses are presented here. The following recently offered courses are generally taken by nonscience majors and they are rated on a 4-point scale where 4 is excellent.

Course	Term	Time	Overall Average
Geos 115	Spring 2002	8:30am	3.27
Geos 115	Spring 2002	9:35am	3.72
Geol 141	Fall 2002	8:30am	3.45
Geol 141	Fall 2002	9:35am	3.55

Notice the difference between the 8:30 and 9:35 times. That is consistent from semester to semester and transcends individual courses. I have also included summary data from my advanced course, Geology 142. This course tends to include more environmental sciences majors. A different course evaluation form was administered. It used a 3-point scale where 3 is excellent.

Course	Term	Time	Overall Average
Geol 142	Spring 2000	9:30am	2.83

I tend to gain the most information from student comments on evaluation forms. As such, I believe that it is appropriate to include a selection here. These are from physical geology (fall 2001) where the overall average for both sections was 2.75 on a 3-point scale.

- "I loved the use of slides during class. Seeing photos of real places helped pull things together. Dr. Henderson's enthusiasm on the subject made learning geology that much better."

- "I thought he presented the material in a clear manner and always backed up his lecture with examples in the environment."

- "He loves his subject with such a passion!"

- "It was great having a professor so enthusiastic about this subject. A joy to come to class."

It is also important to obtain feedback on the long-term effects of your teaching on former students. Therefore, I have included some unsolicited letters from students in *Appendix O.*

Goals for Peer Evaluation of Teaching
The best source for peer evaluation of my teaching comes from colleagues that I have had the enjoyment of teaching and working with over the years. I have given presentations on the campuses of both Oxford and Emory Colleges and guest lectures in a number of different classes here at Oxford. The people who have seen me in action the most are those that I have been out with in the field. They include faculty members in sociology, English, philosophy, and anthropology at Oxford College and environmental sciences at Emory College. I'm sure that most would be willing to write letters for me, especially in regard to my teaching. When they are received, they will be in *Appendix P* and quotes from them will appear here.

Appendices
Appendix A: Course Syllabi
Appendix B: Fieldtrip List
Appendix C: Letters From Elementary School Students
Appendix D: *Emory Report* Article
Appendix E: Representative Slides With Captions
Appendix F: Derivations of Geological Terms
Appendix G: Weather of Oxford Laboratory Exercise
Appendix H: Petroleum Exploration Laboratory Exercise
Appendix I: Distillation of Crude Oil Laboratory Exercise
Appendix J: *Atlanta Journal-Constitution* Article
Appendix K: Sample Essay Questions
Appendix L: Students' Short Stories
Appendix M: Excerpts From Student Journals
Appendix N: Course Evaluation Summaries
Appendix O: Letters From Former Students
Appendix P: Letters From Colleagues

29

THE TEACHING PORTFOLIO
Karen L. Rasmussen
Division of Instructional and Performance Technology
College of Professional Studies
University of West Florida
Spring, 2003

Table of Contents

Teaching Responsibilities

I primarily teach courses in the master's, specialist, and doctoral instructional technology programs. In the past, I have worked with pre-service teachers at the undergraduate level in the area of technology integration in the classroom. Currently, I most frequently teach:

- *Principles of Instructional Design and Product Development* (EDG 5332, 30 students each section, online and face-to-face; required)

- *Web-Based Instruction* (EME 6414, 25–30 students each section, online and face-to-face; required online program, otherwise elective)

- *Advanced Web-Based Learning Environments* (EME 7417, 10–15 students each section, face-to-face; elective)

- *IT Research Design Seminar* (EME 7938, 12 students each section, face-to-face; required research design class for doctorate)

I advise all instructional technology students in the specialist program (approximately 50) and in the doctoral program (approximately 50) until they select a doctoral chair. In addition, I have ten students in active dissertation research and another ten who will complete their preliminary examinations within the next year. Five of my past doctoral students have successfully defended their dissertations and graduated.

Teaching Philosophy

In the discipline of instructional technology, as well as in our technologically driven world, no one individual can have all of the answers to the many possible questions. Students and instructors must be partners in the learning process—with the instructor learning as much from the students as the students learn from the instructor. This partnership facilitates the development of a supportive learning community that is focused on acquisition of new knowledge for all members of the community. The idea of a partnership also requires students and instructors to act as mentors for other students or novices in the content areas.

The learning community forms the basis of my teaching philosophy. Students bring to the learning environment a variety of skills which they already possess that need to be reflected upon and fine-tuned. The learning community is based upon practice and reflection of how those skills can be used in the "real world." My teaching philosophy revolves around the notions that students must be able to apply instructional technology-related skills in a variety of settings as they select appropriate tools to solve instructional problems.

Over the course of my career, I have worked with increasingly advanced students. This progression has led to my developing a different perception of and relationship with learners, which has, in turn, altered my teaching philosophy. In the beginning of my teaching career, I focused on simple skill acquisition with plenty of time devoted to guided and project-based practice. As my students changed, I expanded my philosophy to embrace the idea that students must actively process the knowledge, skills, and abilities of an instructional designer or instructional technologist. The theory of constructivism lends itself well to providing a framework to structure instructional strategies and course assignments. Constructivism provides a framework for both online and face-to-face delivery.

Teaching Methods and Strategies

I use a variety of teaching strategies in my classes. Regardless of the delivery system (online or face-to-face), good strategies transcend the delivery system. I believe that students must be active learners as they participate in the learning environment and community for the community to be successful. As part of this instructional strategy, students need guidance as they develop skills and reflect upon the relevance of the instruction to their professional lives. To align these beliefs with strategies, my classes, whether online or face-to-face are comprised of: lecture-ettes (30 minutes at most), small-group discussion, large-group discussion, games, in-class work groups, debates, and reflections, demonstrations (both by instructor and students).

Face-to-Face Teaching

In face-to-face environments, I structure the class time to meet a series of objectives. PowerPoint presentations are used to both organize the class and to provide students with a class handout that they can refer to at a later point. Students access the presentation via the class web site to give them an opportunity to take notes and then reflect upon the class in a structured fashion during the following week. The presentation contains an advance organizer that outlines highlights from the previous class session as well as all of the activities, in-class assignments, and assignments for the next class session. Use of this presentation technique ensures that the major objectives of the class session are reached; yet there is flexibility to address other issues as they arise. Sample presentations are located in Appendix A.

In addition to the presentation, each class consists of small-group discussion that may, depending on the content and the objectives, involve analysis of a case study, debate, or game. After the discussion, we debrief the content and processes that students have gone through. In production courses, time is spent in the laboratory, practicing technology-based skills.

Online Teaching

Online environments offer special challenges to both the student and the instructor. In the philosophy of our online program, we believe that active engagement in the learning process keeps students motivated and involved in the class—to avoid any isolation that may occur. Instructional strategies that are appropriate for face-to-face delivery can be easily modified and implemented in an online learning environment.

In my online classes, I begin each class with an introduction that outlines the topics for the session (in essence, a week of instruction), highlights the due dates for the week, and details any special activities that might be occurring. In addition, any discussions from the previous week are available for students to review. In the example lesson (see Appendix B), the week begins with an introduction and an overview of the previous week's main topics. *This Week: In Focus* outlines the objectives and major activities for the upcoming week. In this particular lesson, the students worked on a case study in teams to develop a needs assessment. Students are presented with information about needs assessment and processes of needs assessment, and are given some information on tools and techniques for needs assessment. In the next section, students are divided into teams and given an assignment. To help structure their discussion a planning guide is provided. Finally, specific instructions are given on how to begin their activity. The end of the lesson provides additional information on upcoming assignments, a recap of the activities, and a look ahead at the next week.

In online classes, I hold online office hours in chat rooms at least once a week. Some of these chat sessions are open to discuss whatever the students want to talk about. Other chat sessions have a focused topic. Students are encouraged to meet in chat rooms or communicate via email with their groups so that they maintain contact throughout the group activities.

Syllabi

Syllabi outline expectations of students and instructors and detail the knowledge, skills, and abilities that students will be able to attain at the end of the course. In addition, the assignments are summarized. In Appendix C, sample syllabi are presented. As part of my syllabi materials, I create a comprehensive companion web site that specifically details the course schedules, lines to online resources, complete descriptions of course assignments, and rubrics. A sample web site is also found in Appendix C.

Teaching Improvements

During the semester, I make notes on presentations and in course material folders on any activities or processes that need to be enhanced. Then, prior to the beginning of every term, I review those materials and assess the current materials from each class that I will be teaching. Based on the previous comments, feedback from students, including critiques of the activities of the class and student evaluations, revisions are made to the processes, activities, and assessments for the class. For example, in EDG 5332, Principles of Instructional Design, students believed that it was important to see additional instances of work to help them frame their own projects. In conjunction with Pam Northrup, we developed an electronic performance support system, SID (Support for Instructional Designers), which provided additional guidance for students. In EDG 6335, Advanced Instructional Design, students felt that they needed additional practice in the application of instructional models to education and training problems. To facilitate additional practice, I began to use a case-based methodology that facilitated discovery and exploration.

Assessment of Teaching Success

I use a variety of data to help evaluate my effectiveness as an instructor. The data are used to alter teaching strategies and improve the learning environment. Several forms are used to develop this assessment and subsequent evaluation.

Colleague Observation

Colleague observations are practical and expected in our program courses. I, many times, team-teach with other faculty, either face-to-face or at a distance, via online delivery or through the Interactive Distance Learning Studio (IDLS). In Appendix D, a sample evaluation form is presented that could be used to guide the colleague observation. It focuses on issues related to classroom organization, instructional methods, relationships with students, and expectations.

Colleague Review of Teaching Materials

Colleagues from inside and outside the Division routinely use my teaching materials in their own classrooms. Appendix E presents a review of my materials from colleagues who have used them.

Student Course Evaluation Data

Students complete evaluation forms related to the course and instructor at the end of each term. The 20-item form and complete results can be found in Appendix F. Data gathered from students involves student perceptions of organization and teaching ability. Listed below are six items that specifically relate to class and instructor characteristics that are critical to the success of a student and representative scores from three classes.

Web-Based Instruction EME 6414C (online) n=15 Summer, 2000		Advanced Instructional Design EDG 6335 (face-to-face) n=25 Spring, 2000		Principles of Instructional Design EDG 5332 (online) n=15 Spring, 2000	
Excellent	Very Good	Excellent	Very Good	Excellent	Very Good
The course was intellectually challenging.					
75%	25%	83.3%	16.7%	92.9%	7.1%
The grading practices were well documented.					
100%		66.7%	3.3%	71.4%	14.3%
The instructor shows a command of the subject matter.					
100%		100%		100%	
The instructor shows respect and concern for students.					
75%	25%	100%		100%	
What is your overall assessment of the instructor?					
100%		100%		100%	
What is your overall rating of the substantive value of the course?					
100%		100%		92.9%	7.1%

Student comments also provide insight into my performance. Listed below are comments that specifically relate to student perceptions of my classes and instructional styles. Original reports can be found in Appendix F.

- "I have probably learned more in this class than any other class I have ever taken."

- "I found you to have high expectations, yet remain patient and sensitive to the needs of the class participants. The course was well organized and the goals were clearly defined. You modeled a variety of instructional methods. You definitely had the expertise to teach the group and you often exhibited a neat sense of humor."

- "I learned a lot in this class and it was a lot of work. Many new uses for technology were brought to my attention as were design and evaluation criteria that went along well with the Advanced Instructional Design class."

Teaching Honors

In 1998, I was one of the awardees of the university's Teaching Incentive Program (TIP). This program is competitive among the faculty of the university. Only five individuals were awarded TIP in the College of Professional Studies. The award is based on a series of criteria, including faculty productivity, teaching philosophy, student evaluation, and alumni comments. Information about the award is found in Appendix G.

I have been twice nominated for the university's Distinguished Teaching Award. Students make nominations to the university's Student Government Association (SGA). My first nomination was in the 1994–1995 academic year (my first year as an instructor in the College of Education); I was not yet eligible for the award because I was not in a tenure-earning position. I was nominated a second time during the 2000–2001 academic year. Unfortunately, again, I was not eligible because I had been awarded a sabbatical for the term when the observation was to take place. Letters from the SGA can be found in Appendix G.

Evidence of Student Learning

Teaching without learning is not good teaching. To further validate my success as an instructor, my students must also be successful. Reviewing student projects and sharing alumni process can demonstrate this success.

Student Success Through Projects

In Appendix H, student projects are presented. The projects show the process of development, beginning with the student's initial ideas and culminating with the final project. Examples of my feedback provided to the student throughout the life of each project are also included.

- *Instructional Design Project.* In EDG 5332, the first development course in all of the instructional technologies, students are guided through the instructional design process. Feedback is provided to the student after each section and the student revises the design document accordingly. The student then turns the design document into an instructional product. The student completes the project by conducting a formative evaluation with target audience learners and revises the instruction accordingly. The project is submitted along with the revised design document and an evaluation plan.

- *Web-Based Instruction.* EME 6414 extends the instructional design and development process to include the web as a delivery system. Students develop a design document that focuses on the main elements of designing instruction. Sample web-based projects can be seen in Appendix H.

- *Advanced Web-Based Learning Environments.* A theoretically based course, EME 7417, promotes the students' reflective skills on learning communities of the future and the role of technology in those learning communities. Students develop a microworld prototype, based on a theoretical model that they synthesize, based on research literature and technological innovations. As products for EME 7417, students submit the prototype and the paper that supports the development of the microworld.

Alumni Successes

Of the 85 graduates of our graduate program, 84 have IT-related positions. In our first cohort of online students (the first online program at the university), we saw a 96% retention rate—a remarkable rate considering the national average is between 30% and 50%. Below are several alumni and their current positions, careers made possible through our programs.

- Joann Wheeler, Ed.D., Director, Center for Instructional Technology and Distributed Education, Tarleton State University

- Sandi King, M.Ed., online student. Resource Teacher, Beacon Learning Center, Bay County Schools

- Valerie Chubb, M.Ed. (and currently in the specialist program). Physics teacher, Okaloosa County Schools, Teacher of the Year for Okaloosa County, 2002–2003

Curricular Revisions

With the ever-changing nature of technology, curricular revisions are an ongoing process. At the beginning of each new class offering, I review the previous syllabus and revise the assignments accordingly. National organizations which develop national standards and competencies that govern our profession are consulted. If goals and objectives require revision, I begin that process. At conferences and via online bookstores, I review new textbooks or reference books that might be appropriate for the course text. I then review the schedule for the class and revise depending on the term. At the same time, I begin to revise the course web site for class documents. For face-to-face classes, I then begin to revise the presentations. In the online courses, I begin to modify the initial lessons.

Scholarship of Teaching and Professional Outreach

As instructional designers, we continually work toward program improvement and student success. I combine contract and grant work with research and scholarship interests to help improve the teaching and learning process. Recent contracts and grants have permitted my colleagues and me to further investigate online teaching and learning techniques and strategies through product development and implementation (see Appendix I for examples). To report relevant findings to peers, topics related to facilitating innovations in teaching are presented. Recent presentations and publications include:

Presentations

- Rasmussen, K. L., Northrup, P. T., Lombardo, C. (2002). Seven Years of Online Learning. IITSEC.

- Rasmussen, K. L. (2002). Online Mentoring: A Model for Supporting Distant Learners. Ed-Media 2002.

- Online Learning: A Survivor's Guide. (October, 2001). CNET CISO Conference. Pensacola, FL.

Publications

- Northrup, P. T., & Rasmussen, K. L. (2001). A web-based graduate program: Theoretical frameworks in practice. *Computers in the Schools, 17*(3/4), 33–46.

- Rasmussen, K. L., & Northrup, P. T. (1999). Situated learning online: Assessment strategies for online expeditions. *Diagnostic, 25*(1), 71–82.

In addition to these examples of scholarship, I have been involved in a variety of faculty development activities over the years. Over three summers, the faculty of our division worked with other faculty in the College of Education to help them develop strategies for integrating technology into the curriculum. In the first year of the faculty development, faculty were introduced to technology skills and developed strategies for incorporating appropriate technologies into their own classrooms. In the second year, we introduced faculty to creation of web pages and use of multimedia in their learning environments. During the last year's faculty development, we worked with faculty across all colleges to explore how distance learning technologies could be used in their programs and courses.

Professional Goals

In the next three to five years, I have several goals:

- Focus on assessment: Assessment is a critical element in the teaching and learning process. I plan to continue to work to enhance assessment strategies that I use, incorporating rubrics and providing students with additional criteria to guide them in the learning process.

- Focus on feedback: Feedback assists learners in revision and improving the quality of their work. To assist learners in their projects, I will improve both quality and quantity of the feedback that I provide.

- Focus on communication: Communication and interaction with students helps to improve the learning process. Specifically, when I use case-study methods, I want to improve debriefing techniques that refocus the students on the processes and the content inherent in the case study.

- Focus on performance: Invite colleagues to observe my performance in the classroom to offer suggestions for improving my teaching.

Appendices
Appendix A   (Presentations)
Appendix B   (Online Lesson)
Appendix C   (Syllabi)
Appendix D   (Colleague Observation)
Appendix E   (Colleague Review)
Appendix F   (Student Evaluation Data)
Appendix G   (Teaching Honors)
Appendix H   (Student Projects)
Appendix I   (Contract and Grant Activities)

30

TEACHING PORTFOLIO
William J. Robinson
Department of Mathematics
Barton County Community College
Spring 2003

Table of Contents

Teaching Responsibilities

My teaching responsibilities fall into two broad categories: developmental and college level courses.

Developmental courses include MATH 1811 Preparatory Math and MATH 1821 Basic Algebra. These courses are required for any student whose assessment scores require remediation in mathematics. Enrollments of around 20 students per section comprise approximately one-third of my workload.

College level courses mainly include MATH 1824 Intermediate Algebra, MATH 1828 College Algebra, MATH 1830 Trigonometry, and MATH 1829/BUSI 1609 Statistics. The algebra courses are required courses for students seeking an associate degree or transferring to a four-year college. The Business Statistics course is a required course for business majors. Students in other disciplines use the Trigonometry and Elements of Statistics courses to fulfill math/science general education electives. Enrollments of around 25 students per section complete my teaching workload.

Teaching Philosophy

There are two things that help me maintain focus on the teaching of mathematics: a passion for the subject and a love for students. The combination of the two enables me to maintain high standards regarding the material yet not lose the student along the way. This characteristic is evident in a statement made by a 2000 graduating student. The nomination by this student in "The Barton Difference" (Appendix A) reads,

> *He (Bill Robinson) shows great enthusiasm for his genre and this enthusiasm is evident in the classroom. Bill works tirelessly to help students understand mathematical concepts. Bill never turns down an opportunity to help students learn, answering even the most basic questions with great patience and in a manner that is easy to understand.*

I believe my role as an instructor is to minimize distractions to student learning and present material in a way that is exciting, challenging, and understandable to the student. Distractions come in many forms, everything from internal anxieties and attitudes to external factors such as my personal presentation skills or classroom management responsibilities.

For the majority of students, the material is not new. They have seen it before and bring with them baggage, both good and bad. Most of the time the baggage is negative due to failure or difficulty in mathematics, a poor experience with a previous instructor, or excuses like "my mother did not do very well in mathematics, either." The strategies covered in the next section reflect my desire to make the classroom a more positive and purposeful learning environment so anxieties are reduced, attitudes changed, and mathematics learned. As I work on reducing risk factors to learning, I also engage the student in the rigors of mathematical facts, concepts, and problem solving.

I disagree with the idea that says you cannot change other people. I teach to change lives. I believe I do have an impact on students, inside and outside the classroom. A combination of personal care and strategies for learning enable the student the opportunity to be more open to learning not just mathematics but any subject.

I am continually challenged by the question, "When will I ever use this stuff?" If the class is a terminal class for the student, chances are that specific mathematical facts may not be used after the class. I illustrate the bigger picture of how fundamental basics are needed in order to apply mathematical principles to a particular discipline. The greatest benefit for any student in any mathematics class is not so much the learning of mathematical facts, but the ability to systematically solve problems.

I feel the student must respond to the opportunities and open environment I have created in order to learn. I expect students to pay attention in class, take notes, read the text, work problems outside of class, and seek help when difficulties arise. Ultimately the student needs to choose to do something about their learning. As one student put it in a Basic Algebra class evaluation,

> *I have enjoyed this class. It is not an easy class for me but the instructor has given me ample ways and opportunities to learn the material and to do the best that I can, so I can move on to the next level of learning. (Appendix B)*

Teaching Strategies and Methods
Developmental Courses
Academic Systems, a computer-mediated software system, was initiated as a pilot project in spring 2000 as a system to use for all developmental courses at Barton County Community College. This method was introduced as a way to increase the percentage of students successful in developmental courses (C or better), reduce the percentage of students withdrawing from a course, and increase the percentage of students successful in subsequent mathematics courses.

This was quite a challenge for me because the human element and my influence in the classroom to deal with the affective side of learning was at stake. I had to reassess my role in the classroom. By placing the student at the center of learning, I find I am still one of two important parts to the mediated learning model. I provide direction, guidance, and individualized instruction. The computer presents the material in a variety of ways and provides immediate feedback.

Currently, I welcome students to the classroom, hand back any papers, and remind them of the daily schedule. Most of my time in the classroom is spent giving help to individual students, monitoring student progress via the computer, and giving mini-lectures.

For more detail on lessons learned using computer-mediated instruction, see the portfolio section titled Efforts to Improve Student Learning.

College-Level Courses
For most classes, my method of classroom teaching is a traditional lecture format peppered with occasional group activities, questions and answers, computer work, video segments, and graphing calculator activities. I prepare thoroughly for each class. I seek to make the classroom an active learning

environment and strive to continue to improve presentation skills (voice, overheads, legible writing on the board, etc.).

In order to know the characteristics of my students, early in the semester I have students complete a "Student Information Sheet"(Appendix C). Data from this informs me of basic demographic information as well as affective information that is derived from the Math Anxiety Rating Scale questions. I use all this information during the course of the semester to illustrate math concepts for certain disciplines, discuss study techniques for students with various credit loads, and it serves as a reminder to me about the level of math anxiety a particular class is experiencing as I present material. Additional data is added to the form at the end of the semester, including number of absences; averages for homework, quizzes, and exams; previous math grades; assessment scores; and the final exam score. See the Goals section for further discussion on use of this form.

A sample syllabus and schedule in Appendix D reveal expectations I have for the student regarding their learning as well as my personal interest in them. Among the features are avenues for help and expectations for evaluation. A detailed schedule guides the student through the course and prevents surprises. In addition, it makes it clear to the student what they can expect and what is expected of them. The syllabus and schedule also reveal my organization of the course.

Transitions from one concept to another are planned so students can move on with new material. One method of learning basic concepts in mathematics is repetition. Because of this, constant review is an element of the course and exams are cumulative in nature. I keep accurate, up-to-date records and give next-day feedback regarding homework, quizzes, and exams. Bimonthly progress reports are distributed to students.

A student comment in a summer course evaluation for MATH 1828 College Algebra portrays my flexibility and persistence in teaching: "I like this instructor, he doesn't get mad when you don't understand something and he will go over the material until you do understand it" (Appendix E). The various methods used to help students understand the mathematical concepts include explaining the material differently, examples from a variety of disciplines, a video clip, or cooperative learning activities.

My most usual approach for the lecture is to place basic concepts on an overhead, follow this with short dialogue, and then work a related problem. This engages the students' sight, hearing, and writing. In addition, I use cooperative learning activities on a regular basis. This gives the student an opportunity to comfortably voice a question or solution in front of a smaller group. Students can actually learn without me being there!

I have incorporated a computer lab into the statistics course. I feel it is critical that students are introduced to a software package that can be used for data entry, graphical display, and analysis. A handout that explains the mechanics and details the steps is prepared for each lab activity. Due to its wide use and accessibility, Microsoft Excel is used. Appendix F is an example of a statistics lab.

Evidence of Teaching Excellence
Student Evaluations

The Individual Development Educational Assessment form is used by students for course evaluation. The results from a fall 2001 course, MATH 1828 College Algebra, are indicative of the positive response from students regarding my teaching. The results, along with written comments, appear in Appendix G. In this survey, "Explained course material clearly and concisely" received one of the highest marks and was noted as a strength to retain.

The table below is a sampling of scores over several semesters for the item "I rate this instructor an excellent teacher." 1 = Definitely False, 2 = More False than True, 3 = In Between, 4 = More True than False, 5 = Definitely True. Column entries indicate the number of students choosing that response.

I have consistently high scores regarding my excellence as an instructor and equal or exceed school and national averages.

In addition, the following comments in Appendix H reveal how my enthusiasm for the subject and teaching ability affected students' attitude and learning mathematics:

- MATH 1829 Elements of Statistics, Spring 2000

    "Your enthusiasm for the course material was very helpful and enjoyable to see."

    "It is great to have an instructor so excited about his/her area."

- MATH 1828 College Algebra, Fall 2001

    "I understand a lot of the material that I didn't know how to do in high school. He really makes me want to learn because he loves what he does, so it makes you want to love it too!"

- MATH 1830 Trigonometry, Fall 2002

    "He is always excited to teach and he makes class interesting."

Term	Course	1	2	3	4	5	My Average	School Average	IDEA National Database
Spring 1999	Intermediate and College Algebra	0	0	1	2	10	4.7	4.4	4.1
Fall 1999	Intermediate and College Algebra	0	0	1	1	16	4.8	Not Available	Not Available
Spring 2000	Statistics	0	0	1	1	12	4.8	Not Available	Not Available
Fall 2000	Intermediate and College Algebra	0	0	5	5	16	4.4	4.4	4.1
Spring 2001	Elements of Statistics	0	0	0	2	14	4.9	Not Available	Not Available
Fall 2001	College Algebra	0	0	1	3	15	4.7	Not Available	4.2
Fall 2001	Basic Algebra	0	1	1	4	8	4.4	Not Available	4.2
Spring 2002	College Algebra	0	0	2	1	15	4.7	Not Available	4.2

Honors Related to Teaching

In 1994 and 2000 I was honored with the National Institute for Staff and Organizational Development (NISOD) Excellence Award. This award, unique to community colleges, recognizes teaching excellence. Selection is based on recommendations from colleagues to the president of the college. The president then submits the names to NISOD.

In the spring of 2000, I became the 16th recipient of the college's Distinguished Instructor Award. The award recognizes excellence among full-time faculty. Fellow faculty members nominate the instructor and a committee comprised of two Barton County residents, one graduating full-time student, a past award winner, one college trustee, and one Barton County Community College Foundation Board member make the final selection. In the presentation of the award, the dean of Instruction and Learning said, "On a Saturday or a Sunday, I see him out here at the chalkboard with a student."

Evidence of Student Learning

Probably one of the most difficult areas to show but undoubtedly most important is to demonstrate that students have actually learned what I had set out for them to learn. With the current emphasis on assessment on student learning on our campus, I have been challenged anew to think about not so much my teaching but students' learning. Earlier comments by students about their learning in my class are appreciative, but to what degree have they actually learned the material? Is the feeling a student has about learning sufficient to say learning has occurred? From the instructor side, I want to know if the student has mastered and to what degree, the competencies listed in the syllabus.

A strength of the computer-mediated classes is the ability to create and track pre- and post-quiz scores. During the spring 2000 semester, I kept track of students' pre- and post-quiz scores for MATH 1821 Basic Algebra. Appendix K shows that based on a matched pairs test, there is enough evidence to say that the averages for pre- and post-quiz scores were significantly different. Students did learn. In addition, the correlation between quiz scores and hardcopy exams was strong enough to indicate that scores on a hardcopy exam were related to the quizzes. If a student had learned the material well enough for the quiz, chances are he or she could replicate that knowledge on the hardcopy exam.

Another demonstration of student learning occurs within the statistics lab. A final project is given in the class. The project asks the student to collect data, use appropriate technology to graphically represent the data, offer an analysis of the data, and write a report summarizing the process and results. Appendix L is an example of work done by a student who synthesized all he had learned in the class and produced an exemplary report.

Efforts to Improve Student Learning

After two semesters of teaching with Academic Systems, the following strategies for teaching these classes has emerged: provide a detailed daily schedule, plan mini-lectures, monitor students progress via the administrative tracking ability, roam the class answering questions, and create and administer hardcopy, objective-based exams (Appendix K).

Students in developmental classes need structure. The detailed schedule includes sections that should be covered that day, topics of a mini-lecture, dates of quizzes and exams, and homework assignments. The mini-lecture may consist of doing a few problems at the board (either students or myself), a short introduction of the material, or a review of the material in preparation for a quiz or exam.

Data was also collected regarding the affective nature of computer-mediated instruction. At the end of the semester, a survey focusing on the students' thoughts and attitudes toward computer-mediated instruction was distributed. The data was analyzed and used to help frame recommendations for continued use. Appendix M contains the survey.

I have tried and regularly use classroom assessment techniques. A version of the "One Minute Paper" is called the daily quiz. For a College Algebra class, I ask students at the end of the hour, one question about some material we covered that day in class. Immediately the quiz is scored and discussed so students know the correct answer and can ask further questions.

In a Trigonometry class, I ask students to fill out a self-assessment (Appendix N) upon completion of a chapter. The document is a list of competencies from the chapter. Students indicate the level of confidence they have with each competency. I use this in preparing a review by focusing on those competencies students are struggling with the most, and I encourage students to focus on those areas in preparation for the exam.

Future Goals

My ambition is to be a great teacher that produces learning in students. To this end, I have four diverse goals:

1) I will continue collect student examples of the statistics report mentioned in the section Evidence of Student Learning (spring 2003).

2) In order to better understand my students, I would like to perform a multiple regression on all the factors I collect on the Student Information Sheet. Information collected from this would be invaluable in determining what factors are most related to student success (summer 2003).

3) In order to determine if my style, teaching techniques, and personality have a positive effect on reducing math anxiety in the classroom, I need to do a post-test of the Math Anxiety Rating Scale (summer 2003).

4) In order to improve my teaching, I would like to elicit my colleagues' input on teaching materials (notes and exams) and classroom observation. I plan to collaborate further on the mathematics departments' common final exam for College Algebra. By studying results of the past year, I plan to enhance teaching of competencies mastered by my students and change my teaching techniques for competencies where students are struggling (spring 2003).

Appendices
Appendix A: The Barton Difference—2000
Appendix B: Fall 1999 Course Evaluation—Student Comment
Appendix C Student Information Sheet
Appendix D: Sample Syllabi and Schedule
Appendix E: Summer 2001 Course Evaluation—Student Comment
Appendix F: Sample Statistics Lab Worksheet
Appendix G: Fall 2001 Course Evaluation Report
Appendix H: Fall 1999–Fall 2002 Course Evaluation—Student Comments
Appendix I: 1994 and 2000 National Institute for Staff and Organizational Development Programs
Appendix J: Distinguished Instructor Award—2000
Appendix K: Computer-Mediated Instruction Research
Appendix L: Student Example of Statistics Report
Appendix M: Survey for Computer-Mediated Instruction
Appendix N: Example of Self-Assessment

31

TEACHING PORTFOLIO
Janet Liou-Mark
Department of Mathematics
New York City College of Technology, CUNY
Spring 2003

Table of Contents

I. Teaching Responsibilities

My teaching responsibility in the Department of Mathematics is to teach undergraduate mathematics courses. Since the department offers the associate degree (A.S.) in computer science, I advise computer science majors during registration. I teach the following courses:

- *Mathematical Concepts and Applications (MA 180)—four class hours, four credits*

  This class has approximately 40 students. The topics covered in this course are selected topics from algebra, geometry, graphs, functions, inequalities, probability and statistics.

- *Fundamentals of Mathematics (MA 175)—four class hours, four credits*

  This class has approximately 40 students. The topics covered in this course are linear and quadratic functions, plane geometry, intermediate algebra, and trigonometry of the right triangle.

- *Introduction to Mathematical Analysis (MA 275)—four class hours, four credits*

  There are approximately 40 students in this class. Topics from intermediate and advanced algebra including quadratics equations, systems of linear equations, exponential and logarithmic functions are covered. Topics from trigonometry including identities, equations, and the solution of triangles are also covered.

- *Mathematical Analysis (MA 375)—four class hours, four credits*

  There are approximately 40 students in this course. This is a pre-calculus functions course that includes topics from advanced algebra and theory of equations such as solution of polynomial equations, DeMoivre's Theorem, binomial theorem, vectors, lines, conic sections and progressions. A graphing calculator is required.

- *Discrete Mathematics (MA 440)—three class hours, three credits*

  This class has approximately 25 students. Topics of elements of discrete mathematical systems pertinent to computer science are covered. Algorithms, Boolean algebra, and the relation to computer design are taught. Directed graphs with applications to flow charting is also covered.

- *Analytical Geometry and Calculus I (MA 475)—four class hours, four credits*

  Approximately 40 students are enrolled in this course. Topics include functions, limits, differentiation, tangent lines, Rolle's Theorem, Mean Value Theorem, integration, and applications.

- *Analytical Geometry and Calculus II (MA 575)—four class hours, four credits*

  Approximately 40 students are enrolled in this course. This course is a continuation of MA 475. Further techniques of integration, derivatives, and integrals of transcendental functions, polar and parametric equations are covered.

- *Numerical Methods (MA 530)—three class hours, three credits*

This course is limited to 24 students because of the number of computers in the classroom. An introduction is given to solving mathematical problems on the computer using a symbolic algebra program with applications in science and engineering. Topics include roots of nonlinear functions, interpolation, numerical differentiation, and integration.

II. Statement of Teaching Philosophy

An old Chinese proverb states:

> If your vision is for a year, plant wheat.
> If your vision is for ten years, plant trees.
> If your vision is for a lifetime, plant people.

When it comes to teaching mathematics, I believe in "planting" a good foundation for all my students since mathematics is a linear learning process. By my willingness to assist the students in their learning, I believe their understanding of mathematics is enhanced and, more importantly, confidence is developed.

To be a good mathematics teacher, one should:

- Be organized and well prepared. A motivating teacher needs to be well prepared. A good lesson plan should have clear objectives and be logically structured in such a way that the students are able to follow it with ease.

- Take time to explain the material. Mathematics is a subject for which students need a good foundation. I believe if a solid understanding of the mathematics being taught is not established, students will have a difficult time applying the concepts. Therefore, I think it is important to take time out to either prove a theorem so students are able to have a better understanding of the new concept or present more examples, allowing time for the students to solve them individually or in groups.

- Provide good notes. I believe it is important to have and take good notes. The objectives are provided in the beginning of each class session. My notes are written in an outline form, starting with the topic followed by definitions, a summary of the procedures used in solving specific problems, and related examples. Good notes can help students refresh what was taught in class. Moreover, I take a step-by-step approach when calculating a problem so that students weak in mathematics can still comprehend the problem.

- Be a motivator. Since mathematics is considered as a "difficult" subject, I believe that showing you sincerely care about each student's performance helps motivate them to achieve a better grade. I often encourage them to seek answers and challenge themselves.

- Establish vocabulary in mathematics. Mathematics is like a foreign language. Vocabulary is often unfamiliar. I believe students need to use and apply the vocabulary of mathematics in their written responses so that understanding can be achieved.

- Teach students to be teachers. If teachers are constantly learning as they teach, students will also learn when they guide their peers through a difficult concept or problem. The sharing of knowledge can have a profound effect on the student's individual and professional growth. I believe using a collaborative approach (as will be elaborated in the next section) will nurture students to take an active role in their learning.

III. Description of Teaching Methodologies

In addition to the traditional pen-and-paper examinations and quizzes, my teaching methods encompass several other essential components such as journal writing, learning style inventory, cooperative learning, take-home examinations, student portfolios, and technology. Different combinations of these strategies are employed depending upon the level of the class and the topic of discussion.

Journal Writing

Students are required to submit an entry in their learning log after each lecture (see Appendix A). They are asked to reflect on what they have just learned by stating the objectives of the lesson, explaining in detail the procedure used to solve a posed problem, questioning concepts that are unclear, and describing concerns. The reflective segment of the learning log helps them to think through the mathematical concepts and vocabulary they have just learned. This process helps students discern if they actually understood the lesson and encourages them to write down their uncertainties. Furthermore, the learning log is a tool that helps me assess student learning. This feedback allows me to address their concerns immediately.

Learning Style Inventory

Students take in and process information in several ways: by the different combinations of visualizing, hearing, reflecting, analyzing, touching, and reasoning logically and intuitively. The teaching styles of instructors are also varied. Some instructors lecture, others demonstrate or prompt students to self-discovery; some focus on principles and others on applications; some emphasize memory and others understanding.

To avoid mismatches between the learning styles of most students in my class and my teaching style, a learning style inventory is administered at the beginning of each semester (see Appendix B). The purpose is twofold. One reason is for the students to be aware of their own learning styles, and the other is for me to select materials and strategies based on the inventory results. This method helps minimize boredom and inattentiveness in class, poor test grades, and discouragement about the course, the curriculum and themselves.

Cooperative Learning

Cooperative learning is implemented in all my classes through group projects and group work because students need to be dynamic learners. When actively participating in their groups or in pairs, students begin to acquire teaching, communication, and leadership skills. They are encouraged to share knowledge and help one another, thus producing a sense of belonging. this environment is particularly beneficial in freshman classes because friendships and/or study groups can be established. Moreover, working together prepares students for their careers because employers want workers who are team players and can work cooperatively with others.

Take-Home Examinations

Certain topics are learned better when students investigate them on their own. For example, statistics is a subject that is best learned by conducting an actual study. In my MA 180 class, a take-home examination in statistics is given (see Appendix C). Students are required to collect, organize, analyze, and interpret their own data on a predetermined topic. In addition, this project provides students with a basic research experience.

Student Portfolios

At the end of the semester, students design their own portfolio according to carefully determined guidelines (see Appendix D). They have the opportunity to select their best exam grades and quizzes from the semester, include the grade of their group project, add points for submitting homework and writing assignments, and declare points for their learning log entries. This project teaches students to be responsible and organized because students must produce all the pertinent exams, quizzes, and reports claimed in the portfolio.

Technology

Graphing calculators, computers, and the Internet are valuable resources for teaching and learning mathematics. The use of technology allows students to visualize and experience mathematics in a different way. They can engage in real-world problem solving, perform rapid and complex computations, and generate their own representations of their own learning. Furthermore, technology allows students to integrate mathematics with other subjects.

When a graphing calculator is used in Calculus (MA 475 and MA 575), students are able to explore sophisticated examples, visualize graphs instantaneously, and be challenged by specific exercises without being immersed by lengthy and tedious calculations (when appropriate).

Java applets are introduced as early as MA 175. These applets are interactive programs in various web sites that students can manipulate and observe animations that help them to grasp the meaning of mathematical ideas.

By exploring mathematical concepts using a symbolic algebra program like Maple, problems that were previously inaccessible because of computational complexity can now be solved. In the Numerical Analysis course (MA 530), a concentration on the creative aspects of a problem is emphasized (see Appendix E).

IV. Course Syllabi

An extensive course syllabus is given to the class at the beginning of each semester (for examples, see Appendix F). The beginning portion of each syllabus states the administrative information about office hours, required texts, examination format, and grading and homework policy. In addition, the student portfolio requirement is explained in detail. Attached to the syllabus is a schedule that highlights the topics to be covered at a particular day, the respective homework problems, and the tentative examination dates. This schedule is particularly helpful for those students who miss class.

V. Student Learning

One main goal as a teacher is to see students learn. Student learning is measured through various methods such as quizzes, group projects, and test corrections.

Frequent quizzes are often given in all my classes, especially before the students' first exam. These quizzes allow me to gauge their understanding of the materials taught, and at the same time force the students to start studying before a major test.

Another method used to measure student learning is through group projects (see Appendix G). They are designed to foster teamwork, develop writing and communication skills, and show that mathematics is utilized in a practical sense. Each group is required to submit several written drafts which I return with comments for improvement. At the end of the semester, a final draft is submitted. For some classes, a ten-minute group presentation summarizing the results of the project is required. A detailed rubric is used to evaluate both the written and oral reports.

Correcting one's mistakes is another way to measure student learning in mathematics. For each examination and quiz, I give students extra points for correcting their mistakes (see Appendix H). An explanation as to why the mistake was made is required after each correction. These explanations help me to determine whether or not the student understood the problem.

VI. Teaching Effectiveness

Peer Assessment of Teaching

Through classroom observations, my peers have expressed satisfaction with my lectures. Appendix I contains the completed peer evaluations, and excerpts from my colleagues are highlighted below.

> *"Prof. Liou-Mark conducted class in a positive, professional and highly personable manner. Her patience and even temperament promoted an easy rapport with students."*
> (Prof. P. Deraney, spring 2002)

> *"The students in this most interesting class [MA 530] worked actively in pairs and small groups, freely and enthusiastically comparing and exchanging ideas and information. Prof. Liou-Mark moved from station to station providing encouragement, asking pertinent questions, and giving suggestions. Finally, three students were asked to go to the chalk board to demonstrate the results they had individually or collaboratively determined concerning the work of the class."*
> (Prof. E. Hill, fall 2001)

> *"The day's objectives were noted on the board, as was the lesson number. The material was presented in a logical manner, with enough review and spiraling of the material that students' pre-*

vious knowledge was constantly called into play."
(Prof. R. Noll, fall 2000)

"Students were comfortable asking questions. The lecture was developed through motivating questions. The students actively participated."
(Prof. Natov, spring 2000)

Student Assessment of Teaching

Student evaluations of my teaching effectiveness are summarized in the table below. Percentages represent respondents who *strongly agree*. The letter *"n"* indicates the number of respondents. Copies of the complete student evaluation of teaching summary can be found in Appendix J.

Criteria	Spring 2002 MA 175 (n=28)	Fall 2001 MA 530 (n=21)	Fall 2000 MA 530 (n=21)	Spring 2000 MA 575 (n=33)	Spring 2000 MA 180 (n=33)
1. The instructor communicated in a way I understood.	89%	100%	100%	88%	85%
2. The instructor held my interest and attention in class.	71%	81%	76%	85%	76%
3. The instructor took the time to explain the material when students did not understand it.	100%	91%	90%	97%	94%
4. Students were encouraged to ask questions and were given meaningful answers.	82%	82%	95%	76%	91%
5. The instructor treated the students with courtesy and respect.	93%	100%	100%	91%	91%
6. The instructor was available to students for discussions or conferences.	82%	82%	81%	79%	82%
7. Overall the instructor's teaching was effective.	86%	82%	86%	85%	85%

I have selected several quotes from student evaluations and class-given "thank-you" cards (see Appendix K) that support success in implementing my teaching philosophy and methodologies. I am pleased that they recognize my enthusiasm and efforts, and more importantly, that they wanted to learn.

> *"If a teacher gives information to her student she is good. If she enlightens them to new concepts she is even better, however, if she develops within them the want of excellence in pursuit of an education, she has reached an ability most deem too costly to bear… it is the last category of sacrificial giving and dedication to her [Prof. Liou-Mark's] profession that I have come to know her."*
> *(Sapphire Gimenez, fall 2002)*

> *"…I think I am going to learn more about how to become a successful educator from Professor Liou. She showed a good example to me, 'Before you become a[n] educator, you should try to be a successful listener first.' That will remind me of how to go on the correct path for reaching my goal—becoming a teacher."*
> *(Yong Chen, spring 2001)*

> *"Thanks for always showing us the key to the problem and not just saying it."*
> *(MA 180, spring 2000)*

> *"Professor Liou-Mark is an excellent professor. She goes above and beyond her call of duty to make us understand math."*
> *(MA 175, Spring 2000)*

> *"She is kind and motivates us by answering any and all questions we ask—some people ask stupid ones too!"*
> *(MA 440, Spring 1999)*

> *"Your patience and caring ways makes me want to study harder and get better grades."*
> *(MA 440, Spring 1999)*

VII. Teaching Improvement Activities
To be an effective teacher one needs to continually gain new information and skills as well as share experiences with others. Through conferences, I

have learned more techniques on how to assess and evaluate student learning and improve my performance in the classroom.

Conference Presentations

- November 2002: "Teaching Mathematics Using a Hands-On Approach" with Profs. S. Han and A. Taraporevala (American Mathematics Association of Two Year Colleges 28th Annual Conference, Phoenix, Arizona)

- April 2002: "Projects in Mathematics Using a Collaborative Approach" with Profs. S. Han and A. Taraporevala (New York State Mathematics Association of Two-Year Colleges 37th Annual Conference, Binghamton, New York)

- March 2001: "The Teaching Portfolio: A Method for Documenting Teaching and Learning" with Dean S. Jackson, Profs. G. Guida, J. Reid, and P. Russo (Professional Development Advisory Council, New York City College of Technology, Brooklyn, New York)

- January 2001: "Writing and Reading in Mathematics" with Profs. C. Goff, J. Meier, and D. Smith) Mathematics Association of America and American Mathematics Society Joint Mathematics Meeting, New Orleans, Louisiana)

- October 2000: "Using Verbal and Written Activities to Understand Math" with Profs. J. Natov, M. E. Rojas, and A. Taraporevala (CUNY Association of Writing Supervisors 24th Annual Conference, Borough of Manhattan Community College, New York, New York)

Conferences Attended

- August 2002: National Conference on Peer-Led Team Learning (University of Montana, Missoula, Montana)

- June 2002: Faculty Development Workshop: Assessing Student Learning (New York City College of Technology, Brooklyn, New York)

- November 2001: American Mathematical Association of Two-Year Colleges 27th Annual Conference (Toronto, Canada)

- August 2001: Mathematical Association of America, Project NExT/Mathfest (University of Wisconsin, Madison, Wisconsin)

- January 2001: Mathematical Association of America and American Mathematical Society, Joint Mathematics Meeting (New Orleans, Louisiana)

- June 1999: Teaching Portfolio Workshop Conducted by Dr. P. Seldin (New York City College of Technology, Brooklyn, New York)

VIII. Future Teaching Goals

My ambitions as a teacher are to reveal to my students that mathematics is not a difficult subject and that anyone can do math. I want to make a difference in the lives of my students, and a way to achieving this goal is to evaluate and improve teaching methods continuously. Therefore, I have set the following goals for the 2002–2003 academic year:

1) Attend at least two national conferences that can help me improve my teaching.
2) Request an annual peer evaluation of my course syllabi and projects.
3) Learn how to improve the dynamics of working in groups.
4) Improve the rubrics for grading group projects and oral reports.
5) Include more technology in the class that can foster student learning in mathematics.

IX. Appendices

Appendix A: Sample Learning Log Entries
- Fundamental of Mathematics (MA 175): Fall 2002
- Mathematical Concepts and Applications (MA 180): Fall 2000

Appendix B: Sample Learning Log With Learning Style Inventory

Appendix C: Sample Take-Home Examinations for MA 180

Appendix D: Guidelines for Student Portfolios

Appendix E: Sample MA 530 Project

Appendix F: Course Syllabi
- Course Syllabus for MA 175: Fall 2002
- Course Syllabus for MA 530: Fall 2001

Appendix G: Sample Group Projects

Appendix H: Sample Test Corrections

Appendix I: Peer Evaluations
- Prof. P. Deraney MA 175: Spring 2002
- Prof. E. Hill   MA 530: Fall 2001
- Prof. R. Noll   MA 175: Fall 2000
- Prof. J. Natov   MA 440: Spring 2000

Appendix J: Student Evaluations
- Fundamentals of Mathematics (MA 175): Spring 2002
- Numerical Analysis (MA 530): Fall 2001
- Numerical Analysis (MA 530): Fall 2000
- Analytical Geometry and Calculus II (MA 575): Spring 2000
- Mathematical Concepts and Applications (MA 180): Spring 2000

Appendix K: Thank-You Cards

32

TEACHING PORTFOLIO
Kay L. Edwards
Department of Music
Miami University (OH)
Spring 2003

Table of Contents

Teaching Responsibilities
I serve as the general music education specialist in the Department of Music at Miami University. Each semester I teach two sections of MUS 266E, *Basic Music Skills and Teaching Techniques for the Early Childhood Teacher,* a three-credit course for education majors (not music majors). In the spring semester I teach one section of MUS 355, *General Music Teaching Techniques,* a three-credit course for music education majors. During fall semester I supervise student teachers in music education and teach one section of MUS 356, *Secondary General Music,* a one-credit course for music education majors. I teach a graduate course in general music that I developed, MUS 622, *Teaching Elementary Music: Theory and Practice,* every three summers and coordinate/co-teach a general music summer workshop. I also sponsor independent studies for individual students. More information regarding my teaching responsibilities is found in Appendix A.

Teaching Philosophy
The music educator and composer Zoltan Kodály stated, "Music is for everyone." I believe that everyone has the *right* to a wide variety of musical opportunities. Music is multifaceted in its fundamental nature as an aural,

visual, and kinesthetic art and thereby provides multiple ways of knowing and multiple means of expression.

I believe that teaching music is an art that includes pedagogy, musicianship, and scholarship. Pre-service music teachers must study pedagogy to discover the means to provide for each student in their classes through music, to develop a repertoire of successful teaching strategies, and to become familiar with current methodologies in the field of music education.

Pre-service music teachers must be fine musicians themselves. They must demonstrate proficiency on many instruments, understand the complexities and richness of music, yet be able to guide children to experience and understand these aspects for themselves.

Pre-service teachers must be fine scholars in general in the field of music. Additionally, teachers should also be "scholars of life," in order to bring their total life experience to their teaching.

Everyone is musical! Every child—and every person—is inherently musical. I believe that general music (classroom music for pre-Kindergarten through eighth grade) is unique within the field of music education. General music serves every child in a school—not just the "talented" or those who can afford private lessons or instrument rental, not just the typically functioning child. General music teachers have the challenge, the joy, and the privilege to impact the life of every child in a school. For many children, classroom music may be their haven, a place they can participate and feel successful. Music can be the "hook" for exceptional learners or children with special needs. Similarly, university students learn in different ways and music can be a key that unlocks new creative venues for them personally and for their teaching.

Teaching Methods

My pragmatic, eclectic, and humanistic philosophy emphasizes a practical application of learning to teach children and utilizes a comprehensive framework of approaches and techniques presented sequentially and efficiently. I draw upon current music education methodologies such as Orff-Schulwerk, Kodály, and Dalcroze Eurhythmics. I encourage student participation and ownership throughout the learning experience as I strive to bring out the best in students. I facilitate their success by setting clear expectations and being available for help. Group work and reflective teaching practice through micro-teaching (having students teach the class), journals, discussions, private conferences, and self-evaluation all help to build on students' strengths and interests in a collaborative and supportive atmosphere that allows many opportunities for students' creativity. (See Appendix B for syllabi.)

I seek to provide a risk-free and inclusive environment, particularly when working with nonmusic majors in MUS 266E, in order to model for them how to create a positive environment for children in their future classrooms. Through three micro-teaching opportunities these teachers present successively longer mini-lessons to the class, in successively smaller groups, culminating with teaching school-age children alone or with a partner. Participation, practical application, creativity, and personal musical growth are emphasized throughout the class activities and assignments. (See Appendix B for course assignments.)

Progress begins with motivation. Students in my courses are motivated through my example and through interaction with their peers in small groups and with the whole class. I provide many ways to learn through a wide variety of experiences and types of assignments. I endeavor to provide a credible model as well as to be a catalyst to facilitate their own personal, professional, and musical growth. I place great emphasis on doing—through active learning and a type of role playing where the class members experience music as children, then step back and analyze the experience as preservice teachers. The degree and manner in which I do this in my classes is perhaps somewhat different than other music educators. Theory is translated into practice in direct, observable ways in every class session. Just as a sense of ownership in the class can be motivating, a high level of motivation and inspiration can in turn foster more ownership of the learning experience, as students develop more confidence with music and unlock the innate musicality they each possess.

Students are involved in self-evaluation of their micro-teaching and "group processing" of their own small-group work. I balance individual and group work and have found that the small group allows nonmusic majors to feel less self-conscious about playing instruments or singing. After each micro-teaching experience, the class (in addition to the instructor) provides verbal and/or written feedback to the student teacher by identifying the strengths of and suggestions for the presentation. Multiple means of assessment are used in each class; assignments range from demonstrating musicianship skills on various instruments, writing critiques after attending local workshops and music classes in schools, writing reviews on journal articles, to actual teaching with the development of lesson plans and teaching materials. These are further described in the next section. Expectations and grading components/criteria are given for each assignment.

Syllabi: Course Content, Assignments, and Projects
Pedagogy

In the courses I teach, students actively experience concepts and skills developmentally appropriate for early childhood/elementary children. Various approaches such as Orff-Schulwerk, Kodály, and Dalcroze Eurhythmics are actively experienced and discussed in class sessions (see Appendix B for examples of syllabi course objectives and a calendar of class sessions). How to sequence these methodologies through grade levels by "revisiting" them within a spiral curriculum throughout elementary music curriculum is presented and discussed. Undergraduate music majors learn (and demonstrate) methodologies in much greater depth, applying their knowledge through field experiences teaching general music classes in local schools.

Students in all four courses are involved in lesson planning and microteaching, observation in area schools and/or the viewing of videotapes of teaching. Again, the level of proficiency, frequency of these activities, and music complexity varies for each course (undergraduate or graduate music majors in MUS 355, 356, or 622; non-music education majors in 266E).

Musicianship

Students learn to play classroom instruments commonly used in teaching general music such as a recorder, Orff instruments, guitar/baritone ukulele, autoharp/Q-Chord, and piano. They meet specific requirements of proficiency which differ for each course. For example, music education majors are required to meet a higher level of proficiency and to develop a larger song repertoire than nonmusic majors. Music majors are also asked to sing and to lead the class in singing more often than nonmajors. (See Appendix B for Skills Test assignment.)

Scholarship

In addition to readings from the course texts (which differ greatly), students read articles selected from the library reserve then synthesize and apply their learning through specific writing assignments. (See Appendix B for article summary assignment.) Undergraduate students write reports on their field experiences in local schools. The students use personal journals to think critically about readings, about ideas presented in class, or to make observations about children's musical expressions. In all three courses (MUS 266, 355, and 356), students develop a resource notebook that organizes all materials from class; the notebook includes lessons presented by fellow class members and a section developed by each individual student on a topic of his or her choosing. Graduate students in MUS 622 are involved in research on specific subjects in elementary music education and the development of curriculum and assessment projects. (See Appendix B for journal and notebook assignments; see Appendix E for an example of a research paper.)

Everyone Is Musical!

In alignment with my philosophy of teaching, every student in my courses is evaluated through a wide variety of means: learning to play instruments, micro-teaching, writing, participation, creating lessons and original materials. There are many ways to include music in the classroom, and not every student will be successful in every aspect of music teaching and learning. Individual strengths are explored by getting to know my students.

On the first day of class, students in my classes fill out an information card that includes their previous music experience (or primary instrument), their previous teaching experience, and their first or strongest music memory. Some nonmusic majors come to the MUS 266 course with considerable experience studying an instrument, singing in choirs, playing in a high school band, or working with children; others enter the course with little or no experience with music or teaching; still others have the "baggage" of negative experiences with music. I strive to meet each student where they are with music, build on their previous positive experiences, and provide a positive experience and confidence with music where none exists.

Curricular Development and Revision

I have developed a graduate general music course here at Miami that was taught for the first time summer 2002. (See Appendix B for MUS 622 syllabus.) I have also developed a summer general music workshop-course, most notably, an Orff-Schulwerk Level I Certification course first taught in August 2003.

I have also done considerable revamping of course syllabi from what had previously been offered at Miami and added on-site lab experiences to the courses (MUS 266E and 355). (See Appendix D for old and new versions of these syllabi, with highlighted changes.) In MUS 266E, for example, students were given a choice of three options for their final project to vote on as a class. During my first year at Miami, one course section (the 11:00 group) elected to hold a music fair for children ages four and five on a Saturday morning. The other section (the 12:00 class) elected to teach 20-minute music lessons to Kindergarten classes at Kramer Elementary in Oxford. For this project, students could refine a lesson they had presented previously in the MUS 266E course. Comments from students, teachers, parents, and children to both projects have been very positive. (See Appendix E for examples of email thank-you letters.)

During Fall 2002, one section of the MUS 266 class took a physical education/dance class together. I collaborated with their dance professor on two assignments during the semester. One of these involved pairs of university students getting to teach integrated "music and creative movement" lessons to four- and five-year-old children at the new on-campus Child Development Center.

An assignment that I include in my undergraduate courses now that I didn't previously is journaling, or the use of personal course journals. I have found this to be a valuable tool for student self-reflection, observation, expression, and communication with me as the instructor. (See Appendix G for examples of journal entries.) I am able to develop a better rapport and can more quickly address student needs through the use of journaling, in addition to frequent use of email or conferencing.

Evaluation of Teaching: Summative and Formative

My teaching has been evaluated by the following means of summative evaluation: *student evaluation* (including two to four additional questions I added to the standard evaluation form and student written reflection on attainment of personal course goals), *peer evaluation* (by Bob Lee, five observations and review of all course materials), *self-evaluation*, and informal, *ongoing feedback* from present and former students.

Student Evaluation

Student evaluations are administered during the last week of classes each semester and are summarized below. (Evaluations prior to Miami University can be found in Appendix H.)

Scale: 1–4

Q 1 = Instructor Interest and Enthusiasm	Q 9 = Clarity of Class Requirements
Q 2 = Student Interest and Enthusiasm	Q10 = Course Content Meets Objectives
Q 3 = Instructor's Knowledge of Subject	Q11 = Overall Rating of Instructor
Q 4 = Instructor's Presentation	**Questions Added:**
Q 5 = Instructor's Attitude Toward Students	Q12 = Course Content Met Personal Goal
Q 6 = Freedom to Participate in Class	Q13 = Classroom Climate
Q 7 = Instructor's Accessibility	Q14 = Course Application Rating
Q 8 = Evaluation Techniques Consistent	Q15 = Course Value to Career

Teaching Evaluations From Spring Semester 2002, MUS 266E
(Section A: 19 respondents/20 enrolled; Section B: 18 respondents/18 enrolled)

Section	Q 1	Q 2	Q 3	Q 4	Q 5	Q 6	Q 7	Q 8	Q 9	Q 10	Q 11
A	3.9	2.9	3.9	3.8	3.7	3.9	3.8	3.8	3.8	3.8	3.9
B	3.7	2.9	3.6	3.2	2.8	2.8	3.3	3.1	3.4	3.2	3.4
Dept Avg.	3.5	2.9	3.6	3.4	3.2	3.4	3.2	3.3	3.4	3.4	3.4
Section	Q12	Q13									
A	3.7	3.9									
B	3.2	3.6									

Teaching Evaluations From Spring Semester 2002, MUS 355
(6 respondents/6 enrolled)

Section	Q 1	Q 2	Q 3	Q 4	Q 5	Q 6	Q 7	Q 8	Q 9	Q 10	Q 11
A	4.0	3.2	3.8	3.7	4.0	3.8	3.7	3.5	2.8	4.0	4.0

Teaching Evaluations From Fall Semester 2001, MUS 266E
(Section A: 24 respondents/24 enrolled; Section B: 24 respondents/26 enrolled)

Section	Q 1	Q 2	Q 3	Q 4	Q 5	Q 6	Q 7	Q 8	Q 9	Q 10	Q 11
A	3.9	2.8	4.0	3.8	3.8	3.8	3.9	3.6	3.6	3.9	3.9
B	3.8	2.7	3.8	3.5	3.3	3.3	3.3	3.1	3.3	3.5	3.5
Dept Avg.	3.5	2.8	3.8	3.4	3.4	3.5	3.2	3.3	3.4	3.5	3.5
Section	Q12	Q13	Q14	Q15							
A	3.5	3.8	3.8	3.5							
B	3.3	3.1	3.7	3.1							

The following summary was prepared by Professor Rob Thomas, faculty member in the Department of Music. The original copy of his complete summary of students' prose comments from course evaluations is available in Appendix H or upon request.

> *In general the comments were very positive, with student after student mentioning Dr. Edwards' enthusiasm for teaching, her obvious knowledge of the course material, the benefits resulting*

from her own experience as a teacher, and the students' own estimation of the practical value of the course material for their own future work in "my own classroom." Student after student wrote that they always felt comfortable and valued in her class, and that they really appreciated both her depth of knowledge and her general warmth as a person.

Peer Evaluation

The following statement was prepared by Bob Lee, music education faculty member and associate chair of the Department of Music, following his observation of five classes and review of all course materials during 2001–2002 and fall 2003. One of his suggestions was to consider incorporating some singing into every class session of MUS 266 and to be sure that the nonmusic majors in that class can read music independently without my help. His complete peer review document is available in Appendix H or upon request.

During the past year, I've observed Dr. Kay Edwards' teaching and have studied all of her syllabi and course materials. She is an inspiring, enthusiastic teacher who engages her students in active learning and participation, promotes age-appropriate methodologies, models classroom management techniques, utilizes collaborative learning and engaging with other learners, and she works to assure the success of all of her students. Her courses are rigorous, current, and pedagogically appropriate for the overall curriculum. She is a nationally recognized authority on multiculturalism in general music and makes ample use of this expertise in her courses to the benefit of all of her students. She is a model teacher, and her students are cited by general music teachers in Princeton City Schools as the best prepared for student teaching of any they have seen.

Self-Evaluation and Ongoing Improvements

As I analyze and reflect upon my teaching, I am pleased with most aspects. My love, passion, and enthusiasm for teaching music is evident in my teaching style. I create a very positive and inclusive classroom environment for learning. I am organized and provide multiple means of engaging all students in my classes. I show a caring attitude that respects students, yet motivates them to excel and to think creatively. I strive to build on students' strengths, yet challenge them to grow.

I requested a Small Group Instructional Diagnosis (SGID) through Miami's Office for the Advancement of Scholarship and Teaching. This was done in November 2001 and March 2002 by facilitator Gail Johnson, as a midterm evaluation of both sections of MUS 266E. This impacted my teaching in a number of ways. As a result of the SGIDs, student evaluations during fall 2001, and conversations with students in the class, I made changes in the MUS 266E course syllabi and course calendar for spring 2002. These changes included further clarification of the attendance policy, one-half as many journal entries turned in less often throughout the course, and clarification/reorganization of the notebook assignment guidelines. In addition, the Small Group Diagnosis affirmed many good things about the course to continue doing, for example, that I am enthusiastic, that I am a good model of effective teaching, and that I am organized (see Appendix H). For fall 2002 I further clarified the attendance policy and the article review assignment (see Appendix D).

One area I will continue to improve on is making assignment guidelines and grading criteria very clear to students, particularly in MUS 355.

Evidence of Student Learning

Student work provides examples of learning in MUS 266E. For instance, two pairs of students taught a lesson for a micro-teaching segment course assignment, then improved and expanded the same lesson for their final project when they taught a Kindergarten class at Kramer Elementary School (see Appendix E).

Many students could not read music and had never played an instrument before taking the course. All of these students demonstrated proficiency on the recorder, baritone ukulele, autoharp, singing, and Orff instruments with grades no lower than B–.

A written midterm exam is administered in the course with a wide variety of measures: short answer, essay, multiple choice, matching, rhythmic dictation, and essay. Examples of an outstanding and a low-scoring midterm can be found in Appendix C. One of my teaching goals was to pre- and post-test the essay, which I did in spring 2002 (see Appendix C).

Other students in the course commented in their journals that they did not understand the use of learning centers prior to the class; however, having the opportunity to create a learning center and use it with children for a final project was a valuable, "real-life" experience (see Appendix G). Students became more aware of the relative success or cohesiveness of their lesson through the use of videotape while teaching children (see Appendix E). In MUS 355, 356, and 622 it is common practice for students to make revisions to a teaching material they designed based upon feedback from the class and instructor.

Professional Development of Teaching

Personal Development

Some ways that I stay current are by reading journals in my field such as *Music Educators Journal, General Music Today, Teaching Music, Contributions to Music Education* (for which I serve on the Editorial Board), *Bulletin of the Council for Research in Music Education, Journal of Music Teacher Education,* and *Triad.* I also attend conference sessions and workshops such as, most recently, Music Educators National Conferences (April 2002), American Orff-Schulwerk Conferences (November 2001), Ohio Music Education Association Conferences (February 2002 and 2003), and I develop original teaching materials and incorporate them directly into my teaching. Other ways I incorporate my own professional development into my courses is by sharing the content of a particularly relevant article with a student teacher or a class, adding the journal or article to my reserve reading, or by trying out new lessons and materials in my classes. (One of my teaching goals is to document the new information I learn and how I integrate this information into my coursework.)

Another example of my professional development is that I received my Orff-Schulwerk Level III certification by taking a two-week intensive training course at Arizona State University in June 2000. (See Appendix G for a copy of the certificate.) I have utilized some of the information from that course in my MUS 355, MUS 356, and MUS 622 classes.

Contributions to Music Teaching Profession

I also share my ideas and materials through presentations or publication on teaching such as the following most recent examples:

- Edwards, K., & Dendler, D. (2003, Spring). The school song: A unifying force. *General Music Today* (journal published by Music Educators National Conference).

- Erwin, J., Edwards, K., Kerchner, J., & Knight, J. (2003). *Prelude to music education.* Upper Saddle River, NJ: Prentice-Hall. This is a textbook for university freshman and sophomore Introduction to Music Education courses.

- Session: "NOW HEAR THIS: Creative Music Listening for Young Children." Ohio Music Education Association Conference presentation, Cincinnati, OH. February 2002.

- Session: "Multicultural Music in the Private Studio." Music Teachers National Association Conference presentation, Cincinnati, OH. March 2002.

- Beethoven, J., et al. (2002). *Making Music.* and Beethoven, J. et al. (2000, 1995). *The Music Connection.* Parsippany, NJ: Scott Foresman Publishing/Silver Burdett.

- I also share my original lesson materials and strategies as a frequent presenter at local meetings of professional music educators (for example, February and March 2003 and August 2002).

Teaching Goals

I have reviewed teaching goals set previously and redefined new teaching goals to be completed during 2003–2004. My primary goal is to continue to accumulate evidence of student learning, specifically:

- With students' permission, to collect additional samples of student work in the classes I teach, including comments and a broader range of quality.

- To expand the off-site field experiences for MUS 355 and MUS 356 and determine their effectiveness.

A secondary goal is also related to documentation of my own learning, specifically:

- To videotape several classes and self-evaluate.

- To send teaching materials and syllabi to a colleague outside of Miami for written feedback.

- To document specific workshop sessions I attend at conferences and how I infuse the new information into my courses.

- To develop one to three rubrics to more clearly state my criteria for grading an assignment.

Appendices
Appendix A: Section I of Dossier
Appendix B: Syllabi and Assignments
Appendix C: Student Lessons, Assignments, and Tests
Appendix D: Old Versus New Syllabi
Appendix E: Final Projects
Appendix F: Original Materials
Appendix G: Journals
Appendix H: Evaluations and Peer Reviews
Appendix I: Letters and Notes on Teaching and Other
Appendix J: Old Course Syllabi

33

Table of Contents

Statement of Teaching Responsibilities

I teach several courses at the undergraduate, master's, and doctoral levels in the School of Nursing. My foci in all degree programs are professional and contemporary issues in nursing, health care policy and politics, and professional values. I also teach philosophy of science at the doctoral level. In addition, I supervise master's level students in nursing systems/health research projects and advise doctoral students doing nursing/health systems research dissertations.

Baccalaureate

Each fall I teach the entry course in the RN to BSN/MSN program, N481, *Personal Effectiveness in Nursing.* Cohort groups of approximately 20 take this blended online-onsite five-credit hour course, the first in a sequence of required coursework in an innovative RN BSN completion program that I developed four years ago. The program is modeled after Steven Covey's Principle Center Leadership theory, which purports that you cannot manage in a complex system until you can first manage yourself. N481 is designed to resocialize and ready RNs to embrace professional values and identity through self-awareness and effectiveness.

In addition, I teach the health policy content in N483, *Effectiveness in Human Health Outcomes,* and the politics content in N484, *Effectiveness in*

Complex Health Systems, each spring to the same cohort group. In spring of 2003 I also team-taught the two- to three-credit hour required companion clinical course in this program, N486, *Application to Practice.* I had ten students within two cohorts in two area health care agencies doing community service and leadership projects.

Master's

I teach a two-credit hour (soon to become three credits) required master's level course, N514, *Policy, Organization, and Financing In Health Care,* each spring to approximately 40 students, usually within a live telecast format across three campuses. During spring 2003 I worked with the university teaching technology department to develop this course in online format. N514 will be offered this summer to about 30 neonatal nurse practitioner students from around the country and full-time local students.

Finally, each year in the spring I precept one or two N572NE, *Advanced Nursing Practice: Synthesis Practicum in Nursing Education* students. These students, often at their request, are placed with me for the semester in an educator apprenticeship. I spend approximately three hours a week with these nurse educator students, assisting and mentoring them in almost all aspects of my role as a teacher in higher education.

Doctoral

About once a year I teach a required two-credit hour N614, *Health and Social Policy* course to an average of five to six students in the nursing doctoral program. This course focuses on issues of cost, access, and quality in the health care industry and domain. It also contains content relevant to policy research methodology.

I serve on numerous doctoral committees in the School of Nursing (N699, *Dissertation Research*), and also take doctoral students for N694, *Directed Readings.* My skills in qualitative research and my research focus on sociopolitical and gender issues within the health care context have generated numerous student requests to serve on their committees or for advice regarding methodology and readings.

I currently serve as the chair of Kay Luft's committee, "The Lived Experience of Women Undergoing Implantation of Defrillator Devices." I also serve as a committee member for the following students:

- Mary Kinnaman, 2002–present, "Interdisciplinary Collaboration and Power"

- Teri Thompson, 2002–present, "The Politics Behind Children's Health Care Policy"

- Shirley Dinkel, 2001–present, "The Primary Care Needs and Beliefs of Lesbian Women"

- Kandace Landreneau, 2001–present, "Why Aren't Many End-Stage Renal Patients Being Offered Transplant?"

I wrote the qualitative research comprehensive exam questions for Dinkel and Landreneau, and did a three-credit hour directed readings course on critical feminist theory with Kinnaman during the 2002–2003 academic year.

Teaching Philosophy

My philosophy of teaching reflects my belief that the empowerment of professional nurses is good business for all stakeholders (see Appendix A, philosophy of nursing). Thus, I teach for empowerment and civic engagement. I am a confessed critical feminist pedagogue, drawing from traditional and contemporary thought in these areas to assist nursing students in the development of critical thinking and confident engagement within complex systems—health care and society.

Critical feminist pedagogy manifests in the student-teacher relationship and the teacher-context relationship. In my relationship with students I consider myself a coach, guide, mentor, and facilitator, as well as an intellectual and disciplinary expert. I strive to help students identify, develop, and express their beliefs and values, knowing those beliefs and values and the ability and will to express them will profoundly affect application of evidence-based knowledge and advocacy in the care of patients and communities. Although I have more positional and formal knowledge power than my students (as a critical feminist I own that), I believe that their standpoint is valuable and worthy of respect and therefore that the relationship should be reciprocal and mutually respectful.

My expectations and standards are high, as evidenced by the fact that many of my students claim they work harder in my courses than in some others. But I believe that through the expectation of personal accountability and full engagement, I empower my students to acquire high-level knowledge as well as confidence in their ability to think and act critically.

My critical feminist leanings require that as a teacher I engage with the system or context that supports the teaching/learning experience and the discipline of nursing. I feel a moral and ethical obligation to work for social, political, economic, and cultural changes that enhance the learning experience for my students and to address barriers to quality and empowerment. Issues such as class size, admission standards, diversity, course format, economic access, student participation in university decision-making, curriculum, and student stories of their practice experiences are all potential points of entry in my role as a critical feminist educator in relationship to the context of learning and, through their learning, professional practice.

Finally, my goal as a teacher is consistent with one of UMKC's core values: "Unleashing Human Potential." The drive to unleash human potential as an educator is strong within me. It is the very essence of who I am as a teacher and intellect. The most rewarding aspect of my role is the knowledge that through his or her relationship with me as a critical feminist nurse educator, a student or alumnus or a member of the profession has realized his or her potential as a professional nurse, advocate, writer, leader, activist, or teacher.

Pedagogical Style and Strategies

My teaching methods are consistent with my philosophy and are designed to promote shared and authentic interaction as well as student empowerment and civic engagement.

If my class is on-site didactic, I generally try to make the room geographically inclusive, arranging chairs in a circle and seating myself within the circle. If I cannot do that, I walk among the students during discussion, or sit with them. I employ appropriate self-revelation within the context of content application, thus placing myself in a position of mutuality in order to assist in the development of trust and openness—a milieu that is often discouraged and therefore foreign to nurses within their workplace settings. One example of this approach is when I ask students to do a one-minute writing exercise, I do the same exercise and read my response out loud. I often talk about my own experiences in my different nursing roles, employing those experiences within an instructive framework. This strategy also models professional, knowledge-based responses to challenging situations.

I encourage students to find and use their own voice by hooking content to their own experiences as a nurse. I frequently employ case-based learning, facilitating class discussion of a concept as it manifests in a real-life health care system example (see Appendix B, syllabi examples). I use small-group work for case learning and to discuss controversial issues and debate. This strategy is useful for students who might be too shy to speak in the large group, helping to build their confidence and critical argumentation skills and encouraging collegial problem solving.

I also use journaling and reflective writing to enable and encourage students to form their own thoughts about concepts, problems, and strategies, to self-express in a safe venue, and to enhance their writing abilities, which all sadly are often quite undeveloped. In addition, I include learning opportunities for scholarly writing to further formal development of critical thought and reliance upon evidence-based work rather than experience or hunch.

Finally, I demonstrate my critical feminist pedagogical style through openness to student-driven learning strategies and content focus, within the framework of course description and objectives. As primarily adult learners who have so often been "told" what to do in hospitals, providing input into the course content and process helps RN students buy in to their learning experiences and become more personally accountable and empowered.

Curricular Revision and Innovation

I thoroughly enjoy and excel at curriculum work. I have done extensive curriculum innovation and revision at both the course and program level in both undergraduate and graduate programs. At the program level I completely revised the entire curriculum in 1999 for the RN to BSN completion program, and have continued to play a critical role in that curriculum. The program is a fast-track, 18-month baccalaureate program designed for working RNs. The developmental nature of the core content focuses on personal, interpersonal, human health outcomes, and systems effectiveness as a professional nurse. Unique to this program is a strong emphasis on leadership and management of self in teams and within a complex system.

I developed the new BSN completion program in response to the lack of ability and confidence in a majority of practicing RNs to respond fully and professionally to the *context of health care,* resulting in constrained patient advocacy, work satisfaction, and potentially patient safety. I also responded to complaints by administrators within hospitals about the need for RNs with more "systems savvy." Called the "Transformational BSN Program," students work in cohorts to develop the skills and knowledge needed for today's chaotic and demanding work environment. See Appendix C for the program's curricular framework.

I made major revisions to the N514 *Policy, Organization, and Financing Health Care* course in response to the needs of the students (see Appendix D for syllabi comparisons). The content and readings assumed a post-master's level knowledge base, and did not adequately reflect the objectives. Students were often unfamiliar with even the most basic policy concepts and had a fear of in-class discussion about this seemingly foreign discourse and thought. I leveled the content and redesigned the learning and evaluation experiences to enhance student participation.

I am preparing to teach for the first time a two-credit hour online required course, N512, *Values in Health Care Decision-Making,* this coming fall, and am revising the course's learning experiences and evaluation activities, as well as updating the readings, texts, and web site. Enrollment for that course is anticipated to be about 30.

I taught the N605 *Philosophy of Science* course via video network to seven Ph.D. students from the Kansas City–Columbia and UMSL campuses for the first time in fall 2002. This course had a reputation of being the "hardest course" in the doctoral program, and students approached the experience with dread. I redesigned the course prior to teaching it, updating readings, learning and in-class activities, and evaluative strategies. During the course I made immediate revisions based on student feedback and gently encouraged and rewarded open debate and discussion of this difficult content. I tried to remove the fear factor related to philosophy of science content and make it relevant to immediate needs in nursing and health care.

One excellent example of the full student engagement that resulted from this approach was a student presentation on the differences between determinism and free will. She used her talents as a folk guitarist and singer to artistically demonstrate those differences within lyrics. Students not only understood the concept better, but also had fun in the process.

I subsequently did an extensive review of this course for the Ph.D. program committee in 2003 and made substantial evaluative remarks and suggestions in light of program goals, accreditation requirements, and scientific soundness (see Appendix E for documentation of course review). After receiving excellent reviews from students and doing quite a bit of revision work, I hope to teach the course on a permanent basis, possibly rotating with another professor.

Evidence and Evaluation of Teaching Effectiveness

I am a proponent of immediate and interactive evaluation of teaching and curriculum. I use a variety of methods with students and my faculty peers to encourage real-time feedback and adaptation. Those methods include open discussions with students both at the beginning of and during courses about their learning needs, concerns, and level of engagement. I am never punitive and always responsive, employing my philosophy of high expectations in a spirit of reciprocity and empowerment

An exemplar of this type of approach occurred this spring 2003 in my master's level N514 policy course. I could tell from the first day in class that students were not reading and engaging with the content and were resisting in-class discussion. As I noticed these phenomena I shared my observations with the class and got very little response, which I attributed to their unfamiliarity with me and a natural fear and lack of trust. I tried new ways to instill interest in the content, including small-group work and hinging content to their workplace issues, and used positive feedback every time a student contributed to the conversation. These were somewhat effective strategies, but I could still detect that they came to class unprepared, and they still resisted talking.

During the sixth week in class I became quite frustrated (internally) with the visible lack of interest and unpreparedness. So I stopped talking in the middle of class, paused, and openly shared with them my frustration. I expressed my belief in the importance of this content to their ability to survive in the current health care system and my earnest desire to remedy this situation, with their help. I opened myself to criticism and encouraged the students to tell me, without repercussion, what the problems were. They broke through their reticence and gave me a litany of complaints and suggestions, most of which related to their complete unfamiliarity with social and political discourse, difficulties reading the text (which, sadly, was the gold-standard text for baccalaureate and master's students in nursing), and me "making them talk in class."

I had to really humble myself in order to demonstrate my sincerity and openness to their criticisms. Through two-way discussion, we developed a plan right then and there. I agreed to prepare discussion questions, which they would use to help them hone in on salient concepts during their readings. They in turn, for me, agreed to write answers to those discussion questions to bring to class and turn in. Then, to respond to their fear of speaking in class, I had them break into groups and within each group "answer" their discussion question. They then picked a leader in their group to present the response. These strategies worked beautifully. The students began to talk openly and freely and thanked me for helping them and responding to their concerns. I had several students approach me after class and thank me (see Appendix F for written student comments).

A similar approach was used in my N481 course and the BSN completion program this past year. My teaching partner in this program and I had responded to administrative requests to put the program mostly online. This was the first year we taught using online for a majority of the coursework.

After about two weeks into this course, I detected a high level of anxiety and frustration from the students which, upon discussion, primarily related to the nature of the online segment of the course. They did not like it. They felt it was a barrier to their learning and to their development of face-to-face peer relating, and in general, created too much busy work.

I consulted with my teaching colleague in the program and immediately revised the course to remove much of the online content, take out the busy work, and revise the course so that it excited and engaged the students rather than turned them off. In addition, my partner and I did a post-program live review with this same cohort at the end of spring 2003. We gathered tremendous feedback from them regarding the format, content, learning experiences, and assignments. The students were immensely grateful that we valued their input enough to devote serious in-class time to their feedback, and we in turn found the input insightful and relevant. We are implementing almost all their suggestions for the coming year, including removing much of the online format and using it only for support (see Appendix G for evaluation content and format).

My formal student evaluations are usually quite high. In 2002–2003 I averaged 4.5 overall on a scale of 1–5, and in some classes like N481 and N605 I scored a course average of close to 5, on a scale of 1–5 (see Appendix H for original scores and reviews):

Year	Course	Average Score (1 = lowest – 5 = highest)
2002–2003	N481	4.8
2002–2003	N514	4.2
2002–2003	N605	4.8
2002–2003	N486	4.1

In addition, I receive many written comments from students both within formal reviews and unsolicited, regarding my ability to make the content exciting, applicable, and most important to me, that I empower them as professionals (see Appendix I for letters and comments). Doctoral students have told me in the past two years that I "transformed" them into scholars and changed their philosophy and approach to nursing and the health care system.

I have received a few criticisms in my written evaluations. For instance, I seem to have a difficult time remembering names. I always struggle with this because I know how important it is to know who is speaking to me, for evaluation and teaching purposes, and how important it is in helping students know that I value them individually. I try to learn their names each semester in each class, but if I am particularly busy that semester, or the course is time-compressed or large or has multiple sites, I may not succeed in this goal. So it came as no surprise to me when a student expressed their dismay that I did not learn their name. They felt slighted and unimportant. Henceforth, I plan to have them use table-tents with their names on them, and have off-site students send me their picture (we have off-site coordinators who can facilitate this) since I am a visual learner. I am resolved to do better in this area.

Finally, we recently incorporated a value-added comprehensive, nationally normed summative test explicitly for BSN completion students in our BSN completion program. This is the first and only such test to be developed. The scores for the 2002–2003 cohort group were far above the national norms (see Appendix J for composite scores and categories). Especially exciting for me were the scores on political advocacy, professional values, and empowerment. They were almost two standard deviations above the norm, and some students' scores were 100%. These results demonstrate student learning as well as student role-socialization in the areas that I teach. In addition, I believe that modeling these values, skills, and knowledge to students using critical and feminist pedagogical approaches also contributed to student success.

Collaboration and Dissemination

Each year I work with two or three N598 *Directed Research* students on projects either related to my systems research work or to their own systems related research interests. The most recent student work in this course includes the following:

- Andrea Spalter, 2003, "A Concept Analysis of Hospital Workplace Bullying"

- Mary Carley, 2002, "What We Should Be Asking Staff Nurses in Exploitative Hospital Environments"

- Shawn Bunch, 2002–present, "A Concept Analysis of Sociopolitical Activism in Nursing"

- Deborah Whitehead, 2000–2001, "Staff Nurse Satisfaction: A Search for Meaning"

- Jonna Dougherty, 2000–2001, "Determinants of Staff Nurse Satisfaction Related to Workplace Environment"

Spalter, Carley, and Bunch are all works in progress for joint publication with me. In addition, I usually have to turn down two or three requests each semester from *Directed Research* students seeking to work with me due to time constraints (see Appendix K for student request example).

I collaborate in a variety of other ways, including with both School of Nursing faculty and faculty in other units and universities on curriculum, learning needs of students such as writing and APA use, and student affairs issues (see Appendix L for letter from faculty). I have published two articles addressing nursing education issues (see Appendix M) and submitted an abstract to present our BSN completion program at a national conference this fall (see Appendix N).

Future Teaching Goals

I believe that after ten years of teaching in higher education I am approaching master-level teaching ability, as evidenced by my self, peer, and student evaluations. But there is much I still desire to accomplish. My goals include:

- Publishing collaborative works with students, doing national presentations on such topics as our transformational BSN completion program, teaching portfolios in nursing, and critical feminist pedagogical application within nursing education.

- Acquire more experience with development and revision of online course format and online instruction.

- Seek the opportunity to teach the qualitative research course in our doctoral program.

- Refine my ability to critically determine and implement appropriate teaching strategies for various levels of students.

Appendices

Appendix A: Philosophy of Nursing
Appendix B: Syllabi Examples of Learning Activities
Appendix C: BSN Completion Program Curricular Framework
Appendix D: N514 Policy Syllabi Comparison Before and After Revision
Appendix E: Documentation of Philosophy of Science Course Review
Appendix F: Written Student Comments Related to Course Revision
Appendix G: Evaluation of BSN Completion Program: Format and Results
Appendix H: Formal Student Evaluation of Course Scores, 2002–2003
Appendix I: Empowerment Letters and Comments From Students
Appendix J: Standardized Post-Program Scores and Categories for BSN Completion Students

Appendix K: Student Request for Me as Research Project Advisor
Appendix L: Letter From Faculty Member
Appendix M: Published Articles Related to Nursing Education
Appendix N: Abstract for Presentation of BSN Completion Program at
             National Conference

34

TEACHING PORTFOLIO
Curtis C. Bradley
Physics and Astronomy Department
Texas Christian University
Spring 2003

Table of Contents

Teaching Responsibilities

My teaching responsibilities in the Department of Physics and Astronomy have had a very strong emphasis toward introductory undergraduate student learning. I teach a section (~15 to 20 students) of the introductory trigonometry-based sequence *General Physics* (Phys 10153 and 10163). This sequence satisfies degree requirements for students who are majoring in biology, chemistry, geology, kinesiology, computer science, or education, but with a substantial majority in the pre-med program. Also, each year I teach a section (~15 to 20 students) of our calculus-based sequence *Physics* (Phys 20473 and 20483) to students majoring in physics, engineering, chemistry, and mathematics. In addition to these lecture sections I supervise (with ~five graduate teaching assistants) all of the laboratory course sections (Phys 10151 and 20471) corresponding to the first semester of the above lecture course sequences (~120 students in 12 sections). In addition to the above introductory course sections, I have also taught smaller numbers of students in more advanced undergraduate and graduate courses. At the junior-senior undergraduate level, I have taught one semester each of *Electromagnetic Fields* (Phys 40653, five students) and *Contemporary Topics in Physics* (Phys

50173, five students), and have supervised students doing research projects in *Senior Research in Physics* (Phys 40103, two students) or education-related projects and/or activities in *The Teaching of Physics* (Phys 40050, two students). At the graduate level, I have taught *Quantum Mechanics II* (Phys 60313, one student) and *Quantum Optics* (Phys 70903, one student). I also teach in other, less formal, ways: In collaborative research work, I teach (and coach) my graduate and undergraduate students on many levels. I have worked with a large number (about two per year) of undergraduate students on research or science education projects. Several of these have presented papers in scientific meetings. Also, I teach (and coach) in my capacity as the advisor to our TCU Society of Physics chapter.

Teaching Philosophy, Methods, and Strategies

My desire to become an effective university educator is a natural extension of my lifelong efforts to reach out to people, to learn how they think and perceive, and to have an impact on their world view. This lifelong passion is discussed in Appendix G. My philosophy of teaching emerges from my own continued efforts in being, and behaving as, a creative and self-disciplined learner. As I continue along the path of becoming a better teacher, I will always seek out new ideas and techniques that I hope will give structure and functionality to my teaching ideals. Like many other important things in life, evaluating the resulting quality of my teaching will be a difficult task and almost completely my solitary responsibility. It is not easily summed-up like income or published works. It is not easily revealed by a survey of student opinions. To help me in this process, I will need to describe in concrete detail, for my students and myself, what I hope to achieve in the classroom.

In choosing teaching strategies to employ in the classroom and for advising, I have a couple of primary goals in mind. I want my students to learn, how to learn and I want to share the intellectual richness of science with my students. In particular, I want to communicate the specific insights that physics provides for understanding nature. In order for my students to learn how to learn, I will insist that they practice their skills in critical reading, question formation, and information organization. They must learn how to take useful notes and records. They must practice their communication skills by verbalization of their ideas and questions and by writing out descriptions of what they are learning. Finally, they must learn how to organize, coordinate, and associate what they know, in order to allow them to find answers to new problems and to explore new situations. This last part is, perhaps, what makes physics education so interesting, challenging, and so incredibly valuable to students.

Typically, I lecture and ask students to prepare questions for discussion in class. In discussions of certain phenomena and ways of describing physical law, I provide ample demonstration of problem solving and analysis skills, question refinement and articulation, and technical tricks-of-the-trade. For most classes, I provide lectures with rhetorical give and take, physical demonstrations, and as much drama as I can muster in order to make the ideas concrete and my main points understandable, memorable, and persuasive. It is my hope to have an intellectual impact on as many of the souls in the classroom as possible. This can easily be squandered by an overemphasis on details—working out the algebra of numerous derivations—instead of talking in-depth about the "big" ideas involved. Still, sometimes I have overemphasized the big ideas, and not spent the required time on the nitty-gritty (see the section on Efforts to Improve My Teaching).

In my classes students have assigned sets of problems and questions due each week. These sets help to test the students' understanding of the ideas and technical skills that are being developed in the course. These assignments give the students something concrete to think about in order to illustrate the more general ideas and themes of the course, and an opportunity to practice for similarly challenging exams given several times during the term and at the end of the course. In some courses, a written report on some relevant topic may be included. A major part of my teaching is to use online homework (first using Blackboard, then WebCT, and recently trying the online homework service out of the University of Texas–Austin). This has been a huge success in providing students with immediate feedback and encouraging them to continue to work individually and collaborate in their struggle with the material. Also, I tend to provide a lot of small quizzes in addition to tests, since I have noted how these energize and sharpen student attention to the material.

In lab courses, students are expected to record their preparation for (prelab assignments) and involvement in their assigned lab exercises (using journals). In addition, they will write summary reports that demonstrate their understanding of what motivated a particular measurement and then what can logically be concluded from that measurement and subsequent analysis.

Maintaining Relevance

Maintaining general student interest and enthusiasm for the subject and its methods is a challenging task in teaching physics. It is easy to lose the interest and curiosity of students, particularly when it comes to the very detailed analytical and abstract aspects of the subject. Many students require frequent reminders of how the course content is relevant to "real life" (that is, we are not just sharpening the point of some academic stick). In lectures and discussions I try hard to begin a topic with phenomena that students have experienced so as to connect with their direct experiences and to inspire some curiosity about something of relevance. Also, I tend to pick illustrative and commonplace things (when possible) as lecture examples and as assigned questions and problems in order to make a strong connection to everyday experience. As examples, I might ask about the energy consumed by a bread toaster compared to drying your hair with a hair dryer, or how long it will take a tetherball to go around the pole if its tether is two meters long. In the lab courses, I have tried to design lab exercises that are relevant to students' lives and interests and at the same time demonstrate the course content.

Another way that I have tried to integrate the course content with the students' other experiences is that, in some classes, I have asked students to write a course journal. This journal writing is intended to help students document their process of doing assigned readings. I have sometimes tried to insist that students produce reasonable questions about the material before I begin a lecture (this is very tough for most students). It is my hope that this will encourage the active learner habits in my students so that lectures and discussions will be far from a passive experience for them.

I have sometimes also considered (and sparingly used) an extra-credit "free form" project about some aspect of the course. To get credit, students must get preapproval via a project proposal sheet (see Appendix C for an example of the proposal sheet). As I continue to ponder this idea, my hope is that students who have the desire and ability will demonstrate their talents in creative writing, computer programming, essay composition, or sculpting to make a connection with the content of the course in a way that would not otherwise be encouraged. Usually, there is too little time for the work (learning opportunities) that is already available to my students for this type of open-ended project to be very attractive to most.

Student Motivation

For motivation of student effort, I offer a simple fixed-point-based grading system, various forms of extra credit (additional problems, so-called redemption points, test redo assignments, etc.), and my personal charisma. From the very start of my relationship with a class, I try to connect with them by getting to know their names (I make seating charts which they regularly sign in on) and by keeping track of how they are doing in the course assignments (grades are posted online, protected with individual passwords). Through humor and expressive responses, I communicate my frustration and pleasure at what I determine to be their level of effort and attentiveness. If a student is struggling with the course, I always hope to establish a stronger connection with that student in order to discover what the main obstacles are and to give specific advice when and if it is appropriate.

The so-called redemption points (when I offer them) and test revisions are a way of encouraging and rewarding students for going over material that they did not sufficiently understand. The way this sometimes works is that students can turn in reworked problems and questions (sometimes using the solutions that I have handed out as a guide, or using the text, each other, me, or tutors for help) to earn points that contribute to their final grade (generally as extra credit). When I give these opportunities, most students make some effort to improve their grade and help their understanding of the material at the same time.

Student Evaluation of Teaching

In Appendix E, I present the results of TCU Student Perception of Teaching (SPOT) surveys in the form of graphs comparing student survey responses about my teaching to departmental and college averages. Based on the results from 2002, it appears that students generally agree (and sometimes strongly agree) that my courses are intellectually stimulating, that I encourage active participation from my students, that I have been available for consultation with students outside of class, and that I have successfully communicated with them in a courteous and respectful manner. The responses from 2002 can be compared with results from 1999 to 2001 (based on an older form of the TCU SPOT). During these years the students were satisfied overall. Students generally felt that the course was taught well, that course materials were clear, that I was available and helpful, and that grading was fair and consistent. The students were least satisfied with the amount of material that was covered and the pace of the course. I feel this was a fair acknowledgement, on their part, of the ambitious goals of the course and the mathematical and intellectual rigor demanded of these students. Based on the accumulated survey data, it appears that I have made some gradual improvement over these four years.

Efforts Toward Improving My Teaching
Teaching Conferences/Workshops Attended
Over the last four years I have attended a number of teaching, or teaching-related, conferences and workshops. In March 1999, I attended the American Association of Physics Teachers (AAPT) sessions in the Centennial meeting of the American Physical Society (APS) held in Atlanta, Georgia.

From talks at that meeting I was encouraged by the great opportunities for communicating physics by use of new technologies and by including strikingly attractive things, ranging from holograms to a dancer's ballet movements, in course materials. Since then I have:

- Participated in the National Science Foundation Regional Grants Conference, College Station, April 11–12, 2002.

- Attended the spring 2002 National Science Teachers Association meeting in San Diego, where I learned a great deal about the American Association for the Advancement of Science (AAAS) PROJECT 2061. Also, I learned about new teaching opportunities using handheld computers and associated tools.

- Served as a reader and evaluator of FIPSE (Fund for the Improvement of Postsecondary Education) grant proposals. The session was held at the University of Texas at Arlington during the spring of 2001.

- Participated in a WebCT workshop at the University of North Texas (June 22–23, 2000), and developed multiple physics courses using WebCT for interactive online coursework.

- Attended T^3 2000 Conference (March 17–19, 2000) in Dallas, Texas, and learned about the use of new technologies in K–16 education (mostly K–12, so far). Some of this is disturbing. Students (teachers, parents, etc.) sometimes think learning has taken place when it, in fact, has not (learning algebraic problem solving is not only helpful for solving algebra problems).

- Participated in four-day, NSF-sponsored, University of Maryland's American Center for Physic 4th Annual Workshop for New Faculty (November 1999).

- Participation in TCU Teaching Portfolio Program during August 1999 (Center for Teaching Excellence, TCU).

My Response to Student Feedback About My Teaching

When I started teaching I often asked students (those who seemed particularly conversational and open) to compare my teaching style with their other professors or other teachers they had experienced. In this informal way I was alerted to some of my strengths and weaknesses. In one instance an academically strong student initiated the conversation and asked for a change in emphasis in my lectures. She wanted a greater amount of time spent in lectures where I was working example problems, with an emphasis on getting the first steps toward solutions to problems. I made an effort to include more of this in my lectures. A second student revealed that my lectures were very clear and that he enjoyed my emphasis on making sure the basic foundations were well understood by the class. I routinely read the comments written by students on the TCU SPOT surveys and have considered a plan of having students write out answers to a few questions at mid-semester and then at the end of the course (see Appendix F).

Staying Current in My Discipline

I have been building a modern research lab at TCU to do state-of-the-art experiments involving graduate and undergraduate students. The content and implications of this and related work and current developments in other areas of physics are always easy to talk about, particularly as they relate somehow to the course content. Questions are usually stimulated when students visit my lab when they come to see me (or my graduate student) for help with their homework. Other relevant "current physics" discussions occur in response to student questions about something they had seen on television or in other media. I have, for example, shown my introductory (and advanced) classes example volumes of conference proceedings from science meetings to show the immense quantity and variety of current physics research areas. All of these things help to remind students (and others) that the subject is dynamic and continues to grow beyond the scope of their introductory textbook.

As part of remaining current in my discipline, I am a member of the following professional organizations: American Association of Physics Teachers (AAPT), American Physical Society (APS), the Division of Atomic Molecular and Optical Physics (DAMOP), APS Division of Laser Science, APS Forum on International Physics, APS Forum on Physics and Society, APS Topical Group on Fundamental Constants, and the Texas Section of the American Physical Society.

Future Teaching Goals

There are several concrete mechanisms available to me to improve the quality of my teaching. For example, by reading and studying literature about teaching and mentoring I can learn about new issues, strategies, techniques, and technologies.

- I plan to routinely examine published articles on these issues, particularly in the AAPT (American Association of Physics Teachers) professional journal and in the journals published by the National Science Teachers Association (NSTA).

- I will listen attentively to my students in order to see where and how they are struggling.

- I will continue to participate in the self-definition of my teaching philosophy and goals by keeping my teaching portfolio up-to-date and documented.

- I can learn by observing and discussing teaching with other faculty, particularly those that are regarded as very good teachers.

List of Appendices

Appendix A: Summary of Courses Taught
Appendix B: Example Course Syllabi
Appendix C: Example Course Assignments
Appendix D: Letters and Comments From Students
Appendix E: Student Perceptions of Teaching
Appendix F: Student and Peer Evaluation Form
Appendix G: My Teaching Philosophy

35

TEACHING PORTFOLIO
Barbara A. B. Patterson
Department of Religion
Emory University
Spring 2003

Table of Contents

Teaching Responsibilities

As a senior lecturer in the religion department, I predominantly teach undergraduates classes. I also teach the required pedagogy class for our Ph.D.-level graduate students and serve on doctoral thesis committees. Several of my courses are cross-listed with environmental studies. I have three main areas of teaching responsibility:

1) Eco-Theology and Practice: From Feminist, Womanist, and Contemplative Religious Perspectives

   - Religion 329, Religion and Ecology: elective, undergraduate course, 30 students

   - Religion 373, Wilderness Spirituality: elective, undergraduate course, 18–22 students (an immersion course)

2) Practical Learning and the Study of Religion

   - Religion 300, Interpreting Religion: required course for undergraduate majors, 35 students

   - Religion 370, Spiritual Practices and Social Change: elective, undergraduate course, co-taught with Tibetan studies professor, 45 students

- Religion 380, Internship in Religion: elective, undergraduate course, 18 students
3) Christian Feminist Theology and Practices

- Religion 366, Christian Women's Fasting Practices: elective, undergraduate course, 35 students

- Religion 370, Women, Christianity, and Globalization: elective, undergraduate course, 35 students

The Religion and Ecology class is taught from a comparative approach. It focuses predominantly on Buddhist and Christian ideas about nature, the movements of energy from cosmological, philosophical, and spiritual perspectives, and ethical actions advocating for the preservation of nature. Students read and write in response to ancient and contemporary texts, including texts about rituals and retreats in natural settings.

The Interpreting Religion class introduces religion majors to the history of the field and to basic methods and theories used in the interpretation of religion. The course explores a variety of approaches to the study of religion, including history of religions, anthropology, sociology, psychology, theology, and cultural studies. Students directly apply the theories and methods examined in the course through a series of self-designed projects related to their particular interests.

The Internship in Religion class provides a structured and reflective setting in which students, faculty, and community partners can engage, analyze, and interpret the religious and ethical dimensions of public issues, policy, and practice. Students interview with and are chosen as interns by one of a number of supervisors in community-based learning settings. In addition to the work in their internships, students and community partners participate in a weekly seminar using comparative, interdisciplinary, and practical approaches of analysis to emphasize the connections of theory and practice. The holistic assumptions of the class engage and educate participants in ideas and actions drawing from theoretical, emotional, analytical, practical, spiritual, and ethical knowledge.

In the Women, Christianity, and Globalization class, students take a journey through and with the voices and witnesses of Christian women through the ages and from many nations. The narratives explore particular women's searches for a history and place in the tradition, considering issues of language, symbol, respect, authority, power, and justice. The class introduces students to national and international Christian feminist approaches to theology and emphasizes how those approaches helped women reshape traditional categories and blaze new ones grounded in women's faith and activism (see Appendix A).

Teaching and Learning Philosophy

> *"What I propose, therefore, is very simple; it is nothing more than to think what we are doing."*
> —Hannah Arendt, *The Human Condition*

Fundamentally, teaching and learning is a process of evolving discovery, analysis, integration, and action. The movement of this process is elliptical, an elongated spiral pitching through theories, methods, and practices. Each component of the ellipse is equally significant and valued, and all assume regular and structured ethical and personal reflection. The purpose of this teaching and learning process is three-fold:

1) To increase knowledge and understanding holistically, meaning involving all aspects of engagement, including thinking, feeling, spiritual awareness, movement/body, physical location, cultural context
2) To better equip learners and teachers to integrate ideas and methods with practical issues and needs of life
3) To enable discernment about the most effective and meaningful ways of being active participants with others working toward the flourishing of all

Teaching and learning are transformative arts. They assume change not only in intellectual content and method, but also in personal and communal consciousness and understanding. They should effect the ways we think and live on multiple levels. Transformative engagement requires deep attention, including penetrating analysis, critical thinking, and imaginative reflection. The process is co-creative as teachers and learners discover new knowledge and make choices as a result. Because of the engaged nature of transformative learning and teaching, ethical analyses are crucial. We must continually ask ourselves if our work is connecting ideas with what matters philosophically, spiritually, and pragmatically.

Ideally, learners and teachers engage in synthetic work, making connections among classroom learnings, particular disciplines, and contemporary situations and needs or questions. Such learning and teaching, alone and with others, assumes interdependency among all involved. he movements of ideas, strategies, and actions cycling with individual perspectives, communal realities, and concrete desires for change are all interwoven. Students and teachers must be conscious of this interdependency, acknowledging different learning styles, different cultural contexts, and the ways in which processes of discovery are and are not mutually useful. Communities beyond the campus also may be part of this learning synthesis, contributing their own perspectives, questions, and knowledge.

All these contributions intersect, conflict, and combine, creating evolving patterns of communication, convergence, debate, collaboration, and at times, rejection. The results are multiple and dynamic, reflecting contexts, assumptions, interests, and needs. This diversity is valued, though its complexity can be stressful. But it awakens our own passions for learning in the midst of others' passions and also teaches us discernment, humility, and imaginative openness.

To follow such a path of discovery, imagination, and co-creation is risky. That is the nature of transformative teaching and learning. Encouraging teachers and learners to be innovative means a certain loss of control amid known and claimed boundaries. It requires a deep attentiveness to the heart of ideas and their consequences. It calls for a certain kind of vulnerability among learners in order that thinking and doing may occur in flexible and imaginative ways. Teachers are vulnerable as well as they try to express ideas they know and feel passionate about while meaningfully connecting with the needs and passions of their students. The teacher is responsible for setting limits to this vulnerability and risk and must do so with keen discernment. Agreed-upon boundaries, goals, objectives, and in some cases, learning contracts provide substantive grounding for shared discovery.

Risk along the path of transformative discovery also requires compassion, shared deep attention to the process of how knowledge and method also become meaning and purpose. Compassion in teaching and learning opens self and community to think deeply about questions, issues, and pragmatic responses at hand. It encourages serious reflection and discernment of best practices for attaining shared goals, visions of knowledge, usable understandings, and participatory change. Compassionate teaching and learning opens space for new possibilities of intellectual understanding and reflection to emerge because it is comfortable in the waiting and hoping of thinking and doing.

Teaching Methods
My teaching methods revolve around three themes: 1) participatory learning, 2) reflective judgment, and 3) learning as process/evolving.

Participatory Learning
In addition to emphasizing structured discussions and structured small-group work, I design assignments that provide creative room for a student's

own intellectual and pragmatic imagination to be expressed in relation to the theories and methods of the class. Frequently, final projects for my classes are done in the form of creative constructions through narrative, art, or film (Religion 190) and/or social action project plans (Religion 329 or Religion 370) (see Appendix B). In Religion 380, students interconnect classroom theory with their internship performance by structuring their learning plan and goals through a learning contract negotiated with their supervisor and the teacher (see Appendix C).

The subject matter that I teach in religious studies is often in the news and in the lives of everyday people. It is a usual occurrence for me and/or students to bring to class articles from newspapers and popular magazines that relate to specific material we are studying. Soon, students bring their own artifacts of relevant contemporary religious life, including music, images, foods, etc. These materials are usually shared over our in-house server, Learn-link. Students review and respond to each other's contributions before class and after class integrate or challenge online my contributions to the discussion. A student in Religion 370 (spring 2002) wrote, "This class may have had the most student-teacher and student-student interaction of any of my courses in four years at Emory. That increased my understanding."

One specific participatory strategy I have developed is called Analysis, Practice, Reflection (APR). There are three members of an APR team. Each member addresses one letter of the format in relation to a class reading. The analysis report is put online first, with practical and reflective responses being offered the following day. All class members read these reports, enabling a more substantive conversation involving the whole class when the APR team presents. A student from the Freshman Seminar course (Religion 190, fall 2002) wrote, "The learning format of analysis, practice and reflection really helped me develop my personal learning skills" (see Appendix D).

Reflective Judgment
Reflective judgment helps students explore the processes of their learning. Students are encouraged to critically examine assumptions they bring to learning, their styles of intellectual discovery, ways of sharing information and applying it, and ethical uses of knowledge. In the classroom, we pay particular attention to how they identify and assess intellectual problems in order to then examine how they might use their knowledge to solve pragmatic problems. This helps students see the complexity of issues and the difficulties of connecting theory in real-world practice. As their reflective consciousness grows, students more explicitly recognize the effect of context and standpoint on ideas and actions. One student in Religion 190 wrote, "I have

opened my mind and self to a more dynamic perspective . . . to be mindful of individual's context and experiences." This self-reflective work is best pursued in a portfolio format that I use most extensively in the internship class and in classes addressing religion and ecology (see Appendix E).

Emphasizing the Process of Learning

As mentioned above, the Analysis, Practice, Reflection method and the portfolio method of teaching and learning awaken students to the importance and power of their own processes of learning. Many of my students are relentlessly goal oriented, and in the midst of that drive not only the context of a course is lost, but also the process of learning. The goal of "finishing" becomes predominant. Through self-conscious reflection and debate, students retrain their focus and often become more energized about the subject matter of the class. Activities such as rewriting a portfolio entry or debating an analysis of an article in a public forum remind students that their ideas and voices not only count but also have consequences. This is especially successful in the Wilderness Spirituality and Philosophy class, since several of the students come with no wilderness experience. Writing pre-reflection pieces in which they imagine what it would be like to camp out for several days, what experiences and feelings they would have, connections with ideas presented in class, and then returning to those entries after the experience is very beneficial. By returning to an earlier short analysis of a reading from environmental philosophy and then responding to that text again after having more wilderness experiences, students see the changes in their understandings and knowledge.

Teaching and Learning Through Immersion Experiences

I have taught several classes in which the classroom was off campus. Sometimes our learning sessions consist of a two-hour site visit. On other occasions, we work for an afternoon with a community-based organization whose staff members had previously come to our classroom teaching us about the systemic sociopolitical issues effecting their organization. Other times, such as in the Wilderness Spirituality class, we hike and camp for three days in a local wilderness engaging spiritual practices we have studied in class. A student in that class two years ago wrote,

> *Spending significant time together as a class in another setting provided a new structure to my/our learning that brought increased openness in sharing ideas and understandings. For me, these led to a much more integrated understanding of our texts, myself, and our relation/responsibilities to the world.*

Improving Teaching
Student Feedback

Through office hours and Learnlink, I hear specifically what students are most interested in, have questions about, or need. Learnlink is particularly important for the students who do not normally speak in class. This information helps me restructure elements of my courses even while in progress. In a student assessment of our fall 2002 internship class, a student wrote, "I was pleasantly surprised and truly encouraged when the class meeting following our mid-point evaluation exercises resulted in actual changes in the class."

I use two types of midpoint evaluations in my classes. In the immersion classes and in the Internship in Religion class, I use the Midpoint Evaluation: Peer and Self- Assessment. This format asks students to respond to a few basic questions about their peers' involvement in and preparation for the class. Individuals are asked to focus on other individuals and the emphasis is on appreciation and appropriate suggestions for change. Everyone is asked to make suggestions about how the course can be more effective. This last area is the core of the midpoint evaluations taken in all my other classes. That evaluation format focuses on three questions: 1) What are we doing that is helping your learning? 2) What are we doing that is hindering your learning? 3) What can we (you, your classmates, and the teacher) do differently to improve your learning? These tools give me specific feedback on how the course and my teaching needs to be adjusted in content and process (see Appendix F).

In-class writing has been another effective form of feedback. Sometimes I begin class by asking students to write for five minutes in response to the readings of the day. I then use their responses to structure the class discussion/teaching. Often, I will ask students at the end of a class to write (anonymously, if they choose) questions resulting from that day's class. These are handed in to me and I use them to organize a short review or clarification to begin our next class. Periodically in the middle of class, I ask students to take three to five minutes and write a summary of what has been happening up to that point in class. This feedback gives me insight into attention spans, the sequencing of material, etc.

Finally, I have chosen below several categories from the instructor evaluation forms that reflect my fundamental teaching philosophy and long-term strategies: participatory learning and the organization of materials and techniques that clarify the dynamics of theory and practice. This data indicates how seriously I have taken feedback, made revisions, and experienced the positive results.

Scale: 1–9

	Religion 380, Fall 2001	Religion 380, Fall 2002
Course organization	8.23	8.75
Value of Assignments	8.09	8.75
	Religion 300, Fall 1998	Religion 300, Fall 2000
Organized individual classes	8.24	8.29
Course organization	8.12	8.48
Organization of readings	7.54	8.29

My complete instructor evaluation reports are in Appendix G.

Peer Educators

After my first year of teaching Religion 329, I met with a representative group of students from the class. They suggested the introduction of peer educators (my term), current upper-class students who have already success-fully completed the course and therefore could help current students adjust to the Theory Practice Learning approach in an immersion context, wilder-ness camping and hiking. Peer educators met with small groups of students to discuss readings and assignments and to organize our outdoor sessions. They were invaluable teachers helping students make holistic connections with the various elements of the class. They also modeled student empower-ment, organizing students to design and implement time in wilderness according to their learning needs and goals. Finally, in our weekly meetings I receive in-course from the peer educators direct and honest feedback about the effectiveness of course materials and approaches. Some of the peer edu-cators have used this responsibility as a way to test their vocation as teachers.

The Scholarship of Teaching

I have embraced Ernest Boyer's phrase, "the scholarship of teaching" as an important part of my vocation. In addition to directing Emory's program for faculty training in experience-based pedagogies, I write about my learn-ings as a teacher.

Papers and Articles

My first paper on Theory Practice Learning was given at Marquette Univer-sity in spring 1995 as part of the national conference "Instilling Democratic Values Through Community Service." I have attended the National Society of Experiential Education meetings for many years and have often been a presenter. I have produced ten published articles on pedagogy (see Appendix H). More recently, I have presented papers on participatory and experience-based learning at the American Academy of Religion meetings and at a conference sponsored by the Carnegie Foundation entitled, "Moral and Civic Responsibility in Higher Education."

Teaching Honors/Special Recognition

Since 1999, I have received four teaching honors and recognitions. In 2001, I received the Humanities Teacher of the Year from the Emory Center for Teaching and Curriculum. My most recent award, spring 2003, is the Emory College Omicron Delta Kappa Chapter's Faculty Member in Service Award. At Emory, I serve on three committees that review teaching-related grants across the university. I also teach the required pedagogy course for the graduate students of the Graduate Division of Religion of Emory University. I often have to turn away graduate students who want to be a teaching assistant with me. As one graduate student wrote,

> *I sought the opportunity to teach with her knowing of her original reflections on college teaching and her reputation as a master teacher who is able to integrate rigorous intellectual work with practice. After the experience, I am able to report that Bobbi's reputation still does not do justice to the ways in which she enables her students to learn and grow.*

Appendices

Appendix A: Course Syllabi
Appendix B: Sample Assignments
Appendix C: Learning Contract for Internship
Appendix D: APR Instructions
Appendix E: Portfolio Instructions
Appendix F: Midpoint Evaluation
Appendix G: Course Evaluation Reports
Appendix H: Published Bibliography in Pedagogy

36

TEACHING PORTFOLIO
Arthur B. Shostak
Department of Psychology, Sociology, and Anthropology
Drexel University
Winter 2003

Table of Contents

Prologue: On Reading *Izvestia*

While I was fortunate enough to have fine K–12 teachers in my Queens, New York, public schools, it was not until I got to high school that I began to dimly realize and value this.

A teacher of literature who loved the writer Edith Wharton helped a class of mine understand why, and thereby taught me indirectly how wonderful it seemed to have such a love. A teacher of Spanish and another of Hebrew modeled the pleasures one could take in endlessly building a vocabulary where there had been none. A teacher of the science only dummies took, Earth Science, proved how foolish was such a label if the instructor valued the subject.

In retrospect, all of this seems to have readied me for the single biggest impact a teacher ever had on my life, a transformational experience that still causes pause whenever I revisit it.

In the early fall of 1954, on the very first day of my college life, in my very first class, I sat nervous and uncertain with 70 other freshmen in a leaky Quonset hut, the heavy rain outside a welcome distraction from our shared misgivings. The appointed hour came and went, but without a professor at the podium.

Three or more minutes later, the door in front swung open and a middle-aged man strode through absorbed in something he was reading. Without looking he stepped up onto the platform, leaned over the podium, and ... to our great puzzlement ... continued to read. Looking up finally from the publication in his hand, the professor, noticing us for the first time, asked in a loud and commanding tone, "Have you seen what they have to say in this week's airmail edition of *Izvestia?*" He was dead serious, I quickly realized, and I was astonished!

Izvestia, I thought, what in hell is that? And who in hell gets an airmail edition of it? Or of any other publication, for that matter? Certainly nobody I knew, either back home in Brooklyn, or even here on campus. *Izvestia?* Wow! This guy is something else! And he thinks it reasonable to ask us about some Russian newspaper in an English-language translation. Wow!

That unreal, unreasonable, and unexpected question—that utterly unrealistic expectation—changed my entire life. I resolved on the spot (or so I now flatter myself in thinking) to meet that challenge, to learn what in hell *Izvestia* was, and maybe even read the damn thing. I was not going to be dumbfounded by such experiences soon again if I could help it, and I was going to learn the sorts of exciting things this chap seemed to know.

Over the semesters ahead I enjoyed learning with several other Master teachers: Milton Konvitz was drafting a Constitution for a new African nation, and patiently explained to us the rationale behind his proposed Bill of Rights. Alice Cook was helping labor unions recover their lost history and learn how to preserve and honor it. A third, Madame Francis Perkins, earlier a Secretary of Labor under President Franklin D. Roosevelt, shared instructive behind-the-scenes anecdotes. Arthur Mizener, a leading biographer of F. Scott Fitzgerald, mesmerized with his interpretations of literature. Albert Salomon helped me see things in art I had never imagined I might. Others did their part, but there are too many to cite.

While I owe much to this gallery of great teachers, it was one early on, M. Gardner Clark, professor of economic history and a specialist in the Russian iron and steel industry, who first helped this learner "cross a line in the desert," a line I've tried ever since to help others cross.

With this portfolio, I'd like to say, many, many thanks!

Teaching Responsibilities, Philosophy, and Strategies

Since arriving at Drexel University in 1967 I have introduced two courses I have handed off (Race and Ethnic Relations; Urban Sociology), given a third to another department (Social Implications of 20th Century Technology), been "retired" by another college from a fourth (Management and Technology), and become a once-a-year guest teacher in the Honors Program, where I offer a course in autobiographical sociology (reliant on my edited 1996 collection, *Private Sociology: Unsparing Reflections, Uncommon Gains*).

As for my current teaching schedule, six times a year I teach a ten-week undergraduate course in some aspect of sociology. More specifically, and by my choice, I teach an elective, Industrial Sociology, twice a year, a required course, Introduction to Sociology, twice a year, and two electives, Social Change and Futuristics, once a year. With 20 to 30 students from a wide range of majors in each class, few of whom have had any sociology as high school students, I have my work cut out for me.

Having now enjoyed 42 years of annually relearning sociology with over 10,000 young adults, I have come to believe I have six major responsibilities as a teacher.

1) I must model what a well-intentioned educated adult can resemble—I must model the civic involvement, creativity, curiosity, ethical concerns, hope for the future, mutual respect, and open-mindedness that belong in front of impressionable young adults.

2) I must quickly capture and hold the attention of those learning the subject along with me. I must link my material to the authentic and pressing interests of the class members, demonstrating sociology's relevance to their lives, now and hereafter. Only if they rapidly and avidly share my excitement with the subject will we both learn as much as we hope from the course.

3) I must represent the subject as best I can, as it is the life's work of many honorable and well-intentioned people throughout modern history and around the world. While frank about its many shortcomings, I owe it to the discipline to emphasize its significant contributions and enormous potential (and possibly thereby help win it some good recruits).

4) I must struggle to make the subject's complexities clearer, its conundrums a bit more acceptable, and its major theoretical controversies worthy of respect. I must not dumb down the subject or patronize class members, lest they leave with more mis-education than learning.

5) I must employ the latest pedagogical aids, especially those linked to the unfolding Information Age. Young adults are owed a demonstration of the utility of cutting-edge educational tools, such as email and the web, the better to encourage their own willingness to try such advances in their own turn.

6) I must stay loose and allow the unexpected its due. The natural rhythm of an unfolding class session warrants careful nurturing, even when it requires a (temporary) suspension of the scheduled lesson. It is far better to draw out listeners, to engage with them in an unexpected dialogue, than to continue their passive listening.

Philosophy

All of this draws naturally on my philosophy of teaching, which I can sum up using three terms: support, challenge, and respect.

By support, I mean operating from the premise that young adults especially need reinforcement of their fledgling sense of self-worth and potential. Many have doubts about their abilities and worry about whether they can measure up. Drexel students, in particular, forced as they are to choose a major on entering, often flounder when they discover the choice was premature. Accordingly, my philosophy emphasizes helping young adults learn to think better of themselves through doing well in learning situations I deliberately make trying, but manageable.

Challenge is a related philosophical concern. I do not believe in coddling or condescending, albeit the very poor intellectual preparation of many Drexel students makes this very easy to slip into. Instead, I pepper every class with questions about current events or the font of world knowledge I believe reasonable to expect of a college degree-seeker. I boast that I read three newspapers a day, and I indicate I expect enrollees to craft some comparable method themselves of staying abreast of changing events.

Lest I appear far too demanding, I hasten to add that over 40 years of coexisting much of my waking hours with young adults has long ago taught me how much respect they are owed. Their lives today appear far more complex, uncertain, and problematic of success and fulfillment than in many previous decades.

Accordingly, I emphasize in my teaching success stories of members of whatever generation I am teaching, along with success stories of former students of mine, the better to underline my respect for all with whom I share my classroom . . . and my fond hope for their future.

Teaching Strategies

As for strategies beyond what I have already explained, I have seven.

1) I rely on overheads that I have designed to facilitate note taking. Young adults seem to appreciate crisp and memorable phrases, lists of useful ideas, and other aids to remembering something useful from the class. (Occasional use of humorous overheads helps as well.)

2) I rely on videotapes of ten or fewer minutes and also short excerpts from major feature films, the better to heighten interest and demonstrate the high quality of learning possible from the processing of mass media. Scenes from the trial in *A Few Good Men,* the "Greed" speech in *Wall Street,* and the debate scene in *Other People's Money* are especially helpful in making major points in a sociology course.

3) I rely on managed classroom ecology to bolster the learning ambience of the setting. That is, I get to the room before the class begins and rearrange all the seats. I draw them forward into a semi-circle and render inaccessible those in the rear otherwise used by "retreatists" in the group. I try in this way to promote closeness, cordiality, and collegiality. (If necessary, I will also gather up trash and get a wet towel and clean the floor, lest we occupy a setting that insults us.)

4) I rely on short, one-page, open-book quizzes assigned every week that require careful reading of the assigned text material. The quizzes (which I write) include ten true-false questions and two short essay-like questions. They are done at home, independent of others in the course, and have been designed to "stroke" conscientious readers. (Course evaluations long ago established that these quizzes are VERY popular, as they provide the weekly confirmation of learning that many students crave.)

5) I rely on a small number of especially good students to help liven the proceedings. I get to know their names as soon as possible and call on them often for their views, relevant experiences, and especially their puzzlement or disagreement with something I have said or they have read in the course material. I am genuinely thrilled when on occasion a student will provide a transformational moment, an event which, while rare, does happily grace nearly every course at least once a term.

6) I rely on email to help me start the course weeks before it is scheduled to meet. Just as soon as I have the email addresses of enrollees I create a listserv and send out a welcoming note. I include the syllabus and signal early on in this way my 24-hour, seven-day availability to dialogue via email with any and all.

7) I rely on at least one of my own 24 books to help convey the impression that Drexel has faculty who do publish, faculty who do original research and take a stand, and faculty who have pride of authorship. Naturally, I focus on items of special timeliness and relevance.

Students as Co-Learners

Coursing through all of the foregoing is my desire as a teacher to view course enrollees as co-learners, rather than as students. I have come to regard the latter term as demeaning, a concept that implies and invites passivity (tip your head and learning will be poured into your ear).

I much prefer the far more robust notion of co-learner, one who fully shares in the responsibility for crafting a rich learning experience, one who gives as much as he or she takes.

Very difficult to achieve, this status is beyond the grasp of most of the Drexel students I have known, but that does not diminish its value as a goal toward which they can aspire—and one that I hold out as right and proper in my teaching of them.

Accordingly, I applaud every voice that suggests in class a movie, TV show, book, or event from which we might learn much of value. I salute every co-learner who adds something out loud to a class, and I commonly reserve an A grade for them. I explain and emphasize this bias of mine in the opening few classes, and reinforce it with my grading scheme, which I go over on the first day and include in the syllabus.

Syllabi, Assignments, and Exams

My syllabi are cogent, friendly, clear, and encouraging. I keep them short to heighten readability. I keep them friendly to reduce anxiety. I keep them clear to head off confusion. And I keep them encouraging to bolster confidence in one's ability to do a fine job in the course.

Assignments are frequent and "heavy," believing as I do that a lot of good work is far better than little poor work. Co-learners have homework every weekend (the true-false reading quizzes I prepare for each chapter). They are also required to complete a field research team project, an essay-style midterm (take home), two in-class 20-item true-false tests, and an essay linking a film to course texts.

I send many items to co-learners throughout the term (and send to those who ask to be kept on a recipient list long after the course is over). As I am on several active listservs related to the courses I teach, I always have new essays and letters to share with class members, and I encourage them to send me Internet material to circulate that they believe the class would profit from. Especially good student course work is circulated this way (with permission) as I want all to learn from it.

A take-home essay-style final exam is required for those with a grade going into it of C or less. It is optional for B students seeking to raise their grade, and it cannot be taken by those who have already earned an A.

My exams are fresh with every class, as I tweak them to accent aspects of the material I want to emphasize at a particular time. When I use essay questions I always include one which reads, "Write and answer a comparable question of your own—after first clearing it via email with me." While few students take advantage of the option, those who do commonly star.

Until the death in 2003 of my 93-year-old mother, I used to mail her in Florida my true-false quizzes as she enjoyed grading them. This odd practice pleased co-learners especially concerned with the question of what can very old people do that warrants their respect. Many commented favorably, and added cute and endearing notes to the "Thank You" cards I circulated at the term's end.

Teaching Honors
Over the years I have earned several awards for teaching, including the top award possible at Drexel, the Lindbach Award for Outstanding Teaching.

The Lindbach awardee is chosen by a small committee of previous winners who get nominations from department chairs. The award consists of $500, the inscription of one's name on a bronze plaque in the Faculty Club, participation in a ceremony during the annual retirement dinner, and the presence for the school year of a large picture of one's self in the Office of the Provost. (The absence of students from the selection committee has always struck me as a revealing form of hypocrisy.)

I was also chosen for several years in the 1970s to speak at the Danforth Foundation Conferences on Innovation in Higher Education. My topic was "Creativity in Teaching: Having a Good [Teaching] Time," and I enjoyed the notion that I was regarded as a "teacher's teacher."

Teaching Improvement
Eager to try ever better approaches and methods, I subscribe to *Teaching Sociology,* a very fine journal published by the American Sociological Association (ASA).

I also sit in on sessions focused on "teaching via computer uses" when available at the annual meeting of the ASA, or the regional meeting of the Eastern Sociological Society. In 1972, I served as president of the Pennsylvania Sociological Society, and I put special emphasis on the teaching of teaching at the annual meeting.

Lately I have gotten very interested in distance learning (DL), and I recently spoke at and spent two days at a regional conference devoted to DL issues. I learned that DL has its own unique teaching challenges, and I was pleased to be in the company of scores of deeply concerned faculty members.

As I am now only a year or two from retirement I am far more likely to tinker with, rather than overhaul, my teaching, though my interest in DL may yet have me try some radical innovation in that area.

I have saved the best here for the last: Teaching improvement for me has always been rooted especially in end-of-course evaluations. I have designed my own form, and I have improved it over the years. I ask co-learners to assess each and every aspect of the course, paying special attention to any and all ideas they can share for improving it.

Co-learners have urged me to require fewer books, and I have therefore dropped back from five to three texts. They have urged more outside guests, and I have tried to get at least three in over ten weeks (20 class meetings, each of an hour and a half). They have recommended more classroom discussion of the reading material, and I have tried—with uneven success—to accommodate this sound idea. Over and again, they have called attention to some weak or even strong aspect of the course I might not have noticed as such save for their help.

Future Teaching Goals

I would like an opportunity over the next two or so years to contribute to workshops for new teachers. I could emphasize small, but vital matters, like rearranging the chairs in a more relaxed pattern before the class arrives. Using different color chalk to set off different points. Creating catchy and new overheads. Never canceling a class (always have a substitute teacher ready to step in, or a film lodged with staffers that can be suddenly drawn on), and so on.

I would also like to try writing some essays along the lines above, possibly for *Teaching Sociology* or other such journals. Finally, I would welcome occasional invitations to return as a guest teacher after I retire, the better to keep my hand in, and have a fine time while at it.

Public Speaking as Teaching

One of the unexpected rewards from taking teaching seriously has been my second career of sorts, or my role as a professional speaker. Over the past 20 years I have steadily developed a business that nowadays brings me 20 or more commissioned talks a year in the United States or Canada. I speak for church groups as small as 50 and for convention center audiences as large as 7,500.

I regard these talks as *teaching* engagements, rather than as speeches. By this I mean that I never give the same talk twice, as one might a speech that has found favor with audiences. Instead, I ask each client to prepare five or so prioritized questions that I use to shape my custom-tailored remarks. I prepare new overheads for each talk; choose new, short VCR films; and insist on as long a question and answer period as possible.

To help further distinguish my classroom-like talks from formal speeches, I provide the client with a set of my overheads beforehand and urge that they be reproduced and given to all audience members at the outset. I often proceed to "walk" listeners through the overheads, taking care never to read them aloud (a most insulting practice). Above all, in choosing what to emphasize and what to leave out, I try to honor a rule I attribute to the movie character Gordon Gekko in the film "Wall Street": "Tell me something I don't already know."

I am now doing quite a bit of repeat business. I also get invitations from high-powered speaker firms to join their stable of high-priced speakers (which I decline), and, as my evaluations are generally pleasing, on good days I amuse myself by thinking I may have become a "speaker's speaker."

Lessons Learned

Reflecting back on my career as a teacher I am inclined to think there are four positive things I wish I had known when I started out—and that I wish newcomers could somehow be made aware of:

1) Unless I am enjoying myself in class, few others will.
2) Unless I find the material interesting, few others will.
3) Unless I believe the material has off-campus relevance and payoff, few others will.
4) Unless co-learners "buy in," much less than is possible will have occurred.

Were I invited to talk about this to novice teachers, I would emphasize these four upbeat ideas, and yet also note a few more points of a somewhat darker variety.

For example, I would warn against overestimating the intellectual background of young adults, as the education they bring with them nowadays is very spotty, uneven, and incomplete. We must take nothing for granted, as in thinking they are familiar with matters we take for granted, for example, the many "deep" meanings of the Vietnam War or of the Holocaust. These vital topics must be taught afresh and made meaningful to many who regard it all with naïve curiosity, at best.

Second, I would warn not to think that class members are the youngsters we were. Their generation has touchstones, jargon, and a culture all of its own. We must endlessly study their world to better make sense of ourselves in it. Our academic subjects must be "translated," so as to make them comprehensible to "natives" from another "country."

Third, I would warn against thinking the life stage concerns of the middle-aged or older teacher are the same or similar to the concerns of a young adult. While we may be wrestling with a midlife crisis, a first or second divorce, or the ailing decline of an elderly parent, young adults are often far from such concerns. Accordingly, our choice of personal anecdotes and course material should be sensitive to this natural differentiation.

Fourth, I would warn against carrying into the classroom any gossip or other mutterings about faculty-administration tensions, however commonplace or exasperating they may seem. Similarly, I would ban any and all criticism of colleagues, open or veiled, as it is unfair, underhanded, and very poor modeling.

Constructive criticisms of campus matters, however, are quite legitimate, especially when used to encourage co-learners to brainstorm pragmatic reforms—and possibly go off thereafter to champion them. I draw for instructive anecdotes here on my long continuous service on faculty senate, my two years as faculty adviser to student government, and my recent two years as head of the Faculty Senate Committee on Student Life.

Finally, I would warn against dwelling on the dark side of life, on its disappointments, frustrations, and disillusionment. Young adults should make any such sobering (and enervating) discoveries for themselves, and they are owed breathing space as collegians to entertain (however briefly) grand hopes, naïve dreams, and empowering illusions.

In this connection, I think it helpful to share some autobiographical notes that underline whatever success one has had in fashioning a good life from origins similar to those of many class members. Taking care to stay "real" and relevant, a teacher can in this way help indirectly validate the private, high aspirations of ambitious co-learners. More specifically, I tell often of learning adventures I have had while traveling overseas. I talk about celebrities I have met. And I reflect on lifestyle pleasures that can intrigue those just starting out.

All five faults above are relatively easy to write about because they are so familiar: I have committed each more often than I am comfortable recalling. And that helps explain why I would like to think newcomers might be warned early on how seductive are these practices, and also how costly, corrosive, and regrettable.

Epilogue: Looking for *Izvestia*

After I have left the scene, if I am ever recalled, I would hope the memories would be of one whose courses were worth their tuition cost; who kept co-learners awake; who shared laughter and caring; who taught some pretty nifty things; who dwelled far more on the positive than on the negative; and, above all, who inspired quite a few to love learning, and to try to apply it artfully for the good of us all.

Should someone even think to ask if is still possible to get and read an airmail edition of *Izvestia,* all the better.

Appendices
Appendix A: Syllabi
Appendix B: Term Paper Guides
Appendix C: Course Evaluation Forms
Appendix D: Email Samples
Appendix E: Articles
Appendix F: Book Ads
Appendix G: Email From Former Students

37

TEACHING PORTFOLIO
Margaret Mitchell
Costume and Scenic Designer
Department of Theatre Arts
University of the Incarnate Word

Table of Contents

Statement of Teaching Responsibilities

My primary teaching responsibility is maintaining the integrity of the costume curriculum. However, I also teach Introduction to Theatre, and occasionally I teach Scenic Design and Play Analysis, as well as direct in the academic season. In addition to course work, I administer the U.I.W. (University of the Incarnate Word) Costume Shop, which has a student staff. Mentoring student designers when they are assisting in production or when they are designing on the main stage at U.I.W. is also part of the job. Most of the students who are interested in design and technology are my advisees. The Department of Theatre Arts faculty also assesses each theatre arts major in the sophomore and senior years.

Designing scenery or costumes also falls in the category of teaching, as I work daily with the students in the Costume Shop and in the scene shop to produce a show. We produce four main stage shows in an academic year. My contact hours with the students are high during production.

Our B.A. program is intensive and demanding. Our courses are tied to one another in learning communities, in team teaching efforts, and in the marriage of course work and theatrical production. Our curriculum and season selection also link to the core liberal arts curriculum. The theatre arts faculty members take roles of shared responsibility in assessing, revising, creating, and editing curricular choices each year. We collaborate with one another when revising/creating syllabi, and we attempt to balance the overall course work in a given semester in order to support one another's teaching. The following undergraduate courses are the common courses I now teach on a rotating cycle:

- TA 1360 **Introduction to Theatre,** a team taught course for majors and nonmajors that serves as a foundation introductory course to historical genres, theory, performance practices, and play analysis. Required for majors. Average class size is 30.

- TA 2361 **Introduction to Theatre Design,** a foundation course introducing the student to scenic, costume, and lighting design. This is a learning community course with Introduction to Technical Production. Average class size is 15.

- TA 4341 **Costume Design,** an advanced level course that prepares the student to design costumes on the main stage at U.I.W. The course is structured around projects that include all aspects of preproduction work and the creative design process. Average class size is ten.

- TA 4342 **Costume History,** a survey of western costume from ancient Egypt to the present day. This course focuses on the social and economic aspects of clothing expression through slide lectures, discussions, and research projects. The course is required for Fashion Design majors, and it is an elective for theatre arts majors. Average class size is 20.

- TA 3342 **Costume Construction** is the study and application of flat patterning and draping techniques for the stage. This course includes costume crafts, hand sewing techniques, machine stitching, and cutting for the stage. Average class size is ten.

- TA 1191–4192 **Theatre Arts Practicum** is a required course for theatre majors. Students work in the Costume Shop to prepare the productions in the season. Skills include stitching, finishing, cutting and draping techniques, pattern engineering, wardrobe maintenance, dressing, and costume crafts. Average class size for the costume section is six.

Other Teaching Responsibilities:

- Supervision of Costume Shop college work study staff. The U.I.W. Costume Shop has a staff of six to eight students who are interested in job training. These students become the advanced or "senior" construction staff. Their work assignments are in alignment with their ongoing learning, and they also mentor younger practicum students on projects. The U.I.W. Costume Shop is the site of a Learning Community. While technical skills are taught, students learn to live and work and care for one another in a collaborative and creative setting.

- Mentoring student designers. The students who design in the U.I.W. academic season must have a faculty mentor who guides them through the production process. Duties include organizing production schedules, labor distribution, guiding critical thinking, attending production meetings, guiding the student through the collaborative process, and assessing the work. I mentor two to five student designers each year.

- Designing costumes/scenery. When designing for the U.I.W. productions, I attempt to model the positive behaviors and high standards that the students will encounter in the professional world. I mentor an assistant for almost every production. I design three or four times a year.

Teaching Philosophy and Objectives

I believe my role as a teacher is to provide resources and skills so that the student is able to achieve competency in the given subject matter. I also believe I must create an environment where various lines of inquiry may be explored, where risks may be taken, and where the presented material may be challenged and dissected. While I have an outcome/proficiency agenda in the mastery of the material, I also recognize that certain classes have their own chemical learning paths and dynamics. I must divine those paths of change and assess the relationships of pedagogy, content, and the needs of the students. My major objectives are:

- To create an environment where we are all learning together

- To challenge the students beyond their perceived limitations

- To hear and acknowledge all voices

- To support success, confront failures, and learn from both

- To incite the students to take the course material into discussions/work beyond the classroom and to encourage them to connect their theatre course work with other course work

- To connect formal education to everyday life

- To recognize the roles and social responsibilities of artists in our culture

Major influences on my teaching are based in Maori and Native American learning styles. I received training from The Learning Way Education Program based in the Iroquois Oneida tradition, disseminated by Paula Underwood, and adopted by educators in Texas, New Mexico, California, and Japan. In the Oneida tradition and in the Maori culture all learning is a community responsibility.

Description of Methods Used in Courses, Mentoring, and Supervising the Costume Shop

Many of our students are first generation college students, and they often come to us with little family support and with an expectation of failure. U.I.W. services this market, as the institution attempts to educate people who might not be raised with the expectation of participating in higher learning. We believe in educating the whole person. Competencies in training and curriculum thrive best in a person with a clear understanding of his or her identity, belief systems, and values. The mission of U.I.W. also focuses on social justice issues. We wish to graduate students who have an awareness of social responsibility and who are considerate and sensitive collaborators. Through mentoring and modeling behavior, we have a responsibility to give the students this kind of support so that their education will be used to enhance and to improve the theatre profession.

The Course Work

Lecture courses (Costume History, Introduction to Theatre) are organized around themes for discussion. The Costume History course is a slide lecture/discussion course. Students are assessed with papers, research projects, and exams. Discovering why the students are in the class and what they wish to explore are the first steps. Once the basic context of student experience is learned, one can select and develop strategies for engaging them in the material. The group dynamic plays a key role in strategizing engagement. I expose polar points of view in the classes to spur debate, while I reinforce themes and connections in the content. Although I have expertise, it is important to stress to the students that we are all learning together, as each class and further research give rise to new questioning. Good results seem to come when the teacher models learning.

Artistic courses require at least two levels of awareness in teaching. Technical skills and formal aspects of art are easily taught to anyone. As if coaching a sport, I coach them through problems with their drawing and critical thinking. But in any act of creation, the creator is confronted with the self, and this confrontation can be exciting or frightening. Guiding the internal work of the student is the more difficult level of teaching. Typically, the students are confronted with their own problems and perceptions as possible future artists in our culture. I take the students through exercises and writing assignments which allow me to observe their own nurturing and damaging artistic behaviors. I expose and offer solutions to correct the negative behaviors. I also recognize and support the positive behaviors. By the end of the Introduction to Design course, all students should have basic design skills and a basic understanding of the manipulation of visual language. The students should be able to identify whether or not they can work as an artist. They should be able to identify *why* they want to be an artist.

Guiding a student to make artistic choices requires the professor to learn about the students' belief systems, discipline (or lack thereof), critical thinking skills, and communication skills. Students must think about the message of their work in the context of their audience. In keeping with the mission of U.I.W., I confront them with their social responsibilities. They should know why they are making artistic choices, and they must know the audience will assign meaning to those choices. They should understand image-making as a language. They must interpret text, and they must know why they are designing the way they are designing. The intermediate and advanced students have course work organized around projects, both actualized and in paper. These artistic projects have specific criteria in the grading components, self-assessment, and both oral and written defenses.

The Costume Shop as a Learning Community

Technical classes/work study activities are focused on competencies in skills and job training. As much as budget and time will allow, I maintain professional standards in teaching technical skills and in teaching professional behavior. The students making the costumes and preparing the wardrobe experience ongoing tutorials which constantly raise the bar of their proficiency and knowledge. The hierarchical model of our shop mirrors the professional model. In addition to teaching technical standards of excellence, I believe it is my job to instill in my students a demand for safe working conditions and humane treatment; professional costume shops are not always operating in acceptable conditions. Students learn safe practices, and I employ strategies from our wellness curriculum to combat stress.

While jobs in costume shops are defined through a hierarchical structure, I use "circular" approaches based in the Maori and Oneida traditions to manage the shop. Consensual decision-making is used whenever possible.

The students have an awareness of their creative process issues. Collectively they have a shared responsibility and ownership of their work.

The Costume Shop provides yet another space for learning through discussion. As students are working and learning about costume construction, I often ask questions about their core curriculum or theatre course work to extend debate and leaning beyond the walls of the traditional classroom.

Description of Curricular Revisions and Steps Taken to Improve Teaching

I revise syllabi every time I teach. Revisions are large or small, depending upon input and student needs. Methods of input are peer and supervisor evaluations, student evaluations, new research, attendance at workshops, seminars, symposia at national or international conferences, and my own notes to myself as we go through a course. The theatre arts faculty is also focused on integrated curriculum, and this agenda has changed courses structurally.

Specific Examples

Introduction to Theatre Design has retained journal assignments and drawing exercises, but over the years, I have become more efficient in diagnosing problems and the assignments have become more streamlined (see Appendix A). Projects are now tied to the main stage season, so that the rehearsal and performance process can be used as laboratory for discussion and debate. Furthermore, this course is now being taught with a linked curriculum to the Introduction to Technical Production course. The integration of these courses was suggested by the department chair.

The general structure of the lectures and discussions in the Costume History course have changed very little, but the content has improved (see Appendix B). I have added almost 300 additional slide images to the course and a summer of costume research in London in 1997 has given me expertise I could not have obtained in a traditional classroom. I studied in the Victoria and Albert Museum, the London Museum, The Petri Museum of Egyptology, and in the Costume Museum in Bath. The new information I gathered about clothing construction led to a large revision of the Costume History course. For the past two years, students have been allowed to conduct research for class projects in the Witte Museum Textile and Dress Collection in collaboration with the curator.

Both the Costume Design course and the Introduction to Design course are influenced by my exposure to international theatre design and by work with international colleagues. I have exhibited designs at the Prague

Quadrennial in 1991 and in 1999 (see Appendix C). I am a member of the Costume Working Group of the International Organization of Scenographers, Theatre Architects, and Technicians (OISTAT), and I have brought colleagues from Toi Whakaari O Aotearoa, The New Zealand Drama School to teach at Incarnate Word. Our students need to be exposed to the power and functions of theatre in cultural contexts outside the United States. I stress to the students the political, economic, and social implications of art, as opposed to the show biz aspects of possible future employment. This is evidenced in discussions and readings of international work, and in the play selections in the course work.

Service-learning projects are a recent aspect of my course work (see Appendix B). The U.I.W. Service-Learning Task Force published a Service-Learning Guide, and this encouraged me to contact the Witte Museum Textile and Dress Collection and the Tobin Theatre Arts Collection at the McNay Art Museum. Both of these collections are within walking distance from U.I.W. Both collections need help in cataloguing and research, and their needs have been incorporated in the Costume History class and the design courses.

I have recently created web sites for each of my classes through Blackboard software. Class materials, grades, research areas and methods, and examples of "A" student work are included on the sites. Communication has become clearer, and the students are able to access course materials day or night. Internet sites are integrated into the curriculum whenever this is helpful.

Listening to feedback from students and colleagues is essential. I carefully consider the student comments for syllabi revisions. One consistent comment by colleagues and students early in my teaching was that I tried to cover too much material. My department chair helped me focus on quality instead of quantity, and integration became a key factor in making change.

Peer Evaluation of Teaching

I have been evaluated twice by my department chair and twice by two deans (see Appendix D). I team taught Introduction to Theatre, and while no formal evaluation occurred, my colleague and I were constantly evaluating our process. I have also recently taught with my colleagues from New Zealand. Because the earlier formal peer evaluations were largely positive, I did not find them terribly helpful for improving teaching. What I do find helpful are more informal and frank discussions of problems and classroom visits from colleagues when we are focused on a particular problem. For example, several years ago I taught two classes which were particularly difficult because of interpersonal trouble among the students. My normal methods were not working because the students were distracted from the course content. I consulted with the theatre arts faculty and they offered suggestions, which I took. Some worked, some did not, but a change in the process was better than no change at all. Team teaching is also an ideal way of seeing one's teaching from another set of eyes, and problems seem to be solved quickly if teaching philosophies are in alignment. I also learn a great deal from conducting peer evaluations of younger teachers and from watching my wiser colleagues teach and present papers or workshops.

Comments (see Appendix D)

- "Your teaching and work with the students is excellent. Students rate your class above the college mean and value the informality of your presentations, all the while acknowledging the great amount of learning that is taking place."
  Dr. Gilberto Hinojosa, Dean

- "Margaret is a challenging teacher, a team player, and a peer advisor. Margaret has shown herself to be an excellent and dedicated teacher."
  Donna Aronson, Director of Theatre

Student Evaluation of Teaching

Most of the student evaluation data is documented in percentages. Because the format has changed, I am unable to make a consistent table of scores. (See Appendix E for full information.)

Comments

- "This has been the most interesting, time consuming, most classmate-sharing, fast paced, total spiritual self-involving, hypereducational, stress causing overloading, self-examining, fearfacing, loving environmental, life changing course of my entire college career."

- "This class is incredible. I learned more in this single class than all of my college classes combined. The self portrait is an excellent and creative way to tell progress, and all exercises helped in my growth. Thanks."

- "Out of all the classes I've had in the past 15 years, I have to say this one was the most challenging. You can't help but learn something from Margaret. She knows what she does well. I've enjoyed and appreciated her class."

- "Margaret Mitchell is an excellent professor; she is, without a doubt, one of the most intelligent people I know, and the university should consider itself enriched by her presence in the curriculum. This course was a delight—I learned so much, and there is so much still left to be learned!!"

Sample Student Work

The first section of student sample work documents progress in drawing skills. Students draw a self portrait the first day of class as a diagnostic "test." On the last day of class they do the same assignment, and we are able to see a remarkable difference if the student has carried out the journal assignments throughout the semester. The self portrait assignment can serve as a metaphor for the overall growth of the student in the semester.

The second section includes images of student design work and costume construction work. The third section includes sample costume designs from the final project in the Costume Design class in spring 2000. A student costume plot and designs for *Land Dreamings,* produced in 2000, are also included. (See Appendix F for samples of student work.)

Successful Students

Below is a selected list of students who are working in theatre, television, or film. These students are not all design/technical students, but they are students I have mentored closely in their college careers.

- George Miller, designer. George owns his own design firm in Dallas, TX

- Kathy Krueter, freelance design assistant and puppet artisan for Irene Corey Studios, Dallas, TX

- Kent Parker, puppet artisan for Irene Corey Studios, Dallas, TX.

- Tamlyn Wright, freelance scenic and costume designer, Los Angeles, CA, prosthetic and special effects artisan for *Star Trek, Babylon 5, Deep Space Nine*

- Saja Sokel, MFA in stage management from CAL ARTS, production manager for Walt Disney Studios

- Jana Groda, actress, MFA in Acting from American Conservatory Theatre

- Tony Ciarravino, MFA in Acting, University of Minnesota, resident actor at The Guthrie Theatre, AEA (Actors Equity Association)

- James Roberts, actor, MFA in Acting, University of Minnesota, American Shakespeare Festival, AEA

- Nick Colligan, actor, MFA in Acting, Michigan State University
- Laura Grey, actress, MFA in Acting, Illinois State University
- Linda Stouffer, CNN Headline News Anchorwoma n
- Karen Christianson, freelance production manager, Los Angeles, CA
- Andrew Jenkins, freelance lighting and sound designer in Los Angeles and Japan
- Ken Hardy, actor, MFA, Rutgers
- Ricardo Chavira, actor, MFA in Acting, UCSD, *Six Feet Under, NYPD Blue, Kingpin, The Alamo.* AEA

Selected Student Design Awards:

- George Miller, American College Theatre Festival National Costume Award, 1992
- Jason Martin, Best Lighting Design, Alamo Arts Council, San Antonio, TX, 1996
- Rene Garza, Best Lighting Design, Alamo Arts Council, San Antonio, TX, 1997
- Catherine Hundly, Texas Educational Theatre Association Award for Outstanding Costume Design, 1998 Conference
- Freddy Reymundo, Best Costume Design, Alamo Arts Council, 1999
- Tamlyn Wright, Emmy Award for Assistant Scenic Design for the 2002 Academy Awards
- Arnie Maldonado, Vilar Fellow at Tisch School of the Arts, McNair Scholar, and exhibition in the student section of the Prague Quadrennial, 2003
- Amiya Brown, Texas Educational Theatre Associate Award for Costume Design, 2003

Further evidence of good teaching is the fact that U.I.W. design and technical students are employed in theatre jobs both locally and regionally while they are still in school. Our students are currently employed and have been employed at the Guadalupe Theatre, Zach Scott Theatre, The Carver Theatre, the Majestic Theatre, Utah Shakespeare Festival, Texas Shakespeare Festival, and Colorado Shakespeare Festival. I encourage them to begin working regionally or nationally in the summer of their junior year.

Future Teaching Goals

- Continue sister school relationship with Toi Whakaari o Aotearoa/New Zealand Drama School

- Continue to integrate and apply Theatre Arts curriculum to production and core curriculum

- Document student work through papers and drafts, and through visual images

- Create a web site of student design work

- Continue to work with the students and local Native People on original performance material related to themes of culture and identity

Appendices

Appendix A: • Course Syllabi, Introduction to Theatre Design
            • Sketchbook /Journal Assignment

Appendix B: • Course Syllabus, Costume History
            • Sample Research Drawings From The Victoria and Albert Museum and the Petri Museum of Egyptology
            • Course Syllabus, Advanced Costume Construction

Appendix C: • Course Syllabus, Costume Design
            • Designs Exhibited at the Prague Quadrennial, 1999, published in *T,D&T*

Appendix D: Peer Evaluations of Teaching

Appendix E: • Student Evaluations of Teaching
            • Article Quoting Students From *Arts In Motion*
            • Notes From Students

Appendix F: • Student Diagnostic Drawings From Introduction to Design
            • Sample Anatomical Studies From Costume Design Sketchbooks
            • Sample Copy Project Assignment, Costume Design
            • Student Production Designs and Construction Work
            • Sample Student Designs, Final Exam, *Our Country's Good*, Costume Design
            • Student Costume Plot and Designs for *Land Dreamings*

Appendix G: Images of Theatrical Production Processes on the Conceptual Medicine Wheel

Bibliography

Barkley, E. F. (2001). From Bach to Tupac: Using an electronic course portfolio to analyze a curricular transformation. In B. L. Cambridge, S. Kahn, D. P. Tompkins, & K. B. Yancey (Eds.), *Electronic portfolios: Emerging practices in student, faculty, and institutional learning* (pp. 117–123). Washington, DC: American Association for Higher Education.

Barrett, H. (2001). Electronic portfolios = multimedia development + portfolio development: The electronic portfolio development process. In B. L. Cambridge, S. Kahn, D. P. Tompkins, & K. B. Yancey (Eds.), *Electronic portfolios: Emerging practices in student, faculty, and institutional learning* (pp. 110–116). Washington, DC: American Association for Higher Education.

Boyer, E. L. (1990). *Scholarship reconsidered: Priorities of the professoriate.* Princeton, NJ: The Carnegie Foundation for the Advancement of Teaching.

Cambridge, B. L. (2001). Electronic portfolios as knowledge builders. In B. L. Cambridge, S. Kahn, D. P. Tompkins, & K. B. Yancey (Eds.), *Electronic portfolios: Emerging practices in student, faculty, and institutional learning* (pp. 1–11). Washington, DC: American Association for Higher Education.

Cerbin, W. (1994). The course portfolio as a tool for continuous improvement of teaching and learning. *Journal of Excellence in College Teaching, 5*(1), 95–105.

Cox, M. D. (1995). A department-based approach to developing teaching portfolios: Perspectives for faculty and department chairs. *Journal on Excellence in Teaching, 6*(1), 117–143.

Cox, M. D. (1996). A department-based approach to developing teaching portfolios: Perspectives for faculty developers. In L. Richlin & D. DeZure (Eds.), *To improve the academy, Vol. 15. Resources for faculty, instructional, and organizational development* (pp. 275–302). Stillwater, OK: New Forums Press.

Cox, M. D. (2001). Faculty learning communities: Change agents for transforming institutions into learning organizations. In D. Lieberman & C. Wehlburg (Eds.), *To improve the academy, Vol. 19. Resources for faculty, instructional, and organizational development* (pp. 69–93). Bolton, MA: Anker.

Cox, M. D. (2003). Proven faculty development tools that foster the scholarship of teaching in faculty learning communities. In C. M. Wehlburg & S. Chadwick-Blossey (Eds.), *To improve the academy, Vol. 21. Resources for faculty, instructional, and organizational development* (pp. 109–142). Bolton, MA: Anker.

Designing a teaching portfolio. (1997). University Park, PA: Pennsylvania State University, Center for Excellence in Learning and Teaching.

Edgerton, R., Hutchings, P., & Quinlan, K. (1991). *The teaching portfolio: Capturing the scholarship in teaching.* Washington, DC: American Association for Higher Education.

Eison, J. (1996). *Creating a teaching portfolio: The SCRIPT model.* Tampa, FL: University of South Florida, Center for Teaching Enhancement.

Glassick, C. E., Huber, M. T., & Maeroff, G. I. (1997). *Scholarship assessed: Evaluation of the professoriate.* San Francisco, CA: Jossey-Bass.

Hatch, T. (2000). A fantasy in teaching and learning: Imagining a future for 'on-line' teaching portfolios. Paper presented at the Conference of the American Educational Research Association, New Orleans, LA.

Haugen, L. (1998). *Writing a teaching philosophy statement.* Ames, IA: Iowa State University, Center for Teaching Excellence.

Hutchings, P. (Ed.). (1998). *The course portfolio: How faculty can examine their teaching to advance practice and improve student learning.* Washington, DC: American Association for Higher Education.

Kelly, M. (2001). Wired for trouble? Creating a hypermedia course portfolio. In B. L. Cambridge, S. Kahn, D. P. Tompkins, & K. B. Yancey (Eds.), *Electronic portfolios: Emerging practices in student, faculty, and institutional learning* (pp. 124–129). Washington, DC: American Association for Higher Education.

Knapper, C., & Wright, W. A. (2001). Using portfolios to document good teaching: Premises, purposes, practices. In C. Knapper & P. Cranton, (Eds.), *New directions for teaching and learning, No. 88. Fresh approaches to the evaluation of teaching* (pp. 19–29). San Francisco, CA: Jossey-Bass.

Schön, D. (1983). *The reflective practitioner.* New York, NY: Basic Books.

Seldin, P. (1997). *The teaching portfolio: A practical guide to improved performance and promotion/tenure decisions* (2nd ed.). Bolton, MA: Anker.

Seldin, P. (2003). *The teaching portfolio.* Paper presented at the American Council on Education Department Chair Seminar, San Diego, CA.

Seldin, P., & Associates. (1993). *Successful use of teaching portfolios.* Bolton, MA: Anker.

Seldin, P., & Higgerson, M. L. (2002). *The administrative portfolio: A practical guide to improved administrative performance and personnel decisions.* Bolton, MA: Anker.

Shulman, L. S. (1993, November/December). Teaching as community property: Putting an end to pedagogical solitude. *Change, 25*(6), 6–7.

Tompkins, D. P. (2001). Ambassadors with portfolios: Electronic portfolios and the improvement of teaching. In B. L. Cambridge, S. Kahn, D. P. Tompkins, & K. B. Yancey (Eds.), *Electronic portfolios: Emerging practices in student, faculty, and institutional learning* (pp. 91–105). Washington, DC: American Association for Higher Education.

Zubizarreta, J. (1995). Using teaching portfolio strategies to improve course instruction. In P. Seldin & Associates, *Improving college teaching* (pp. 167–179). Bolton, MA: Anker.

Zubizarreta, J. (1997). Improving teaching through portfolio revisions. In P. Seldin, *The teaching portfolio: A practical guide to improved performance and promotion/tenure decisions* (2nd ed., pp. 37–45). Bolton, MA: Anker.

Index